Praise for

The Renaissance Soul

"Lobenstine has identified a situation rarely addressed by self-help books, and her advice is sensible, concrete and do-able."
—*Publishers Weekly*

"Here's one self-help book that is exactly as advertised, well thought out and offering sage advice . . ."
—*Boston Sunday Globe*

"Can't decide which life or career path is right for you? Maybe you don't have to! In *The Renaissance Soul*, Margaret Lobenstine offers inspiration, advice, and practical tips for people with more than one burning passion."
—*Laurence Boldt, author of Zen and the Art of Making a Living*

"I'm so grateful this book has finally been written! I need, my clients need, the world needs this incredibly helpful, practical, life-changing guidebook for those of us with a multitude of passions and aptitudes. Please, get this book into the hands of every person you know who is a Renaissance Soul. You could change their lives!"
—*Jennifer Louden, author of Comfort Secrets for Busy Women and other books in the bestselling Comfort Book series*

"*The Renaissance Soul* will help highly innovative and creative people find ways to make their many dreams come true. I've already begun using its wonderful ideas and practices with clients."
—*M. J. Ryan, author of This Year I will*

CALGARY PUBLIC LIBRARY

DEC - 2013

"Wow! Where was *The Renaissance Soul* when I needed it during my five career changes? This is a fabulous guide for people who find themselves constantly tap dancing from job to job. Benjamin Franklin would be proud!"

—Julie Jansen, author of *I Don't Know What I Want, But I Know It's Not This*

"Sure to speak to Boomers and older people who have done many things well yet feel sidelined by a culture that rewards consistency and focus. Margaret Lobenstine makes the world safer for the multigifted of any age who are well served by her wit and wisdom. Bravo!"

—Marika and Howard Stone, coauthors of *Too Young to Retire: 101 Ways to Start the Rest of Your Life*

"*The Renaissance Soul* is welcome news for individuals who just can't make up their mind 'what they want to be when they grow up!' Career coach Margaret Lobenstine shows how you can have it all and create a structure for yourself that blends your many talents, abilities, and intelligences into one vital and satisfying lifestyle."

—Thomas Armstrong, PhD, author of *7 Kinds of Smart: Identifying and Developing Your Multiple Intelligences*

"Finally the multigifted have a champion. But anyone feeling that they only need a little sunshine in order to blossom will find this book bursting with light—it has all the creative and practical ideas they need for getting life on toward its purpose."

—Elaine Aron, PhD, author of *The Highly Sensitive Person* and *The Highly Sensitive Child*

CALGARY PUBLIC LIBRARY

DEC 2013

"With this long-overdue book, Margaret finally reveals that the constantly evolving people among us are actually the ones most equipped to thrive in a world where adaptability, creativity, and emotional awareness are the qualities that make all the difference in career/life success. It's about time we acknowledged that the career track has been replaced by the career trampoline. As a career counselor and coach and former director of a career office working with people ages eighteen to eighty, I know that Lobenstine's message will be welcomed both by Renaissance Souls searching for twenty-first-century career advice and by the professionals hoping to provide it."

—Dr. Barbara Reinhold, author of *Free to Succeed: Designing the Life You Want in the New Free Agent Economy* and former director of Smith College Office of Career Development

"For all the people who have a multitude of passions, this book's for you. The life journey we take to answer to our own Self may be different from the 'norm.' Margaret Lobenstine is a wise guide on that journey, offering help and inspiration as you develop fully into the Renaissance Soul that you are meant to be! This book will be a cherished traveling companion."

—Marilyn Tam, former president of Reebok Apparel and Retail Group and international-selling author of *How to Use What You've Got to Get What You Want*

"*The Renaissance Soul* accurately solves what has long been an unsolvable problem—how people with 'too many' talents and interests can manage their diverse passions. With warmth, insight, and helpful exercises, Lobenstine helps these souls find their way to making a contribution . . . and finally feeling complete about what they're here to do."

—Suzanne Falter-Barns, author of *Living Your Joy*

"This amazing, inspiring, and practical book encourages us to take joy in our dazzling array of legitimate life choices and to make those choices boldly and fearlessly. The book is perfect to use with clients in my empowerment-coaching practice."

—Helena Judith Sturnick, PhD, executive and empowerment coach for twelve years and former president of several campuses

"Many of my coaching clients are individuals searching for more meaningfulness in their life and work, and organizational leaders who have made it yet are unable to figure out why they feel lost. Margaret Lobenstine has developed a breath of fresh air, along with a model of liberation for people who have felt that they don't fit in their life and work. *The Renaissance Soul* is an inspiring and easy-to-use approach that helps me guide my secret Renaissance Soul clients."

—Bernie Saunders, consultant for Fortune 500 companies, foundations, small manufacturers, and health-care providers

"The Renaissance Soul is the consummate Social Artist, embodying the complex interests and open hearts that are needed now in the global world. Today, when the world mind is taking a walk with itself, we require a consciousness that can encompass the multiple realities we face. This work gives us tools that enable that needed growth in consciousness."

—Jean Houston, PhD, author of *Jump Time* and senior consultant to the United Nations Development Programme

"At once illuminating, practical, and visionary, *The Renaissance Soul* is an invaluable resource for all of us who can't be confined to one path. If you want to build a satisfying, textured life based on multiple interests and passions, treat this as your textbook and Lobenstine as your trusted advisor."

—Marci Alboher, author of *One Person/Multiple Careers: The Original Guide to the Slash Career*

The *Renaissance* SOUL

How to Make Your Passions Your Life— A Creative and Practical Guide

MARGARET LOBENSTINE

THE EXPERIMENT
NEW YORK

THE RENAISSANCE SOUL: *How to Make Your Passions Your Life—A Creative and Practical Guide*

Copyright © 2006, 2013, Margaret Lobenstine

Published by arrangement with Harmony Books, an imprint of the Crown Publishing Group, a division of Random House, Inc.

All rights reserved. Except for brief passages quoted in newspaper, magazine, radio, television, or online reviews, no portion of this book may be reproduced, distributed, or transmitted in any form or by any means, electronic or mechanical, including photocopying, recording, or information storage or retrieval system, without the prior written permission of the publisher.

Many of the designations used by manufacturers and sellers to distinguish their products are claimed as trademarks. Where those designations appear in this book and The Experiment was aware of a trademark claim, the designations have been capitalized.

The Experiment, LLC
260 Fifth Avenue
New York, NY 10001-6408
www.theexperimentpublishing.com

Note: Many of the cases in this book are based on a composite of the author's professional experiences. Where cases are based on individuals the author has encountered in her coaching practice, she has changed names and characteristics to protect the subjects' privacy. Where cases are based on individuals who have granted her permission to use their full names, she has done so.

The Experiment's books are available at special discounts when purchased in bulk for premiums and sales promotions as well as for fund-raising or educational use. For details, contact us at info@theexperimentpublishing.com.

Library of Congress Cataloging-in-Publication Data

Lobenstine, Margaret.
  The renaissance soul : how to make your passions your life--a creative and practical guide / Margaret Lobenstine.
      pages cm
  Updated edition of the author's The Renaissance soul : life design for people with too many passions to pick just one, published in 2006.
  Includes index.
  ISBN 978-1-61519-092-8 (pbk.) -- ISBN 978-1-61519-184-0 (ebook)
1. Career development--Handbooks, manuals, etc. 2. Vocational guidance--Handbooks, manuals, etc. I. Title.
  HF5381.L585 2013
  650.1--dc23
2013016735

ISBN 978-1-61519-092-8
Ebook ISBN 978-1-61519-184-0

Cover design by Howard Grossman | www.12edesign.com
Cover illustration © Designer_things | VectorStock
Author photograph by Ellen Cohan
Book design by Nicola Ferguson
Typesetting by Neuwirth & Associates, Inc.

Manufactured in the United States of America
Distributed by Workman Publishing Company, Inc.
Distributed simultaneously in Canada by Thomas Allen & Son Ltd.

First printing of the paperback edition September 2013
10 9 8 7 6 5 4 3 2 1

This book is dedicated first and foremost to Renaissance Souls the world over, whose multitude of interests and talents are a gift to us all; to my late parents, who would have been thrilled to hold it in their hands; and, with such profound gratitude, to my husband, Geoff, and my daughters, Heather and Lori, who have been on this journey with me so lovingly from beginning to end.

CONTENTS

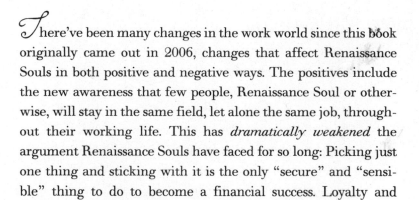

PREFACE

*T*here've been many changes in the work world since this book originally came out in 2006, changes that affect Renaissance Souls in both positive and negative ways. The positives include the new awareness that few people, Renaissance Soul or otherwise, will stay in the same field, let alone the same job, throughout their working life. This has *dramatically weakened* the argument Renaissance Souls have faced for so long: Picking just one thing and sticking with it is the only "secure" and "sensible" thing to do to become a financial success. Loyalty and longevity in one job equals financial security? Not anymore!

Given how long people are out of work, or at least out of their field, another positive for Renaissance Souls is that resumes with *gaps or work in a variety of fields* are more common. Ironically, in fact, those who focused on "climbing the ladder" while working are now told they're "overqualified" when they try to return.

Yes, today's economy offers advantages for today's Renaissance Souls, but still things aren't easy. Any job opening draws hundreds of applicants, and jobs that stay here, such as retail, can be dead ends and pay terribly. Even many young people who get that "all-important" degree aren't "rewarded by the system." No, they're likely to end up deep in debt, with only entry-level (or even no) jobs waiting for them.

Even so, reading this book will show how you, *as a Renaissance Soul*, can make effective use of college years, gap times, early jobs, and unpaid work to end up being the one hired! Even if a need for benefits binds you to a job that's not you, for longer than you'd ever want to be bound to anything, the J-O-B concept offered here may save your sanity!

You can read this book in whatever order works for you. For example:

+ If you already identify as a Renaissance Soul, read the first few chapters and consider skipping ahead to Part III before you work with Focal Points. Understanding the difference between a job and a J-O-B may free you to identify your passions unhampered by financial panic.
+ If you were glued to this book as soon as you got it, but then put it aside with others you "meant to finish," spend some serious time with Chapter Twelve. There may be underlying reasons you're doing this that will be important to uncover before moving forward.

In any event, regardless of where, in what stage of life, or in what order you read this book, I hope that understanding you're a Renaissance Soul will make your life feel like *yours*!

Margaret Lobenstine
Belchertown, MA, 2013

INTRODUCTION

Are You a Renaissance Soul?

+ Do you feel a pang of envy when you hear someone
  say, "I've always known exactly what I wanted to do
  ever since I was a kid"?
+ Do you get down on yourself for being a "jack-of-all-
  trades, master of none" because you are fascinated by
  many subjects but have never become an expert in
  any of them?
+ Or are you an expert in one or more areas but feel
  trapped by other people's expectations that you will
  stay in your current field for the rest of your life?
+ Are you frustrated by career books or advisors who
  insist that you identify just *one* passion or goal?
+ Do you enjoy following a diverse and ever-evolving
  set of interests but feel thwarted by family members
  or friends who ask, "Why on earth can't you find
  something you like and stick with it?"

If you answered yes to any of these questions, read on! Chances are you're a Renaissance Soul, a person who thrives on a variety of interests and who redefines the accepted meaning of success. And chances are you're struggling—maybe a little, maybe a lot—because not everyone in our culture understands your approach to work and other pursuits. Take heart. With the advice in this book, you can transform this aspect of your personality into a powerful tool for designing a vibrant, fulfilling life.

PLEASE DON'T MAKE ME CHOOSE!

*H*ow do I define Renaissance Souls? In a nutshell, we are people whose number-one career or hobby choice is "Please don't make me choose!" We're much more inclined to pursue a slew of interests than to narrow our options to a single one. Renaissance Souls love nothing better than to take on a new problem or situation and then dig into it . . . until we master the challenge we've set for ourselves. And then, with fresh enthusiasm, we move on to another passion. We are lucky people who, if left to our own devices, are never bored for long.

Yet sometimes Renaissance Souls don't feel so lucky. Despite a long and proud history of Renaissance Souls who've negotiated treaties, invented revolutionary machines, written great novels, and led victorious armies, our culture often insists that we are defective. In fact, it's common for new clients to sink into my office rocking chair, sighing, "What's *wrong* with me? Why can't I get my act together?" or "Why doesn't anyone 'get' me?"

Marcie: Stuck at the Bottom of the Ladder

Marcie, for example, came to me after a hectic day working as a receptionist for a busy medical practice. She was late because her ancient station wagon had broken down again and she'd needed to borrow a car. "That's the bottom-line reason why I'm here," she told me. "I need to earn more money. I need to find a career and get moving. I can't be scheduling pediatric appointments for the rest of my life unless I want to be a bag lady when I retire!"

When I asked Marcie what else she'd done with her life, she went on at length. After working herself silly in college, pursuing a double major in astronomy and French and also vigorously participating in theater, she had taken a break by traveling abroad for a year. And then she'd worked as a nanny to pay off the money she'd borrowed to travel, and then she'd worked as a set person in off-off-off-Broadway productions, and then she'd worked in a travel agency, and then . . . "Well, you get the picture," Marcie said. "My parents are getting tired of explaining to people, 'Oh, Marcie just hasn't settled down yet.' And it's true. I'm twenty-seven years old and I have never picked just one thing and stuck with it. How could I? Every time I come up with a potential career, I think of at least two other possibilities. So rather than zeroing in on the perfect career choice, I go on filling my time with dead-end jobs, like the one I have now."

Craig: "Too Many" Successes

Unlike Marcie, thirty-five-year-old Craig had successfully developed many of his talents without pressuring himself to choose just one. But he felt unfairly dismissed by other people who couldn't see the value of his unconventional credentials.

When I met him, Craig was a published poet and the leader of a popular local band. He arrived at his first appointment feeling stuck and very angry. "I just don't get it," he practically yelled. "I have letters of reference that would turn most people green. But just because I've done lots of different things, just because my resume is unconventional—the woman I interviewed with yesterday called it a 'hodgepodge'—no one wants to hire me! I've gotten really intrigued by financial planning management. But even when I say I'm willing to take on an entry-level position, everyone keeps asking me if I took any business courses in college or whether I've ever 'been in sales.' '*Everyone* in the art world is in sales,' I say, but they just don't get it. I never even make it to the second interview . . . Is it a crime to be multitalented?"

Jim: At the Top and Hating It

Another client, Jim, had an extremely "respectable" resume, but like Marcie and Craig, he also was feeling stuck when he scheduled his first appointment with me. Wearing an elegant three-piece suit and driving a shiny black Lexus, he exuded success. He had entered the family construction business as a young man and shown great flair for the financial, construction, and human resources sides of the enterprise. By the time I saw him he was running a hugely expanded corporation. As he approached his forty-fifth birthday, everything seemed to be going his way. Except . . .

Except that Jim was now avoiding going to work. Avoiding placing outreach calls. Avoiding working on the upcoming five-year plan. Not answering his phone. His wife was concerned and referred him to me. What was the matter?

"To put it bluntly, I'm bored to death!" Jim finally blurted out. "I just cringe inside when I think of spending the rest of

my life on proposals and bidding and merging and schmooz-
ing and hiring and firing. I know I'm good at it all, and I know
most people would love to be in my shoes. But I'm not most
people. In fact, I feel like I don't fit in my own shoes."

Jim talked about how he had enjoyed the first five years of
his career, learning the business and developing his talents.

"But, between you and me, I hadn't even been there for
five years when it began to go stale. Now and then something
like computer blueprinting would come along and I'd get
jazzed for a bit. But basically I knew even then I had lost the
spark. That was the period when I got all interested in the
green revolution in agriculture, and picked up Italian too—I
love learning new languages! Anyway, I wanted to leave and do
something else. But that isn't what grown men do, certainly
not any men I know, not any responsible men. . . . So I stayed.

"But now I am about to be forty-five, and I just can't do it
anymore. My family thinks I'm nuts to want to walk away
from success, but I'm just shriveling up inside. This can't be all
there is to my life. There's too much else I want to try."

*J*im, Marcie, and Craig are not alone, and neither are you. Your
only problem is that your unwillingness to pick one specific path
and stick with it shouldn't be labeled a "problem" in the first
place. Let me reassure you right now: *your desire to follow many
(and frequently changing) interests is one of the best things about
you.* This book will help you understand your Renaissance Soul
and introduce you to many others who share it. It will offer you
numerous time-tested methods for helping you harness those
interests and create a dynamic life whether you are currently
without a job, aim to keep the job you have, or plan to strike out
on another path. Because Renaissance Souls often fear that by
jumping off the career ladder they'll find themselves on a path

to the poorhouse, this book will also show you how to nourish your passions in a way that is economically viable.

WHAT'S IN A NAME?
A FRESH VIEW OF YOUR PERSONALITY TRAIT

*M*y use of the term "Renaissance Soul" is inspired by the centuries-old concept of the Renaissance man. From the early fourteenth century to the late sixteenth century, the Renaissance era ignited Europe with its exciting emphasis on human individuality and expression. Renaissance thinkers rejected the dominant philosophy of the Middle Ages, when a person's highest purpose was to pray for his eternal soul to ensure life in the hereafter—and to accept his lot in life while on earth. The Renaissance fascination with individual potential stimulated a spirit of inquiry and experimentation. Its brightest stars made brave forays into uncharted lands; experimented with new forms of government; conducted scientific studies on plants, animals, and the elements; invented technologies such as gunpowder and the printing press; and reached dizzying heights of artistic endeavor.

The Renaissance demanded a new kind of person, one well suited to the era's invigorating atmosphere. This new ideal emerged in Italy from the writings of Leon Battista Alberti (1404–1472), an architect and art theorist who stated boldly that "a man can do all things if he will." Alberti dubbed this versatile, highly capable type of human *Uoma Universale*, meaning "universal man," but the phrase that has survived in our history books is "Renaissance man." To say that the Renaissance man was well rounded would be an understatement. Renaissance men were expected to develop their understanding of natural sciences and philosophy (these two goals alone would be a mighty stretch for most of us today) *and* exhibit accomplishment in athletics, artistic pursuits, and the courtly art of conversation.

Some Renaissance men (and women) really *did* seem to embody Alberti's edict to "do all things." The first person who comes to most people's minds is Leonardo da Vinci (1452–1519). Sure, he's the genius behind the world's most famous painting, the *Mona Lisa*, and the glorious fresco *The Last Supper.* But he also studied geography, hydraulics, music, sculpting, and botany. He built canals and designed bicycles, musical instruments, cutting-edge weaponry, and machines for flight. He advanced the understanding of human anatomy to an astonishing degree.

Another wonderful example is Isabella d'Este (1474–1539). It wasn't enough for this Renaissance woman to display her great political talent when she became the chief of state for the Italian city of Mantua upon the death of her husband. Isabella d'Este also founded a school for young women, established an impressive art collection, played the lute, and spoke Greek and Latin. And the nearly two thousand letters she wrote on such subjects as politics and war brought her as close to earning the title historian as any woman of that era could have hoped to come.

Then there's Sir Thomas More (1478–1535). He was torn between his religious calling and the political life. So he did what comes naturally to many of us current-day Renaissance Souls: first he did one, and then he did the other. After spending several years cloistered in a monastery, he emerged to become a brilliant civil servant. As undersheriff of London, he served as a patron to the poor, helped resolve disputes about the wool trade, and was instrumental in quelling a 1517 London uprising against foreigners. On the side, he published several major works of translation and his famous *Utopia.*

RENAISSANCE MEN AND WOMEN THROUGHOUT HISTORY

This short list includes just a small number of the Renaissance Souls who have made a name for themselves throughout history:

- Imhotep (circa 3000 B.C.): Architect of Egypt's Step Pyramid; high priest; astronomer; scribe; and physician who is reputed to have written the *materia medica*, a set of papyri that codified the ancient Egyptians' medical knowledge.
- Aristotle (384–322 B.C.): Logician; theologian; scientist; ethicist; and rhetorician.
- Abū 'Alī al-Hasan ibn al-Haytham (965–1039 A.D.): Hydraulic engineer; astronomer; optician who established a theory of vision that was accepted until the seventeenth century; and artist whose stunning copies of mathematical manuscripts are still displayed in Istanbul.
- Hildegard von Bingen (1098–1179): Benedictine abbess; visionary; theologian; advisor to popes and kings; composer; and student of medicine.
- Mary (Sidney) Herbert (1561–1621): Patron of the musical and literary arts; poetry editor and translator; writer; multilinguist who spoke French, Italian, Latin, and Greek; and mother of four children.
- Sir Robert Dudley (1574–1649): Navigator; cartographer who compiled the first world atlas of sea charts; mathematician; engineer who drained

Eventually More was beheaded for his refusal to acknowledge King Henry VIII as the leader of the Church of England. In 1935, this Renaissance Soul took on yet another role beyond the grave when Pope Pius XI canonized him as a saint.

But you don't need to have been born during the Renaissance to be a Renaissance Soul. One of my favorite the swamps outside of Pisa, Italy; and privateer who sponsored pirate raids.

- Thomas Jefferson (1743–1826): An author of the Declaration of Independence; Southern gentleman and farmer; owner of a nail-making business; diplomat; founder of the University of Virginia; architect of UVA and his home, Monticello; president of the United States; and bibliophile (his book collection became the foundation for the Library of Congress).

- Florence Nightingale (1820–1910): Nursing pioneer who formalized her profession; reformer of medical sanitation methods; writer; and statistician.

- George Washington Carver (1864–1943): Chemist and agriculturist who developed synthetic sugar, mayonnaise, and instant coffee, among many other products; educator; businessman; medical worker; artist; author; and social reformer.

- Winston Churchill (1874–1965): Leader of his country during a devastating war; orator who delivered the finest speeches of his generation; painter whose watercolors now hang in the Metropolitan Museum of Art, the Smithsonian, and the Royal Academy in London; and winner of the Nobel Prize for Literature.

- Woody Guthrie (1912–1967): Singer and songwriter who galvanized America's folk-music scene; social critic; soldier; sailor; cartoonist; mural painter; memoirist; avid hitchhiker; and homespun philosopher.

Renaissance men is actually from the American colonial era: Benjamin Franklin. As a printer, inventor, scientist, author, and diplomat, he blended the perpetual curiosity of the Renaissance man with the down-to-earth, can-do spirit of America. We'll come back to Ben often in this book.

When I began my practice as a life and career coach over

two decades ago, I was not yet thinking about Ben Franklin, Leonardo da Vinci, or any others who upheld the Renaissance ideal. In fact, the idea for my practice began when my bed-and-breakfast business expanded to become the country's first apprenticeship program for would-be innkeepers. At the end of the weeklong program, the apprentice and I always sat down to talk about why he or she was interested in this particular career. As I listened to apprentice after apprentice, I was astounded by the number of people for whom innkeeping was not a serious business proposition but an escape fantasy, the way other people dream of opening a little restaurant in their favorite vacation spot or starting a bookstore on a quaint city corner. In these sessions, we began talking about what the apprentice was trying to escape and what was happening in his or her life back home. I discovered a talent for listening, and for asking provocative questions that led to swift, creative problem-solving. I began to dream of my own life-coaching business, and in 1992, after closing up the bed-and-breakfast and studying this new field, I hung out my shingle.

My clients came from a broad swath of American life: they were doctors, lawyers, architects, writers, restaurateurs, therapists, artists, acupuncturists, and business owners. Some delivered the local paper as their only source of income, and others received a nice big check from a trust fund every January 1 whether or not they got out of bed in the morning. I noticed that a significant number of these clients tended to have trouble choosing—whether that choice was a career path or activities outside the realm of paid work. Their problems felt bigger than "What should I do to earn a living?" They felt almost philosophical, even existential. "Where is all this going?" they'd ask me in frustration. "Why can't I make up my mind? If I could, my life would be so much easier!"

These laments certainly sounded familiar to me. Through

the years I'd often asked them of myself. I worried that I'd never amount to anything or be able to support my family if I followed my divergent interests. I felt this way even though I managed to pursue a series of fascinating—but completely unrelated—careers that produced a good income. Once I even faked an illness so that I wouldn't have to explain to uncomprehending friends why I was making yet another radical career change! So when I began counseling and my clients started talking, I listened carefully and asked questions. I started to hear recognizable patterns in their stories of multiple interests, pressure from family and friends "to pick an interest and stick to it," money worries, and general frustration. The more frequently I encountered these patterns, the bolder I grew in my assessments.

"Would you mind if I played a hunch here?" I'd ask certain clients. "I'm going to describe a couple of personality characteristics and I want you to tell me if they resonate with you." I'd talk about the ability to become excited by several

---

FIVE SIGNS THAT YOU MIGHT BE
A RENAISSANCE SOUL

1. The ability to become excited by many things at once, often accompanied by difficulty choosing

2. A love of new challenges; once challenges are mastered, easily bored

3. A fear of being trapped in the same career or activity for life

4. A pattern of quick, sometimes unsatisfying flings with many hobbies

5. A successful career that has left you bored or restless

things at once, the fear of being trapped for life in the same career or activity, and the boredom that sometimes appeared after the challenge of a new task had been met.

"That's me!" people would often exclaim. "How did you know?" As I described these personality traits further, and how many other people shared them, the person in the chair across from mine would respond viscerally, either visibly relaxing or nearly leaping out of his or her chair in excitement. This concept clearly touched some of my clients at the core. They were thrilled to find out that they were not alone. There were other, wonderful people out there with the same personality trait—people whose flourishing lives could light their own unique paths.

Over time, I began to call these people—and myself— "Renaissance Souls." This new term helped people like Marcie, Craig, and Jim, the three clients I described at the beginning of this Introduction, reframe their personality trait in a positive way. People who had long suffered under the labels "dilettante" or "flake" or just plain "failure" could now glance backward toward a time—the Renaissance—when people who pursued many different interests were held in the highest esteem.

I was surprised—and thrilled—at how quickly the word spread about Renaissance Souls. "I heard about you from my coworker," a new client would say. "She says that her son is a Renaissance Soul and that I might be, too. And that you help people like us get moving." Some clients were drawn in as soon as they heard the words "Renaissance Soul" from their friends: "Finally I have a name for how I feel," they'd tell me. Parents called my office, wanting to buy Renaissance Soul gift certificates for their children. And I was having a marvelous time, helping Renaissance Souls "get unstuck" from low-paying jobs, from a pattern of quick, unsatisfying flings with dozens of hobbies, or from careers that left them bored and restless. Soon I began giving Renaissance Soul workshops and talks. I gave my first programs at the University of Massachusetts, and soon I was receiving requests from organizations that wanted me to present Renaissance Soul information to their members. I've spoken to groups ranging from the Boston Center for Adult Education to the international headquarters for the SYDA Foundation to meetings of

THE RENAISSANCE SOUL APPROACH

The Renaissance Soul coaching I do is not limited to career planning. It is about life design as well. At times my clients have realized that the job they have has served its purpose and they find they are ready to move on to a new challenge or challenges. Other clients learn to see their paid work in a new light when they realize they can design a life of multiple passions around the job they already have. Some Renaissance Souls have chosen to pursue fresh career interests sequentially, and others have chosen to follow multiple interests at once.

Wherever they end up, Renaissance Souls usually find that they have to tackle three challenges in order to get where they want to be: focus, money, and time. The challenge of focus is to avoid being paralyzed by the seeming need to choose among many paths. The challenge of money is to link your passions to a source of income. And the challenge of time is twofold: how to avoid "starting all over again" each time you switch interests, and how to organize your time in a way that works with your Renaissance Soul rhythms. You will learn how to clear each of these hurdles en route to a successful new life design in the chapters that follow.

life coaches from around the country who want to know more
about their Renaissance Soul clients.

HOW THIS BOOK CAN HELP

I've worked with about two thousand Renaissance Souls,
and along the way I've developed many strategies for "getting
unstuck" and making the most of this personality trait. I've
written this book to share the secrets I've discovered and to put
these strategies directly into your hands.

Part I, "Claiming Your Renaissance Soul," guides you toward
rethinking your personality type, so that you see it as healthy and
full of rich potential. It debunks some of the crippling myths
about Renaissance Souls, including that we are doomed to
poverty or that we suffer from Attention Deficit Disorder.

After you do the preparatory work in which you locate
your deepest values, Part II, "Thriving on Many Interests
Without Feeling Scattered," shows you how to pursue a variety of passions without becoming overwhelmed by them.
Here you'll learn the critical difference between the paralyzing restrictions of *choice* and the freeing concept of *focus*.

At this point, most Renaissance Souls are excited about
their newly discovered identity but wonder about its practical
implications. Part III, "Practical Realities: Career Design for
Pursuing Your Passions" shows you ways to link your passions
to a source of income and avoid starting on the bottom rung
of the ladder each time you switch interests. It also provides
you with suggestions for describing your Renaissance Soul
approach to life to family, friends, and coworkers. (By the end
of this section, you'll have mastered your answer to that
dreaded cocktail-party standard, "What do you do?") Since
Renaissance Souls may need more rounds of education or job

training than will other people, we'll look at alternatives to spending time and money on graduate programs.

CAREER OPTIONS FOR THE RENAISSANCE SOUL

1. Different career paths, pursued sequentially

2. Umbrellas—one job title that embraces many interests

3. Two for one—two jobs that may be pursued simultaneously and that often complement one another (i.e., banker/financial journalist, stay at home mom/activist)

4. A J-O-B—paid work that serves one's interests

5. A singular career path with improved life design to accommodate many interests

Part IV, "Successful Life Design for Renaissance Souls," recognizes that traditional planning techniques don't always work for Renaissance Souls. The chapters here delineate new strategies that will unlock your capacity for commitment, setting goals, and managing time. These tactics work with, rather than against, your natural way of operating.

The book concludes with Part V, "Going Deeper." It offers extra help for those of you who encounter deep-seated fears or self-doubts as you forge your new life.

The first tool I can offer you is this short quiz, "Are You a Renaissance Soul?" This quiz is based on a list of characteristics that I've refined over years of coaching and leading workshops. If after taking the quiz you are still unsure whether you meet the criteria, try reading the first chapter of this book, where I describe the Renaissance Soul concept in more detail.

QUIZ: Are You a Renaissance Soul?

Answer the following questions with your first, from-the-gut response:

1. Are you capable of becoming passionately excited about a wide variety of subjects?

    Yes ☐   No ☐

2. Do you have a hard time choosing between one interest and another?

    Yes ☐   No ☐

3. Do you find yourself interrupting yourself, dropping one task to pick up another before it's done?

    Yes ☐   No ☐

4. When you really understand how something works, or master a new activity, do you feel bored and ready to try something new?

    Yes ☐   No ☐

5. When you were a child, did you have many answers to the question "What do you want to be when you grow up?"

    Yes ☐   No ☐

6. Do friends and coworkers seek out your opinion on a variety of topics (even outside your field) because they

like the way you see connections between apparently unrelated subjects?

Yes ☐   No ☐

7. When you come up with an idea, do you prefer to delegate or hire out the tasks of turning that idea into a reality?

Yes ☐   No ☐

8. Do you ever describe yourself as a "dabbler" or a "dilettante"?

Yes ☐   No ☐

9. Are bookstores and libraries like candy stores to you, places where wonderful and intriguing items are on display at every turn?

Yes ☐   No ☐

10. Do you find it almost impossible to answer the question "What do you picture yourself doing in five years?"

Yes ☐   No ☐

11. Do friends suggest that you become a contestant on game shows because you know "something about everything"?

Yes ☐   No ☐

12. Do people say that they enjoy talking to you because of your enthusiasm for their plans and activities?

Yes ☐   No ☐

13. Are you skeptical of traditional time-management and business tools, such as long-range plans or detailed schedules?

Yes ☐   No ☐

14. If you went to college, did you look for interdisciplinary or multiple majors?

    Yes ☐   No ☐

15. If you specialized in a particular subject in school, did you move into a new field after your education was complete?

    Yes ☐   No ☐

16. Are you competent—even highly successful—at your job but feel there's something else you'd rather be doing, even if you're not sure what?

    Yes ☐   No ☐

17. After a year or two of doing something, do you feel the itch to move on to something else?

    Yes ☐   No ☐

18. Do family members offer this kind of advice: "You ought to settle down and get known in one field, rather than switching from one career to another"?

    Yes ☐   No ☐

19. When friends or family members describe you to others, do they often say, "Oh, _____ just hasn't settled down yet. _____ is always trying something different. I wish _____ would just figure out something s/he's interested in and *stick to it!*"

    Yes ☐   No ☐

20. Do you distrust your own decision-making ability because you "definitely knew" you wanted to be an *X*, and then you "definitely knew" you wanted to be a *Y*, and

then you "definitely knew" you wanted to be a Z, and then . . .

Yes ☐   No ☐

If you checked yes for nine or more of these questions, you can proudly identify yourself as a Renaissance Soul. In fact, given that no short quiz can be perfectly accurate, if you answered yes to even three or four of these questions, but felt very strongly about those answers, you too may well learn more about yourself within these pages.

Part 1

Claiming Your Renaissance Soul

ONE

Renaissance Souls: Who You Are—and Who You're Not

When my sister told me about Renaissance Souls, I got so excited. But when I tried telling my partner this was why I don't finish all the projects I start, he just laughed and said I was lazy. And when I tried to tell my realtor friend Janet this was why I hadn't picked one field and stayed with it like she had, she said I didn't need a new name for myself, I just needed discipline. Are they right? How do I know I really am a Renaissance Soul?

—Tracy, twenty-five

ven if you've taken the quiz in the Introduction and identified yourself as a Renaissance Soul, you probably still have some questions. *Can I be a Renaissance Soul even though I'm not a genius like Leonardo da Vinci? What if I've successfully climbed one career ladder but still feel like a Renaissance Soul?* You may also long to hear more about the characteristics you share with so many others, especially if you've experienced a lifetime of feeling different. *Why* do *I have so many interests?* you may wonder. Or even: *Why do I still feel so alone?* In this chapter, I'll take you on a journey deeper into the Renaissance Soul.

WOLFGANG AMADEUS MOZART . . . OR BEN FRANKLIN?

The Continuum of Interests

Wolfgang Amadeus Mozart —————————— Benjamin Franklin

One Passionate Lifelong Interest   *A Great Many Varied Interests*

*P*icture a line representing the continuum of human interests. At one end, you have people like Mozart. To say that Mozart chose one interest and stuck with it is an understatement. He made his career choice at age three, when he begged for piano lessons and spent his playtime performing on make-believe musical instruments. And he continued to eat, breathe, and sleep music, playing for royal courts as a youngster and then composing his masterpieces practically up until the minute he died. Mozart would *never* have needed a self-help book or career workshop to pinpoint his interests and help him figure out what to do with his life. (He could have used one of my money-management workshops, but that's another story. . . .)

Now look at the other end of the spectrum. There, with his multitude of changing interests, stands Ben Franklin. (I warned you he was my favorite example!) Just for fun, let's imagine that Ben is alive today. How might his friends and family react to his revolving-door approach to careers? Having played his key role in the drafting of the Declaration of Independence, they might expect him to head for a tenured position at the Kennedy School of Government at Harvard. But what about his strange fascination with kite and key experiments? Fine, his wife might say. Why don't you go to MIT and pursue a nice stable career in science? But no, it turns out that Ben *also* wants to go abroad to study French culture and language! Okay, his friends suggest, he can work for the United Nations or Berlitz. But wait——he also has plans to design a post office, invent bifocals, and print his *Poor Richard's Almanac*! Looking at Ben's life this way reminds us that a life can look scattered and fragmented while it's unfolding but still go down in history as a smashing success. (This viewpoint can also help keep complaints from family and friends in perspective.)

In my workshops, I often use "Ben Franklin" as a kind of shorthand for the Renaissance Soul, because most people immediately understand him as a kind of goodwill ambassador for the multitalented. Afterward, people will often tell me of the moment during the workshop when they realized, "I'm not a weirdo——I'm a *Ben Franklin.*" Their relief and pride are written on their faces.

Not every Renaissance Soul takes the concept of versatility quite as far as Ben Franklin did, though. Those people who are closer to the middle of the continuum often have a foot in both camps. Some, like my client Matt, may even have one foot on Mozart's side of the line. A brilliant Harvard Medical School graduate, Matt turned down the opportunity to work in one of Boston's high-pressured teaching hospitals for a far less remunerative rural family practice, because it allows him time to pursue his other passions. While Matt will be happy being a doctor all his life, he can't live without time for his horses, his softball team, his oboe playing, and his million different fix-it projects. Matt, too, is a Renaissance Soul.

THREE CHARACTERISTICS OF THE RENAISSANCE SOUL

*Y*ou may find yourself more toward the middle of the continuum, or you might be jostling Ben Franklin for elbow room toward the end of the line. But what all Renaissance Souls have in common are the following three characteristics. Some Renaissance Souls demonstrate them more than others, but most will feel a warm sense of recognition and belonging upon reading this list.

Characteristic #1:
A Preference for Variety over Single-Minded Focus

The most obvious trait shared by Renaissance Souls is our love for variety over concentrating on just one thing. This doesn't mean that we can't concentrate on what we're doing! Quite the contrary—when we're working at peak performance, we are as absorbed and detail-oriented as neurosurgeons. (Which is a good thing for those Renaissance Souls who happen to *be* neurosurgeons.) But we do love variety, and there are many ways in which Renaissance Souls express that love.

Many Renaissance Souls pursue several interests simultaneously. Caroline, a client of mine, is both a professional clown and a Holocaust educator who gives talks on the lessons of Auschwitz. Mark, a college student, is majoring in economics and English with a minor in piano performance. Guess how my client Ellen combines her passions for urban history, commerce, textiles, and women's issues? She spends part of her time showing visitors from Europe the hidden joys of Atlanta and the rest of her time importing and selling handmade rugs from women's cooperatives in Turkey.

One particularly dynamic way to practice several interests

at once is to combine them under one title—what I call an *umbrella*. Take Dan. When Dan set out to create a second career after running a successful restaurant, his wife suggested he get trained as a social worker. After all, she knew that Dan wanted to help troubled kids. When his friends heard that Dan dreamed of finally spending time rock climbing and white-water rafting, they suggested he start a business to take outdoor enthusiasts on wilderness trips. Did Dan choose between these two career tracks? No! Instead, he is now the happy owner of a beautiful camp in wild northern Maine, where he can share the outdoor activities he loves with paying customers *and* inner-city kids. (I'll come back to the subject of umbrellas later in the book, when you're ready for specific life-design strategies.)

Others pursue their varied interests on a rotating basis. Betsy, with her love of gardening and quilting and helping others, changes her activities with the seasons. During the winter she makes unusual baby quilts to sell over the Internet. In early spring she offers quilting workshops for seniors, using materials specially adapted with Velcro for arthritic hands. From late spring through early fall she has a position developing outdoor gardening and landscaping projects with prisoners. Come late fall she again gives quilting workshops for seniors.

Then there are Renaissance Souls who do just one thing at a time . . . until they move on to their next interest, so that each distinct passion reads like a chapter in a fascinating book. A Renaissance Soul I interviewed, Bob Lodie, is a great example. What are the chapters in his life? After seven years as an Air Force aviator, he became a sales executive for a Fortune 50 company. After about a decade, that lost its charm. So Bob spent the 1980s chasing sweat equity in the personal computing industry, moving from company to company. Currently, he's engaging his new love of speaking and writing as an executive at a corporation that provides planning and training tools to businesses worldwide.

As a Renaissance Soul, it doesn't matter whether we engage in our multitude of interests simultaneously, on a rotating basis, or sequentially. What's important is that we honor our delight in variety, rather than forcing ourselves to choose just one thing. Our multi-interest way of life is the one we *prefer*, and it's one to which we're entitled.

Characteristic #2: A Working Style
That Emphasizes Growth and Evolution Instead
of Rigid Adherence to a Plan

Renaissance Souls tend to enjoy a working style that doesn't follow a linear, predictable process. We're not like career academics, for example, who relish the process of starting out in the college of liberal arts, then choosing an English major, narrowing *that* down to Elizabethan literature, narrowing *that* down to Shakespeare, narrowing *that* down to tragedy, narrowing *that* down to *Romeo and Juliet*, then narrowing that down to dialogue within *Romeo and Juliet*, until they can clearly define their doctoral thesis topic. What to them feels like a satisfying sense of narrowing in on one clear choice can feel to us like a straitjacket.

This don't-fence-me-in feeling can confuse friends and family, especially those who are smitten with a favorite technique of college advisors and career counselors: the five-year plan. In the five-year plan, you describe exactly where you'd like to be in five years and then outline specific actions you'll take to get there and a timetable for taking them. Now, Renaissance Souls are certainly *capable* of creating and executing a long-range plan, if one of our current enterprises requires it. But in general the Renaissance Soul chafes at being strapped down to a rigid set of long-term goals and actions.

Renaissance Souls much prefer a work process that's less restrictive, one that allows us to grow and evolve. We need lives and—yes—*flexible* plans that allow us to change direction and to respond eagerly to new possibilities. We enjoy stretching in directions we had no idea we'd turn. My client Katherine, for example, was growing a business that helped individuals and corporations record their histories. Then the tragic events of September 11, 2001, occurred, and like so many of us, Katherine felt a new call to help the victims. What is Katherine doing now? She's following that call by heading Modern Memoirs, a national organization of volunteers who document the life stories of 9/11 victims. Instead of riding her first business down a fixed path for life, she let that experience evolve into an entirely new option when circumstances changed.

If I were to envision the Renaissance approach to life, the traditional career metaphors of a highway to follow or a mountain to climb wouldn't come to mind. The Renaissance approach to life looks more like a tree branching out in myriad directions, some branches overlapping, some intertwining, and some just finding their own merry ways to the sunlight.

This organic process applies to our daily activities as well. When given the choice, Renaissance Souls prefer to be governed by our own energy rather than by a schedule, calendar, or "to do" list. We may *write down* an activity in our planner, such as going to the library or doing research on Thursday morning. When Thursday comes, if we *feel like* doing research, we'll be dynamite at it. But should we *not* feel that energy, in two seconds flat we'll be out chatting up clients, developing a new system for our files, walking the dog, or doing any one of the other million and one things we find interesting and worthwhile. Even *we* may find this go-with-the-flow process frustrating at times. Nevertheless, it's a plain truth about how many Renaissance Souls operate.

Characteristic #3: A Sense of Success That's Defined by the Challenges We've Mastered, Instead of How Far Up the Ladder We've Climbed

You are probably already familiar with the learning curve, the graph that demonstrates how long it takes to master the new information and challenges that arise in any given situation. As you begin learning a task, you push your way up the learning curve's steep incline. Eventually, as you understand this new environment or task, the path begins to level. It's easier going now that you're over the hump, and you become more efficient and productive.

Most people dread the difficult time spent moving up the front end of the learning curve. Not the Renaissance Soul! We are most fully engaged when learning something new and discovering how it works. Because we love a good challenge, we tend to define success and completion differently from other people. Once we've mastered a particular problem, we're done—and ready for a different set of problems to solve. Jim, the construction-company owner from the Introduction, is an example of a Renaissance Soul who felt trapped by other people's definitions of success. Jim's family and peers felt that he should have been intoxicated by the rarefied air at the top of the business ladder, especially since those first few rungs had been difficult to climb. But to Jim, it was those first years of business that he looked back on most fondly, as a time when all his faculties were fully absorbed.

It's this love of new challenges that causes Renaissance

Souls to opt for change—not continuation—in the face of success. What would most people do if they had a shoe store that, after years of grunt work and staff turnover and inventory mistakes, finally became highly profitable? They'd carry on. Maybe they'd relax into a routine with their current store, or perhaps develop a chain, with each new outlet looking much like the previous ones. But what about Renaissance Souls? The instantaneous response from my Renaissance Soul workshop participants is inevitably: "Sell! Do something else!" I often think that "been there, done that" is an expression we could have invented.

Some lucky Renaissance Souls come to this understanding early in their lives, before spending years in a career that has lost its luster. When my client Annie had her first session with me, she was a caterer with a stellar reputation and a profitably packed schedule. Her colleagues were encouraging her to cater bigger and bigger parties, or maybe open a carryout restaurant that sold her most popular dishes. To them, success was defined by continuity and expansion. But these scenarios left Annie feeling flat. Having figured out what to her were the hardest parts of the business (logistics, staffing, menu planning, and so on), she felt, well, done. The last thing she wanted was more of the same! What Annie craved now was the fresh adventure of travel, so she happily left the catering field to work internationally as a representative for a major dictionary publisher.

Not everyone will understand your desire to move on to new challenges. You can always remind these people of Leonardo da Vinci. Nowadays, he'd probably be considered a failure because he left the *The Last Supper* unfinished, or because he was satisfied simply with having designed a helicopter instead of having his flying machine mocked up, market tested, and sold to the public at a fifty percent markup. It takes a brave person to redefine success, especially in a time when money and status seem to be prized above all else.

WHAT THE RENAISSANCE SOUL IS *NOT*

My Renaissance Soul client Robert shuffled into his second session with me, his mouth in a tight line of tension. I was concerned, because Robert had nearly bounded out of his first appointment, eagerly looking forward to telling his wife that all his "eccentricities"—his leap from architecture school to a master's program in business, his penchant for inventing new gadgets on paper with no intent to manufacture them—could be mined as a source of both profit and pride.

As it turned out, Robert explained to me, he *did* go home and enthusiastically describe Renaissance Souls to his wife, Sarah. "Oh," Sarah said, "I get it. You have ADD." And now here Robert sat, deflated and worried.

Robert did not have Attention Deficit Disorder. But he did experience something that happens quite frequently to other Renaissance Souls: he ran smack into one of the misconceptions that others often harbor about Renaissance Souls. To help you more fully understand your Renaissance Soul, let's debunk some of these myths right now.

Myth #1: Renaissance Souls Have Attention Deficit Disorder

Attention Deficit Disorder (now officially known as Attention Deficit/Hyperactivity Disorder) should never be confused with healthy Renaissance Soul behavior. Characterized by chronic inattention, impulsivity, and an inability to focus or to sit still, ADHD is a psychological disorder quite separate from a desire to follow diverse pursuits. And the impulsivity of ADHD is nothing like the Renaissance Soul's rational choice to leave a project after mastering a particular challenge. ADHD can affect *anyone*, no matter where he or she stands on the continuum of interests. In fact, Edward Hallowell, one of the world's foremost ADHD researchers and author of *Driven to Distraction*, has famously made the case that Mozart himself suffered from this disorder!

Myth #2: Renaissance Souls Are Superior to Other People

Your Renaissance Soul represents a key aspect of your personality, but not your *entire* personality. Being a Renaissance Soul does not indicate whether you are neat or messy, or whether you promptly file your taxes in early January or procrastinate well past April 15. People on one side of the continuum of interests are no more or less likely to be intelligent, famous, successful, healthy, or loved than those on the other side.

Myth #3: All Renaissance Souls Are Geniuses

Many of my clients say to me: "But Margaret, how can I be a Renaissance Soul? I'm no genius like Ben Franklin!" My response: It's true that the most famous Renaissance Souls are geniuses like Leonardo da Vinci and Ben Franklin ... but that's the reason they're famous in the first place! We've heard of them *because* they're shining examples of human potential, and we've heard of Mozart and other single-passion people for the very same reason. Renaissance Souls are not required to be brilliant or to master every interest they choose to pursue. After all, we don't expect everyone on the Mozart side of the continuum to be a child prodigy.

Myth #4: Renaissance Soul Behavior Is an Avoidance Mechanism

We all know people who avoid their problems by staying busy, busy, busy. They schedule themselves around the clock, making sure they never sit down, never stop, and never have time to confront life's difficult challenges. There are also people who avoid making choices because they're fearful of making a mistake.

This behavior has nothing in particular to do with Renaissance Souls. Your difficulty choosing is not about avoiding personal problems. If you have a hard time making up your mind, it's because many activities glimmer with fascination—and because you relish a host of good challenges. You engage your many passions out of a nature that is curious and alive. Yet I've known clients who wonder, or whose families wonder, whether such versatility is an "avoidance mechanism." In fact, the opposite is often true. Acknowledging your inner Ben Franklin when you're surrounded by Mozarts can require a healthy dose of courage and clear-sightedness.

Myth #5: All Job-Hoppers Are Renaissance Souls

You probably know someone like my friend Alex, a born salesman. From when he was a kid selling lemonade on the street corner up through his graduation from business school, everyone knew Alex would go into sales. And he has, but what a wild ride it has been. In the last eleven years, he has changed companies four times. Why? In two cases, he read the writing on the wall and saw that the firm he was working for was losing market share. In another instance, the company he worked for fell victim to a merger and the entire sales team was let go. And once he got a call from a headhunter who wooed him away with a better offer.

Alex is a talented and ambitious man, but he is not a Renaissance Soul. Like many people these days, Alex eschews the old role of loyal company man. Instead, he sees himself as a free agent, one who will leap nimbly from job to job in search of greener pastures—but he remains in the same field of sales. A Renaissance Soul loves change not just for the economic opportunities it may provide, but as a way to stake out broad new territory.

SWANS LIKE US: THE GIFT OF ROLE MODELS

One reason so many of these myths still prevail is that Renaissance Souls lack explicit role models that can serve as reality checks. In fact when I'm working with Renaissance Souls who feel terribly lost—who wonder aloud, "Why do I feel so alone?"—I remind them of Hans Christian Andersen's story "The Ugly Duckling." The story begins when a swan's egg is inadvertently left in a duck's nest. As the swan grows, surrounded by ducks and with no adult swans to admire and imitate, it desperately tries to conform. The ducks see the swan as a failure. By duck cultural standards, the long-necked, all-white creature just doesn't fit in. The poor swan feels hopelessly ugly and flawed—until one day it spies some other swans flying overhead and its vision of life's possibilities is dramatically transformed. Suddenly, the shortcomings of an "ugly duckling" are recognizable as the strengths of a normal swan.

This charming story holds an important lesson for Renaissance Souls. Those who focus on an exclusive pursuit or career track are often seen as the socially acceptable ducks of our culture, while those who delight in a diversity of passions can feel like the out-of-step swans in the children's story.

Being cast in this negative light can lead Renaissance Souls to
a lifetime of self-criticism and self-doubt. Unless you, like the
swan in the story, can see others like yourself in successful
pursuit of their many interests, you may continue to feel
deeply flawed.

I've already mentioned several historical examples of successful Renaissance Souls, including Leonardo da Vinci, Sir
Thomas More, and, of course, Ben Franklin. But I think it's
particularly helpful to hear from Renaissance Souls who have
joyfully walked the earth with us more recently. Consider this
woman, whose resume ticks off the following accomplishments:

- Serving as a journalist in Ghana and Egypt
- Composing songs for popular singers like Harry
  Belafonte
- Lecturing to packed auditoriums and appearing on
  innumerable talk shows
- Acting, both on camera and on stage
- Receiving nominations for both the National Book
  Award and the Pulitzer Prize
- Working with Dr. Martin Luther King, Jr. for civil rights
- Singing jazz
- Holding a professorship in American studies
- Dancing in the opera *Porgy and Bess*
- Speaking eight languages
- Serving as America's poet laureate

Her name? Maya Angelou! Here's what she has to say, one
swan to another: "I think we've done a real disservice to young
people by telling them, 'Oh you be careful. You'll be a jack-of-
all-trades and a master of none.' It's the stupidest thing I've
ever heard. I think you can be a jack-of-all-trades and a

mistress-of-all-trades. If you study it, and you put reasonable intelligence and reasonable energy, reasonable electricity to it, you can do that."

The world is a better place because Maya Angelou eagerly pursued her many interests. The same is true for Dan (who ran his successful restaurant before developing his wilderness camp), Betsy (the quilter/gardener/teacher of senior citizens), and Ellen (the rug importer/city docent/women's advocate). Throughout this book, I'll continue to highlight contemporary Renaissance Soul role models. I hope these lives will show you that it is possible to live a much richer life—bestowing on those around you the gifts of your many talents—when you give full rein to your Renaissance Soul.

TWO

Yes, But . . . : Common Doubts of the Renaissance Soul

As soon as I took the Renaissance Soul quiz, I knew I was one. That
made me happy the whole weekend. But when Monday morning
rolled around and I was back at work, I went into a panic. How
can I have any sort of economic security if I keep changing interests
all the time? Deep down I think I really count on that regular
paycheck, the promotions, and having a pension.

—José, forty-eight

It's not that I want to totally change who I am. I value my passion
for playing the clarinet, and I don't want to give up my work with
organic farmers or my involvement with our state's literacy
initiative. But I look around at my friends who are steadily making
progress in one particular field, receiving accolades and honors,
and I wonder if being a Renaissance Soul is worth this feeling that
I'll never get to be an expert in anything.

—Jed, thirty-two

*L*et's assume that the three characteristics of the Renaissance Soul laid out in the previous chapter accurately describe your approach to work and other activities. You've realized that you've been swimming for years in the duck pond—and now recognize that you are a swan. It should be easy to fluff up those downy feathers with pride and proclaim your true identity to the world. Right?

Well, maybe. After the initial excitement and sense of recognition lights up my Renaissance Soul workshops, the room quiets down. Then I hear deep sighs and a buzz of *Yes, but* among the participants. I'm never surprised. Ever since our well-meaning kindergarten teachers asked, "What do you want to be when you grow up?" we've been conditioned to think that when we grow up we're going to be only one thing. You may have invested years or decades trying to find your one true bliss (or at least sticking with one well-paying job). Changing perspectives isn't always easy, even when that perspective casts you in a more flattering light. You may have a jumble of questions. So in preparation for the down-and-dirty work of designing your new life, let's look four of the most common doubts about the Renaissance life straight in the eye.

COMMON DOUBT #1: BUT IT'S TOO LATE
FOR ME TO START SOMETHING NEW

A classic lament from newly identified Renaissance Souls is, "Oh, *why* didn't I learn this about myself sooner! It's too late for me to go out and start pursuing all my interests."

The funny thing is that I hear this complaint from people in *every* age bracket. When I give workshops, the twenty-somethings start mooning over all the time they wasted in college trying to adhere to just one major and pursue a single dream career. When I question them, they say, "Oh, for me to follow my Renaissance Soul interests now would require learning X or finding out about Y, and it's much too late for me to do that. I've already spent four years in college and another three paying my dues doing entry-level work." Meanwhile, the folks in their thirties, forties, fifties are sighing over these fresh-faced kids. "I wish there had been a workshop for Renaissance Souls when I was just a few years out of school," they say. "Now it's too late to get really involved in anything new." And the retirees are casting envious glances at their middle-aged comrades, muttering, "If only I'd understood Renaissance Souls at *their* age, I could have done so much more."

The truth is that we all have more time than we think. If you want to see this for yourself, take a few minutes to complete the "Give Me Time!" questionnaire below. It won't actually grant you extra time on the planet, but it *will* give you the gift of fully accounting for that gold mine of time you're perched on top of right now. For many people, performing this exercise is the *Aha!* experience that frees them to take on the Renaissance Soul challenge with true gusto.

GIVE ME TIME!

A. Quickly jot down the age to which you expect to live. _____

B. Write down your present age. _____

C. Subtract the answer on line B from your answer on line A. _____

D. Now write your present age again. _____

E. Subtract the answer on line C from the answer on line D. _____

The answer on line E (and it may be a negative number, such as −20) is your **final answer**.

What does this math have to do with how much time our Renaissance Souls have to blossom? The answer on line C shows you how many years stretch ahead of you. To put some perspective on that number, check out your final answer. That number looks in the other direction. When you were the age of your final answer, you had the very same number of years to go until your present age.

Let's look at an example from Barbara, age forty-four.

A. Quickly jot down the age to which you expect to live. <u>80</u>

B. Write down your present age. <u>44</u>

C. Subtract the answer on line B from your answer on line A. <u>36</u>

D. Now write your present age again. <u>44</u>

E. Subtract the answer on line C from the answer on line D. <u>8</u>

According to her estimate, Barbara has thirty-six years for satisfying her Renaissance Soul. "Interesting," Barbara might say, in a somewhat noncommittal fashion. But let's tell Barbara to turn her attention to her final answer and the age there. Looking forward, there are exactly as many years *ahead* of Barbara as there are *going back* all the way to when she was eight years old. That's only third grade! Think of all the things she's learned and done since then. Long division . . . grammar . . . tales of the American Revolution and the Civil

War . . . field trips, hobbies, part-time jobs, relationships. In all
the years since Barbara was eight, she's had far more experiences and honed far more skills than can possibly be enumer-
ated here. And here's the revelation: *Barbara has as much time
left to experience, learn, and do as she's had between the time she
was eight years old and now.*

But, you say: My final answer is a negative number! Not to
worry. Take a look at how John, just out of graduate school,
filled out the questionnaire.

A. Quickly jot down the age to which you expect to live. <u>85</u>

B. Write down your present age. <u>26</u>

C. Subtract the answer on line B from your answer on line A. <u>59</u>

D. Now write your present age again. <u>26</u>

E. Subtract the answer on line C from the answer on line D. <u>-33</u>

John's estimate is that he has fifty-nine years remaining.
Going the other way, John wasn't even alive fifty-nine years
ago. In fact, he would be −33 years old. In other words, he'd
have thirty-three years to "blow" before he was even born!

Finally, let's look at the questionnaire for Irene, age sixty-
four.

A. Quickly jot down the age to which you expect to live. <u>88</u>

B. Write down your present age. <u>64</u>

C. Subtract the answer on line B from your answer on line A. <u>24</u>

D. Now write your present age again. <u>64</u>

E. Subtract the answer on line C from the answer on line D. <u>40</u>

Irene has twenty-four years ahead of her. Going back the other way takes her to age forty Does that seem like a long time ago? I asked her that very question. "Oh my gosh," she said, "that seems so far off I can hardly remember! I guess one of my girls was still in high school. I hadn't even taken a painting class. No, I was studying Italian back then!"

"Oh, but what if I don't make it to eighty-eight?" Irene protested. So she decided to knock her predicted age back ten years. That put her final answer at age fifty. What had she been up to then? Had she felt it was too late to start anything new at that age? "At fifty I was taking my first watercolor class. And I was loving it! And I was thinking of signing up for a creative writing seminar offered by the local college."

Irene had one other concern. "What if I get sick?" she asked (as so many people do). "What if I start going downhill?" So, just to be safe, she took a few more years off her maximum age to allow for disability, putting her answer on line A at seventy-three. In this scenario, she'd *still* have nine years for all her projects.

But Irene looked concerned. Nine years seemed paltry compared to the other answers she'd received. I suggested she think of it this way. Nine years equals 468 weeks. How many weeks are in, say, a long vacation? Two? Four? Or the whole summer—around ten weeks? If Irene were suddenly offered a 468-week vacation, wouldn't she feel that she had plenty of time to explore her interests? It would be like having almost fifty summers' worth of possibility! You should have seen Irene's face when she contemplated *that.*

How about you? What have you done with your life since the age that appeared as your final answer? Have you been to college, served in the military, had a family? Learned to type or surf the Internet? Grown your own food, or your own business? Joined a church, business club, co-op, fraternity? Been a member of a dance troupe, political party, writing group? Enjoyed learning musical instruments or foreign languages? Remember, there are as many years *going forward* between your present age and the age to which you expect to live as there are *going back* to the age listed as your final answer. No matter what your age, you are young enough to relish your Renaissance Soul.

Like Irene, you may worry that your answer in the Give Me Time! work is skewed because it doesn't reflect the possibility of illness and disability in later years. Fair enough; if you're worried about this, you can always bring down your numbers accordingly. But don't make the mistake of assuming that age *itself* is a disability. Who's to say when, as Irene put it, we start "going downhill"? Was Yeats going downhill when he published his *Last Poems* and *Two Plays* at age seventy-three? How about Michelangelo? He'd just begun designing the monumental dome of St. Peter's Basilica at seventy-two. Two of the most revered Stradivarius violins were crafted when their maker was in his nineties. Helen Keller still had the energy at seventy-five to publish *Teacher*, a book about how Anne Sullivan helped her overcome being blind, deaf, and mute. Opera writer Giuseppe Verdi composed *Othello* at seventy-four, and *Falstaff* at eighty.

And we can't forget the "Honda Honey," an eighty-year-old Michigan woman who rode 2,800 miles on a motorcycle in 1989. She also took up waterskiing at fifty-seven, acting on her belief that people shouldn't just sit and relax, but rather should seek out and respond to new challenges.

"Oh, but Margaret," someone in my workshops inevitably says, "maybe it's always possible to take up waterskiing or riding motorcycles, but what if I told you I wanted to be a doctor?" There are many ways to respond to ambitious goals such as getting an MD. A few careers really are stamped indelibly with expiration dates: Anyone donning their first pair of toe shoes after the ripe old age of fifteen probably isn't going to dance for the Joffrey. If you're over forty-five, I'll wager that you won't make it past the first cut of NFL training camp.

But many big dreams remain surprisingly within reach. Consider Robert Lopatin's story. A son of a garment manufacturer, he knew, even when he was in college, that he was headed to work for his father's business. Even though he dreamed of going to medical school, Lopatin majored in sociology while also studying Spanish, French, and art history. He put those interests on hold as he took over the family company. In the spring of 1992, he left the business a successful man. Still searching for direction, he took calculus and Shakespeare classes, then departed that summer for an archaeological dig in Belgium. Then, on the Sunday after the dig was over, Robert attended a wedding in Switzerland and struck up a conversation with a medical student. Old passions were stirred, and he knew what he had to do: become a doctor. So at forty-eight this man who, with his father, had built a multimillion-dollar garment company, started down the road of medical school. By age fifty-eight he was in his first year of residency, working eighty- and one-hundred-hour weeks. In some cases, patients confided symptoms to him that they would have felt uncomfortable revealing to younger residents.

Thoughtlessly assuming that "it's too late" may just keep us from enjoying our Renaissance souls to their fullest!

ON BIOLOGICAL CLOCKS AND GOLD WATCHES

Renaissance Souls can feel that they're "too old" at any age. But a few groups are especially likely to make this objection.

Women in their late thirties and forties tend to be extra-panicked by the sense that their time's almost up. As their biological clocks wind down, women are just gearing up for some of the most exciting and productive years of their lives. But although they *say* they plan to enjoy many more decades of exploration and possibility, many of them betray their own words by telling me, "By the time my last kid is out of high school, I'll be practically over the hill," or "Yes, now that I *finally* have the chance to pursue what I want, I'd better not slip up."

Why would women feel themselves in the clutches of time at this relatively early age? Well, for centuries women were told that bearing children was their main—and perhaps only—task. Giving birth and raising little ones to independence was often a woman's only way to leave her mark on the planet. Coming to the end of her childbearing years was akin to closing down the productive, useful part of her life. Her work here was done! Now, of course, the thinking has changed, at least for most of us. But that "time's up" feeling lingers like a bad aftertaste. Women who intellectually understand that they have many decades stretching ahead of them may *unconsciously* feel a

COMMON DOUBT #2: BUT I REALLY WANT TO BE
AN EXPERT AT *SOMETHING*

*C*an't you hear that old taunt—*jack-of-all-trades, master of none*? In our culture, we often assume that to be passionate about a certain subject means to be unswerving in our focus. We may recall the classic Disney movie *The Absent-Minded*

need to stake their claim in a hurry. If they don't figure out their lives soon, they think to themselves, they'll have blown their last shot at getting it right.

If it's the fortieth birthday that hits women hardest, Renaissance men have a tougher time when they're facing age fifty. It's at this age when our culture says that men should be at their peak of accomplishment, with one hand grasping for that top rung of the ladder. If women are scared to hear the fading tick of their biological clocks, many men at this age are attuned to another sound—the winding up of that fabled pocket watch given during retirement ceremonies. They may talk about sailing full-steam ahead well past the official retirement age, but inside they feel those ultimate ten or fifteen years of work are their last chance to do anything really significant.

And if a man in his fifties decides to follow his latest and truest interests, his courageous act of change is often written off as a midlife crisis. He finds himself the brunt of jokes about trophy wives and red convertibles. If the change involves a dramatic drop in status or salary, he rarely receives adequate support or understanding. Most men who are contemplating how to free their Renaissance Souls can foresee this unkind response, and it can add to their feeling that time is putting the squeeze on them.

Recognizing the source of anxiety can be a relief for many people in these two groups; these fears about time running out often fade when they are identified and examined consciously.

Professor, in which a fanatical scientist is so absorbed in his rubbery, bouncy invention that he forgets to attend his own wedding—twice. Or we imagine the obsessed writer pouring out her soul in a garret, oblivious to the cold and unwilling to stanch the flow of words long enough to eat her meager crust of bread. Implicit in these images is the idea that expertise is achieved only through exclusivity; that in order to commit to any of our own strong passions, we will have to give up all the other things we love.

This is absolutely *not* the case. Not only do Renaissance Souls have loads of interests; they are often capable of bringing a passionate level of intensity to several of them at once. My client Isaac, for example, finds that by rotating through his interests, he can maintain a high level of engagement with each one: "I love both my sculpting and the sales challenge of connecting with the world of art connoisseurs who are interested in what I do, but these are two completely different interests. So some weeks I devote myself completely to sculpture—living, eating, sometimes even sleeping in my studio— while other weeks I one hundred percent enjoy getting out there and hustling, to put it bluntly. And then, of course, there's the pedantic business side of things—paying bills and all that. If you saw me then, you'd think I was born to be a secretary. I use that as a break between the other two activities, which are so intense." It's variety that allows Isaac to stay fresh enough to develop expertise in three disparate activities.

It is true that if you want to develop a specialized skill or knowledge base, you'll have to practice a particular activity over time. But if you don't want to devote yourself to a single activity for a long stretch, so what? You can always develop your expertise on a timetable of your own making. What about the Renaissance Soul who loves karate? He may dedicate many hours each week toward his black belt—while he also develops his psychiatry practice and studies French. It might take him longer to earn his black belt than it would a person with nothing else on his plate, but he isn't any less an expert when he gets there.

If you're the kind of Renaissance Soul who gathers interests under one umbrella, it's possible to gain expert status as quickly as anyone else. You may remember the concept of umbrellas from the previous chapter: they are professions or hobbies with a single name that cover enough different activities to delight a Renaissance Soul for a long time. Consider the Renaissance Soul with a passion for documentary filmmaking. She can develop her reputation as an expert filmmaker—while making films about all the other topics (high fashion, Roman history, subatomic physics) that fascinate her. I was able to happily hang on to a career running a bed-and-breakfast for almost a decade. Under the umbrella of "innkeeper," I could be a storyteller, interior decorator, publicity person, landscape gardener, gourmet breakfast chef, finance person, historian, travel guide, and workshop developer!—*and* I became enough of an expert that a major television network flew me across the country to share my knowledge with their viewers.

Remember, too, that expert status is not automatically conferred on anyone who pursues one single interest. There are many, many secretaries and plumbers and travel agents and cello players who do one thing their entire life without gaining any particular recognition as experts in their field. Expertise comes when a person is so turned on that he'll go that extra mile or risk trying a new idea. I would have been just one innkeeper among hundreds if I hadn't thought to develop the first national apprenticeship program for prospective bed-and-breakfast owners. The fact that I had as much "ham" in me as hostess allowed me to thrive on the public speaking opportunities that other innkeepers, wired more like Mozart, saw only as distractions to be avoided as much as possible. In fact, Renaissance Souls who enjoy stepping outside their routine to write, teach, demonstrate, or promote their business often discover a surprising result. We move into the realm of respected expert *ahead* of our more narrowly focused peers.

Renaissance Soul Marilyn Tam has been president of the Reebok Apparel and Retail Products Group and vice president of Nike, Inc. She respected her varied interests from the first day she began working in the garment industry. In doing so, she cultivated a special expertise: "From my very first job I didn't just focus on the areas the other management-track people were focusing in on. I started asking about the accounting/receiving and distribution/advertising parts of the business, and, of course, the more I did that, the more I learned. So then I'm making my part of the product better, because I've already learned what the other departments need. Then, if there didn't happen to be a new opening in my particular area as soon as I wanted one, that did not stop me. I just built on what my curiosity had allowed me to learn and moved into another area. Similarly, when I felt a company wasn't moving me fast enough, I looked to other companies." The result was an expertise—not in one aspect of the process, such as distribution, or in one product, such as socks—but in business management.

For Renaissance Souls, the surest means to expertise is honoring our passions instead of stifling them. Any other approach will backfire. If we're not motivated, we will eventually stop paying close attention and slide into bitterness. Under these conditions, we're far more likely to burn out than to boast the "expert" label.

COMMON DOUBT #3: BUT I CAN'T EARN A LIVING UNLESS I STICK TO ONE THING

Before you disown your Renaissance Soul out of a fear of financial instability, let's clear up one big misconception. So you think the grass is greener on the other side of the fence—the

side with the career ladders and the so-called steady paychecks? I say: That grass looks pretty parched and brown to
me. Let me tell you why.

You may have grown up hearing, "If you want to make
money, go into business, or become a lawyer, or a plumber, or
a chemist, chef, doctor, whatever—pay your dues and then
stick to it!" We're taught that once we've chosen our professional ladder, started at the bottom, and then proceeded step
by linear step to the remunerative top, we will make ourselves
rich and our families proud. And yes, there was a brief period
in the history of time—basically, the latter half of the twen-
tieth century—when a person could be hired fresh out of
school by a large corporation and steadily climb that corporation's ladder to more and more money and perks, until he (and
sometimes she) retired with a good pension and absolutely no
financial concerns. Almost everyone who worked hard and remained loyal was basically guaranteed a certain level of economic success, with no fears of ending life as a Bowery bum
or a bag lady.

But that little economic blip on time's radar screen has
vanished. The economy has changed, and I m not just talking
about how the stock market behaved in one particular year or
whether jobs were lost or created during another. The economy will always experience cycles that are punctuated by periodic downturns and exuberant swings upward. When we (or
our parents) were forming assumptions about the world of
work, we took those cycles into account. Back then, the pre-
vailing wisdom was that if you *did* lose your job during hard
times, you'd be rehired when the economy perked back up.
But the last few swings up and down haven't landed us where
we were before. They have sculpted a dramatically different
economic landscape.

One new reality is that many jobs are going away—

permanently. In some instances, low wages and tax loopholes have enticed corporations to move their businesses offshore. In the last few years, millions of factory jobs in the United States have packed up and moved abroad. Jobs in the service industry and information technology are leaving permanently also. Some of my clients have had to suffer the indignity of training their own replacements overseas, knowing that the result of their efforts will be the elimination of their own position at home. These jobs aren't the victims of periodic dips in the economy, and they aren't coming back.

What about those supposedly stable white-collar jobs? They're being gobbled up by greater technological efficiency and new management styles that squeeze more out of each worker. And most of us know that companies no longer feel loyal to their employees. We've all heard—or lived—horror stories about employees who sacrificed thirty years to a corporation, only to be sloughed off a few years before retirement. I think of one client, a single-career man named Frank, who has lost his job in the medical-equipment industry three times in the last fifteen years, thanks to downsizing or mergers. Now Frank is in his late fifties, unemployed again, and hoping to find a position that he can ride out until retirement age—a number that he's had to push back from sixty-five to sixty-eight to seventy as his savings have shrunk. William J. Morin, a veteran career manager for executives, put the new white-collar reality in stark terms for the readers of *Fortune*, asking, "What do you expect? You do understand that the old social contract between US companies and their employees has expired, don't you? Surely you no longer believe that unconditional loyalty, or even doing a good job, guarantees employment. . . . change has become an accepted fact of life and reengineering is no longer an emergency exercise" (12/9/96).

And should we talk about pensions and benefits? Some

companies change their retirement or health plans so that they're much less advantageous, leaving their employees with two options: accept the new terms, or find a new job. Some businesses have quietly reduced or even eliminated the health benefits they'd promised their retirees.

Yes, the news is gloomy. But it's *liberating* to pose this question: Do I really want to pursue one interest for life, in search of financial security that is essentially a mirage? If you can accept that there's no real link between economic security and the one-career life, you can spare yourself the nagging feeling that you'd do better by fencing yourself into a one-career pasture. The grass really isn't greener over there, so learn to enjoy the eats where you are!

Passion Is Your Power

When you decide to work with your Renaissance Soul nature rather than fighting it, you actually welcome distinct economic benefits into your life. One advantage you acquire is passion, a force that attracts others to you. Let me explain.

Question: When there's heavy competition among qualified people for scarce positions, who's more likely to land a job—Renaissance Souls or people who've held steady to one career?

Answer: Neither.

Whether economic winds blow you out of a job, or whether your changing interests send you in search of a new position, what matters when you're looking to get hired isn't necessarily a long track record in one career. What matters is whether your performance sparkles with passion.

Here's an example. A few years ago, three hospitals near my town merged and consolidated their staffs. Dozens of nurses received pink slips instead of paychecks, and over the course of several months I saw many of them (as it turned out, they were all women) for career counseling. A few of these nurses were Renaissance Souls who had stifled other interests to pursue what they felt was one of the most secure lines of work around. "There will *always* be jobs for nurses," parents and teachers had advised them. Now these women were having a terrible time finding new jobs and suffering through long stretches of unemployment.

I also worked with women who'd gone into nursing because they loved the job. Some were the Mozarts of their profession, who'd dreamed of becoming nurses since they were old enough to wrap bandages around their sick teddy bears. Others were Renaissance Souls who'd joined the profession more recently, as a result of following their latest passions. They ate up its combination of hard science, common sense, and compassionate caregiving. They thrilled to their busy schedules. And do you know what? *These* nurses, who thrived on what they were doing—no matter whether they'd been on the job for a lifetime or a few years—found new jobs within a relatively short period of time, for two primary reasons.

First, their love of nursing had naturally led to professional development. While their less enthusiastic coworkers had settled for the easiest, most convenient way to fulfill their continuing-education requirements, these nurses were the first to sign up for demanding conferences on nontraditional nursing practices in pediatrics or seminars on new care strategies for hospital patients with Alzheimer's. While attending conferences, instead of cutting out early and heading for the nearest beach with their bored and burned-out colleagues, they eagerly stuck around to ask questions of presenters and panelists.

And second, whenever their excitement led them into a

discussion with another health professional, these nurses strengthened their network of contacts. Every day that they exhibited dedication and enthusiasm on the job, they built up their reputation with supervisors and coworkers. So when the merger occurred, these women—Renaissance Souls and non-Renaissance Souls alike—had dozens of contacts to call on, the kind who could say, "Hmmm . . . I've heard that a nurse in the neonatology ward at St. Francis might retire soon. You took that class on nontraditional pediatrics practices, right? Let me place a phone call on your behalf." They had a solid leg up compared to the nurses who had ignored their passions to squeeze into the nursing box—those nurses who weren't doing what they loved—and it showed. When it came time for them to drag out their resumes for a job search, their support networks were flimsy. As a result, they had to rely on responding to stale want ads and cold-calling.

The people who are most secure are *not* those who pick one career and stick with it. They are the people who follow their passion—or passions. This is true for both the ducks and the swans among us. Some of the saddest clients I have worked with are those who "ate their souls to fill their bellies," choosing traditional fields such as computer science, business management, nursing, or teaching, not because those fields were a good fit for their particular passion(s), but because they thought of work as a ticket to security. When they found themselves unexpectedly cast out by economic forces, they were unable to compete for scarce jobs with those whose enthusiasm led to glow-in-the-dark recommendations.

The moral of the story? Trying to squeeze your square peg into a round hole is a bad idea, even in the virtuous pursuit of job security. Only by staying in tune with your passions will you acquire the glowing references and kindred-spirit networking contacts that will pull you through times of change,

---

ECONOMIC ADVANTAGES TO BEING A RENAISSANCE SOUL

1. Passion makes your performance sparkle, giving you an edge over "lifers."
2. An ability to embrace change is valued within today's corporate world and in the new "free agent nation."
3. You're more likely to be a successful entrepreneur when you thrive on wearing many hats.
4. Love of variety makes you a great project manager and troubleshooter.
5. People who enjoy learning new languages and exploring many cultures are highly valued in the global economy.

whether that change is imposed from without or within. For the Renaissance Soul, "security" means creating a life that goes with, rather than against, your Renaissance nature.

In Times of Change, an Ability to Embrace Change Is in Demand

Another economic benefit of accepting your Renaissance Soul is that your love of variety is a marketable asset. The new economy requires an ability to stay light on one's feet, to adapt quickly to change. For some, this means accepting the trend toward outsourcing work and setting up shop as a free agent. But change is now a constant within the corporate world as well. An engineer who has spent the last two decades designing propellers alone in her office must now become a team player, working in tandem with employees from sales and marketing. A therapist accustomed to working with patients over the course of months or years must now find ways to ferret out a client's major problems—and produce solutions—within the ten or so sessions allowed by a corporate HMO.

For people who cling to the familiar, new work requirements are frightening. They stand at the base of the learning curve and moan at the thought of the uphill climb ahead of them. But for Renaissance Souls? Why, we thrive on that steep portion of the learning curve—and we go into new situations with a more positive psychology than many of our counterparts.

Susan Hawkins, who spent nearly twenty years as a human resources professional at several large American companies and now works as a career consultant, offers this analogy: "Think of it this way. On the one hand, there are employees who have basically followed the old one-track career ladder, staying in pretty much the same position at the same company for years. They're like drivers who travel the same route to work each day, knowing exactly where they're headed and where they're going to park; they're practically on automatic pilot. On the other hand, there are employees who have been at a variety of companies, worked in a variety of different positions, maybe taken time off to travel or run their own business. In today's highly competitive constantly changing work environment, more and more companies want people like this. Why? Because they are much more adept at listening for change and noticing what needs to be done differently and more creatively inside the department, the company, or even the market that the company is maneuvering within."

Savvy Renaissance Souls learn to highlight this quality in their resumes. Instead of apologizing for their many talents, they say with confidence, "I can move from one role to another with ease." Department of Labor statistics predict that the current crop of college graduates will change jobs between eight and ten times over the course of a lifetime; many will cross from one field to another at least once or twice. To many employers, a varied, multidimensional resume displays flexibility, not immaturity. Says Laurie Jadick, vice president for human resources at a major information technology firm, "If I [am considering] the 'organization professional' and the professional who has built a variety of experiences into their dossier—even taking time off to study a language or paint, I will look at the nontraditionalist first. . . . To be an industry leader, a business needs to attract and hire people who have sought out change and embraced it and grown from it."

Carole Brown is the managing director of the Thinking Team, a consulting firm whose clients include Citibank, Shell, and Deutsche Bank. She says: "To put it bluntly: in today's business world, adaptation is the name of the game. In order to succeed, organizations have to realize that. Once they do, they recognize the need for employees who adapt quickly and easily. And who are these people? They're the ones with the broadest range of skills and employment experiences. People who are not limited to working in only one corporate culture."

Bernie Saunders, an organizational and leadership development consultant and coauthor of *Ten Steps to a Learning Organization*, notes that companies are increasingly willing to teach technical or other skills to applicants who offer an attractive mix of flexibility and openness to change. He believes that companies look for a "right attitude" toward challenge. When I asked him to describe this attitude, he gave an answer that should make Renaissance Souls smile: "a lot of agility, adaptability, a natural propensity toward curiosity, an insatiable appetite for that and this and this and that!"

If you aim for the very highest corporate level, you may experience a range of responses to your background. Renaissance Soul Steve John says, "I've been a senior director in a global pharmaceutical firm, senior vice president in a financial services firm on Wall Street, and a principal in a big consulting firm. But I don't believe I'll ever get to the tip tip top of an organization. . . . The closer you get to the top of the pyramid, the more loyal you have to be to 'the cause.' People sense that I don't march to the beat of that drum."

But Marilyn Tam, the woman we met earlier in this chapter, who held high positions at both Reebok and Nike, believes otherwise. "As an Asian woman, I am not the stereotypical top-level executive," she says. "But I made it to 'the top' because over and over people saw that I have a very wide and deep experience in a lot of different areas. In today's complex and interrelated world, CEOs can't have a narrow base of knowledge: they have to understand and appreciate every aspect of the business and the world they're doing business in. Understanding the many facets of today's international and fast-changing workplace is critical. So who gets promoted? The person with the most diverse interests. And who's that? People like us, the Renaissance Souls!"

Not *every* company or industry is ready for Renaissance Souls. Bernie Saunders points out that "even now, places like NASA probably look for lifelong astrophysicists." Susan Hawkins reminds us that old-guard insurance companies are less accepting of change, and so are certain departments, such as accounting, across the business world. Hawkins suggests that Renaissance Souls train their sights on what she calls "agile" industries that put a premium on change. Retail, information technology, medical-supply companies, electronic services, and consulting organizations are just a few. Even within the more staid industries, departments such as marketing and product development need people who, as Hawkins says, "can bring a variety of flexible and multifaceted skills to the table."

"I CAN DO WHATEVER I WANT":
PORTRAIT OF A RENAISSANCE SOUL

Like many musicians, Ric Cherwin struggled to make ends meet. When a chance encounter exposed him to the world of art auctioneering, he thought—in typical Renaissance Soul fashion—*I could do that!* Auctioneering became financially as well as personally satisfying, and soon he was making five figures per auction.

Ric then found himself drawn to a newly opened progressive law school. He helped put himself through those three long years of study by producing nightly entertainment for a major Manhattan hotel. After graduating from law school, Ric gave his attention to the small legal firm that hired him. He didn't love the paperwork and dry court presentations, but he *did* love helping women obtain child support from deadbeat dads. The firm soon offered him a partnership. Was he interested? Full-time? Forever? No way.

Instead, Ric continued to practice his activist legal work on a part-time basis. In his free time, he grew his own business: the Ric Cherwin Agency. An extension of his production work, the agency booked entertainment for the World Series, the US Open, and the Tribeca Film Festival.

By following his passions, Ric has become financially secure. He enjoys the outward trappings of success—a Manhattan apartment, a second home in the country—but he's most grateful for the freedom he enjoys. "Now I can do whatever I want," he says. He can afford to be choosy, taking on only those law clients who interest him the most, and accepting invitations for only the most intriguing art auctions. He still sings and performs whenever he feels like it. And are you surprised to hear that he got a master's in social work and now has a small but thriving psychotherapy practice?

This book won't teach you how to spin Renaissance Soul straw into gold and instant fame. You'll have to work just as hard as anyone else at making a living. But the idea that everyone on the Mozart end of the continuum will be financially successful and everyone on the Ben Franklin end will inevitably suffer is absolutely false. Let's not forget that it was Mozart who was buried in a pauper's grave, while Franklin died a successful and wealthy man.

COMMON DOUBT #4: BUT WHAT IF I DON'T WANT TO BE A RENAISSANCE SOUL?

*O*kay," you may be thinking, "I've taken the test and I know that I'm a Renaissance Soul. I get that Renaissance Souls are like the little swan in 'The Ugly Duckling' story. They are beautiful in their own way, and they can make money, and they can become experts, . . . but what if I just don't want to be a swan? What if I *want* to be a duck and just settle down and do one thing for the rest of my life?"

If you're still asking these questions, I'll bet you've spent your life desperately wanting to please a parent, or a spouse, or a voice inside your head saying *You're not a grown-up until you decide on one career!* And that's what you may have hoped to find in this book: how to figure out your singular, for-the-rest-of-your-life path. You've believed that there *is* such a road out there for you, and if I'd just point the way, you'd pack your bags and doggedly follow it wherever it leads. This is perfectly understandable. The cultural messages about what constitutes legitimate success and adulthood are strong. But you cannot change who you are.

If you feel a sense of loss as you move to a new understanding of your Renaissance Soul, it is important for you to honor that grief. Whether you feel that your grief is "rational" or not is immaterial. What *is* critical is to define the feelings that you presently have. Ignoring them makes them no less present, and while they are present but not dealt with, they will prevent you from fully embracing your Renaissance Soul. Most of us have developed our own ways of processing difficult feelings: writing in a journal, talking with friends, taking time alone. I hope you'll take some time to engage in that process.

"Just as a duck can't force its neck to grow longer to please the swans of the world," I frequently remind my clients, "so a swan cannot will its neck to be shorter to match that of a duck parent or to fit the needs of a duck career counselor, spouse, or partner." In order to get anywhere truly satisfying in our lives, we have to be true to who we *are*, not who we might wish to be. If we can accept our swan selves, we open ourselves to what life can truly hold.

The Pulitzer Prize–winning author Studs Terkel, who has interviewed thousands of Americans from all races, religions, and walks of life, offers an observation meant for everyone but with a particular poignancy for Renaissance Souls: "Most of us have jobs that are too small for our spirits." With all our different interests, we definitely can't allow ourselves to get stuck in *that* trap: We need to design a multifaceted life big enough to accommodate our Renaissance Souls.

Next, I'll introduce you to the principles that give you room to lead that big life, one with plenty of space for both your basic values and your multitude of passions: Part II will show you how to thrive on many interests without being too scattered; Part III will address the practical realities of making money while pursuing your passions.

Part II

Thriving on Many Interests
Without Feeling Scattered

THREE

Panning for Golden Values

As a Renaissance Soul, of course I get so excited about so many things. I just wish there were some kind of a litmus test I could use to tell which of all my enthusiasms it makes sense to follow.

—*Felix, sixty-two*

iners who pan for gold don't overload their backpacks with every stone that happens to catch their eye. No, to be really successful they have to distinguish between fool's gold and the rocks whose essence is truly valuable.

This chapter is a course in mining your own fertile terrain. You'll dig down deep in search of your purest beliefs; you'll examine them to see which form the bedrock for your creative, intellectual, and spiritual lives. Given how many things compete for your attention, it's worthwhile to develop the gold-rush skills of sifting through raw matter and recognizing those elements that are truly precious. And remember, we Renaissance Souls are constantly changing. When you emerge from this very personal work, you'll have a clear sense of the values that really matter to you *at this stage of your life*. What values do you want to live by *now*? Not what you valued, or were valued for, in the past. Not what you hope will be the values of your future. But what do you value *today*? These values will form the basis of the decisions you make about your career and life design.

This process is crucial because so many Renaissance Souls have difficulty trusting their decisions. For example, my client Richard, a mid-level employee at a local university, came to me because his life felt "helter-skelter." He decided during our first session that he wanted to focus his current energies on four interests: fathering, playing the flute, fixing things, and collecting farm implements. He left feeling quite chipper, but when he returned the following week, he was no longer so sure of himself. "How can I be certain I really want to take up *these* interests?" he wondered. "Couldn't I just as easily have chosen four others? I don't feel as if I've been struck by lightning." Much to his surprise, I agreed.

Like many other Renaissance Souls, Richard wanted to believe that there was a lightning-bolt litmus test out there that could assure him that *this* time he was definitely, absolutely, positively on the right track. That's what we imagine eight-year-old Bill Clinton felt when he suddenly knew he wanted to be president. And maybe he did. But you will never be so uninterested in all the other options out there to be sure without the shadow of a doubt that your choices are the best ones.

I've heard Renaissance Souls who have been coached in the language of talk shows and self-help books knock themselves for their "inability to make good choices." They don't understand that the choices they've left behind could well have been good ones they've simply outgrown. If you lack confidence in your own decisions, you may have a long history of beating up on yourself when you dropped one passion for another. You may have fallen into the trap of thinking that your *different* choices must have been the *wrong* choices. This is usually far from the case.

One of the best ways to dispel uncertainty is to clarify what you value. When Renaissance Soul Barbara couldn't decide which of her many interests to pursue, she made a confession. "I'm embarrassed to say this," she admitted, "but what's *really* important to me is being famous." It turned out that Barbara was the middle child in a large family. She had three older siblings and three younger ones. When her parents wanted to get her attention, they often rattled off three or four other names before finally coming up with the correct one, and most outsiders couldn't remember her name at all. As Barbara and I talked further, it became clear that she wasn't so much interested in national fame as in personal recognition: "When I walk into a room, I want everyone to know my name!" She ended up having a ball by volunteering at an elementary school and then eventually becoming the children's librarian in a small town. "Now whenever I walk down the street, children run up to me, yelling, 'Mrs. O'Hare! Mrs. O'Hare!' I love it. They know exactly who I am."

The work you'll perform here is an act of preparation. The three exercises you'll be doing (Five from Fifty, Many Circles, and Throw Your Own Birthday Party) are tools that many Renaissance Souls before you have been grateful to have. The values you discover will guide the decisions you'll make about how you'll earn income, manage your time, and select your current favorites from the activities that interest you. Values are not some abstract concepts reserved for Sunday school or other times we set aside for thinking about being better people. I promise you this: If you separate your actions from your integrity, you will end up sabotaging yourself.

Martha came to me a few months after her husband, Nick, landed his first significant job in a law firm. Just after he began the new job, they bought a house in a somewhat pricey neighborhood. Martha immediately set herself to the task of decorating their new home from top to bottom. In addition to caring for her young son, her days were full of meetings with interior designers, measuring for drapes, and combing boutiques for just the right end tables. When she called me for a session, she felt strangely drained. She was overwhelmed by the circus of ongoing design projects, often overlooking important details, yet she wasn't particularly happy when any one of the projects was completed. Only when we looked at how this decorating activity fit in with her values did Martha figure out what was wrong. She confessed she was redecorating to keep up with the exacting standards of the neighborhood. In fact, she said that she'd much rather be spending her precious free time pursuing her interests in music and environmental science. "I'd really rather put my time and resources there than in tile for my foyer!" she said.

People who aren't fully committed to the values that their activities represent sputter through life, pulled in one direction by their commitments and in another by their spirits. Like Martha, they feel vaguely dissatisfied but they're not sure why. They notice that nothing seems to *move* for them in the way that it does for others. When people who are stuck like this tune into their values, they locate a source of abundant energy and they learn they can be carried forward by their own motivation.

The three exercises I'm about to show you won't necessarily establish a direct link between your values and the actions you'll take later. Instead, they form a series of prospectors' tools, designed to help you see which choices are aligned with your deepest and most genuine motives. You may find that they point to an area of your life that matters to you but has been neglected. Or you may realize that your plans to start up a new business aren't *your* plans at all. They belong to a parent or spouse or someone other than you.

I find that sometimes my clients resist identifying their values at first. They feel they already understand their morals and principles, or they believe thinking about these concepts isn't "interesting" enough. Yet it is often these same people who, upon completing this work, are electrified by their new sense of mission.

FIVE FROM FIFTY

*I*n the following list you'll see fifty abstract concepts, all of which can be held as important values. In fact, I'd be willing to bet you're likely to say that most or even *all* of these concepts are integral to your personal values system! And that's precisely what makes this exercise so challenging—and so clarifying. I'm asking you to read the list of fifty values and choose the five that are most important to you *right now*.

You don't need to assign an order to the five values you choose. But chances are you'll have to think very hard to narrow down your list. Will it be creativity, for example, that makes the cut, or community? Since most of us are not asked to examine our values very often, you may find that you need an evening or even a few days to mull over your choices. It's perfectly fine to take as much time as you need.

Don't worry about whether you have the "correct" understanding of each term; use whatever definition makes the most sense to you. You may find that two or more of the terms are very close in meaning. That's an intentional element of the exercise, one that will force you to think sharply about which one matters more to you. I've left additional space for you to add values you feel are important but that do not appear on the list.

FIVE FROM FIFTY

Choose the five values most important to you *at this moment.*

Achievement	Health (emotional)	Privacy
Affection	Health (physical)	Recognition
Appearance	Home	Relationships
Approval	Honesty	Religion
Arts	Integrity	Reputation
Authority	Learning	Respect
Beauty	Leisure	Risk Taking
Career/Employment	Love	Security
Community	Loyalty	Social Acceptance
Creativity	Meaning	Socializing
Environment	Money	Solitude
Expertise	Openness	Spiritual Development
Fame	Patriotism	Status
Family	Personal Growth	Winning
Freedom (personal)	Pleasure	Wisdom
Freedom (political)	Popularity	
Generosity	Power	

As you went through this exercise, did any interesting information emerge? Did "family" make it into your top five, for example? If so, be sure that your future decisions regarding careers or interests allow you to practice your emphasis on family. Perhaps, like Richard—who identified being a good father as one of his interests—you'll want to reflect family in the activities you'll decide to pursue. Or maybe you'll need to double-check that your plans aren't so demanding that they negatively affect the family you value so highly.

Did Career/Employment make your top five? Was it accompanied by Security, Status, Money, or Power? This can give you a clue about how important paid work is to your sense of identity. Consider Lou, a lawyer and Renaissance Soul who had set up his own practice to escape the rigid hierarchy and enforced specialization of a law firm. He was surprised to find that at age fifty, security made it into his top five values. He realized that he was ready to commit to a nine-to-five job as a lawyer for the city Department of Transportation in order to gain the retirement benefits he craved. He was delighted to discover that he was working far fewer evenings and weekends than when he ran his own business, and that he had more time to pursue his passion for Italian cooking and his sideline as a night court judge.

Consider Amy, a Renaissance Soul whose goals had long included winning a Northeast archery championship. Amy knew that most champions at this level of competition practiced for several hours a day, every day, for years before their first win. Yet she had never managed to begin a serious training program. Amy began to doubt herself: Was she incapable of the immense physical effort? Was she lazy?

It wasn't until she identified her values that Amy realized the problem: This rigorous training was in conflict with the way Amy expressed her value of "family." She'd have to cut back too much on time with her husband, and there would be far fewer long weekends spent traveling to visit members of her beloved extended family. As she considered the issue, Amy decided that she'd much rather spend time with her loved ones than become the sole archery star of her entire region. Instead, she decided to train at a less intense level, one that would help her gain *eligibility* to compete in the archery championship. She'd leave the winner's podium to others.

It's so easy for Renaissance Souls to say, "I *want to* do *X* because it's interesting and I *want to* do *Y* because it's satisfying. . . ." and so on. Taking time to evaluate your values is a rigorous challenge that helps you feel more confident about the precision with which you have defined your *want to*'s.

A second way to examine what you value is via the Many Circles exercise shown on the following page. This exercise asks you to think about values in a more concrete way, requiring you to rank ten broad areas of life in order of their importance to you. Take a look at the circles pictured here. Now, here are ten possible life goals to think about:

+ Continuing personal growth and healing
+ Earning respect from my colleagues
+ Improving spiritual balance
+ Increasing competence
+ Maintaining physical health
+ Making a contribution
+ Moving my business to a new level
+ Opening communication
+ Securing finances
+ Sustaining interpersonal relationships

(Students can adjust a couple of the goals to better suit their circumstances. "Moving my business to a new level"

MANY CIRCLES

Look at the list at the lower right. Pick any of the titles that interest you. Match circle titles with the circle sizes as you think appropriate. The more important the title is, the larger the circle you assign to it. You can use as many of the titles as you wish, and can replace any with one(s) more important to you.

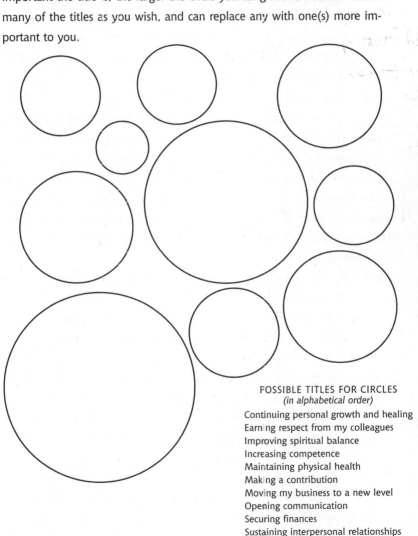

FOSSIBLE TITLES FOR CIRCLES
(in alphabetical order)
Continuing personal growth and healing
Earning respect from my colleagues
Improving spiritual balance
Increasing competence
Maintaining physical health
Making a contribution
Moving my business to a new level
Opening communication
Securing finances
Sustaining interpersonal relationships

could become "Graduating with honors"; "Earning respect from my colleagues" easily changes to "Earning respect from teachers/fellow students.")

Now take another look at those ten circles. The goal that is most important to you *right now* goes into the largest circle, the second-largest circle gets the second-most important goal, and so on. You'll label the very smallest circle with the goal that is least important to you at this moment. If you would like to replace any of the goals I've listed with one of your own choosing, by all means do so.

What was that exercise like for you? Did you perhaps find the biggest and littlest circles quite easy to label but have trouble with the "middle" ones? I've had clients share with me that the very struggle they went through making those less obvious choices gave them an idea they might not have otherwise considered. Once, a participant in one of my workshops wavered about whether to put "Sustaining interpersonal relationships" into one of the bigger circles or into a smaller one. She was surprised that the topic asserted its importance at all. She got along well with her new love and her stepson and had a great relationship with her mom and stepdad. But even as she said this, she realized, "Hey, I've been both a stepdaughter and a stepmom. And I've been frustrated at times in both situations because there wasn't a Dear Abby advice column for people in my shoes. I bet that's something I'd have a ball doing! Writing a column like that might be really interesting. . . ." She then proposed a question-and-answer column for blended families for her local paper, which snapped up the idea.

Sometimes it's the combination of exercises that produces a surprise. This was the case for Janet, a Renaissance Soul in her early thirties who worked for an investment bank. "I had no idea creativity was a value I considered very important," she said. "Not that I considered it *un*important, but I just had never given it much thought. And yet, try as I might, when I did the Five from Fifty Exercise, I just could not seem to kick it out of my top five. My *top five*! It was like it had a mind of its own. My other four values were Achievement, Expertise, Power, and Security, so you can see how out of place creativity seemed. At least if you think of it as painting and novel writing and all that. They're not me at all."

Then Janet went on to the Many Circles Exercise. "You know what came up there? 'Increasing competence' even beat out 'Securing finances' for the largest circle. And when I thought about what these two exercise outcomes were saying, I realized that I was thinking about how to be more creative at work! That's what I wanted, and that's the competence I wanted to increase. I'd like to develop creative training materials for people who need to improve their sales. I've never done that, but I'd love to learn! And I'd like to try my hand at ways to make boring stock information more user-friendly and appealing."

THROW YOUR OWN BIRTHDAY PARTY

A classic task handed out by career counselors suggests you write your own obituary. You are asked to list the kind of accomplishments you'd want to have under your belt before the end of your life. But I find that this exercise breeds a starchy, somewhat predictable "to do" list. Most entries end up looking something like this: *He was a fine, upstanding citizen who climbed to the top of his department, went to all his kids' soccer games, and was a respected deacon in the city's largest church.* Instead of focusing on what *really* matters, this entry screams: *Please approve of me! Have I earned my gold stars yet?* For

Renaissance Souls who have come to doubt their own instincts in the first place, this kind of exercise sucks them right back into the vortex of other peoples' values, usually the ones held by their parents' generation or the culture at large. Let's adapt this old chestnut to suit our needs.

Instead of picturing yourself in need of an obituary, imagine that you've lived eighty healthy and vigorous years (with more to come!) and are throwing a big birthday bash in celebration. You've asked four people who know the *real* you to make toasts in your honor:

+ a family member
+ a friend
+ someone you've worked with
+ a person from the community (perhaps your neighborhood, the gym, volunteer group, or place of worship)

Of course, each person will have seen a different side of your personality and accomplishments. Some may tick off your achievements; others may praise less tangible qualities, such as kindness or commitment. Take some time to think about what you *genuinely* hope each of these people would say about you, and write out their "toasts" on a sheet or two of paper. If you are very young and find it simply impossible to imagine life at forty, let alone eighty, you could instead imagine asking four people who know you well (your parents? a roommate?) to write about you in your school yearbook.

After writing out the toasts, it helps to highlight or spell out in the margins the underlying values described or implied. For example, if you have your colleague describe your ascent to the vertiginous heights of the corporate boardroom, you might write "Success and commitment." If someone talks about how much she enjoyed visiting your beautifully decorated home during the holidays, you might write "Giving pleasure to others through the domestic arts."

Nearly everyone finds that some toasts are more challenging to write than others. Was there a category for which you struggled to imagine a person who might give the toast? Don't let this discourage you; many people stumble across this realization as they ponder their toasts. For example, someone may believe that community is an important value, but then discover that he doesn't know his neighbors. This person will then need to ask himself: Is community really one of my most deeply held values? If I wanted to design a life so that I could participate more fully in a community, what would that life look like?

You may discover other food for thought as you clarify your values. Take Roberto, a father in his late forties who ran a computer-programming business. He confessed that he'd done the Five from Fifty exercise almost by rote. "Of course I listed my top five values as family, patriotism, religion, respect, and risk-taking," he said, smiling. "What else would a good Hispanic Catholic ex-Marine entrepreneur choose?" His Many Circles exercise reflected the same "obvious" pattern.

"But you know what? You know what got to me?" he asked. "The Birthday Party question about what I'd like a member of my family to say about me! To be honest, it brought me up short. When I thought of what my three sons would say, it hit me real hard. I knew I *wanted* them to say that we had a much closer relationship than I had with my dad. I *wanted* them to say that I spent time with them and gave them lots of praise and helped them to think about their futures. Heck, my dad didn't do any of that. But you know what?" And here Roberto went silent for a minute, struggling to get his emotions in check. "If they spoke the truth, based on our lives right this minute, today, they wouldn't say *any* of that! Because I've been so caught up in making my company grow. Making the money my father never made, yes, but . . ." Roberto couldn't go on and sat down abruptly. I knew that by the end of the process, Roberto would create a life more congruent with his values than he would have otherwise.

WHEN YOUR VALUES ARE "EMBARRASSING"

Some values are easy to identify but hard to own up to. Barbara O'Hare, the middle-child-turned-librarian from the beginning of this chapter, was unusually up front about her desire for fame, even though she was embarrassed by it. Did *you* turn up a value that you think is embarrassing or somehow wrong? Do you want to be rich, famous, in charge, admired, or popular—and wish that you didn't?

Our culture worships the wealthy and famous. But then it turns around to admonish the rest of us to be good, modest little worker bees. "And just who do you think *you* are?" is a belittling and common challenge that can stunt the development of wealth and genius. Even kids who are pushed toward fame by stage mothers or hockey dads are taught to say that they love the "hard work," not the limelight, of stagecraft or sport. They're supposed to be the *humbly* talented, whose stars shine through a becoming cloud of modesty.

Look, if you want fame or fortune or adoration, it makes absolutely no sense to kid yourself about it. There's no use trying to ignore these values in favor of other, secondary values that you think look more impressive on paper. You're looking here for your primary motivators, the ones that power your biggest dreams. At the very least, lying to yourself about these values will divert some of that power. At the worst, it will sabotage your efforts. And *so what* if you want to be rich? Maybe you grew up poor and intend to leave poverty far, far behind. Maybe you crave the beauty (expensive artwork) and adventure (your own sailboat) that money buys. Maybe you just like money! If these are *your* intrinsic motivations, you need to work honestly and joyfully with them.

Are you worried that cash and fame will make you a bad person? Aristotle believed that Greek citizens could not be fully virtuous *without* lots of money to fund neighborhood play festivals and other good works. If you want to, use your wealth to buy a fabulous sailboat—and let the Make a Wish Foundation know that should a dying person wish for a sail up the East Coast, your boat and your energies will be available. Let your fame call attention to the causes that make sense to you. Think of Diana, Princess of Wales, who made the world care about the land mines that were killing children throughout Asia.

If an embarrassing value really bugs you, maybe it's time to check it for authenticity. Is this value you're having trouble claiming really yours? In my family, my father made "Be famous!" a directive for all of us. For years, if I loved something but felt I couldn't become the best in my field—and thereby famous—I tended to write it off. I didn't want to become a failure at famousness. What eventually got me going? Identifying my true values, the ones that took priority for me, such as spreading the word about Renaissance Souls.

Or have you mistaken one value for another? Barbara O'Hare said she wanted to be famous. That was an overstatement of the personal recognition she sought from her local community. I know other people who have panicked, thinking they were bad, greedy people because they named "wealth" as a value. Mainly, though, they just wanted to avoid the deprivation of their childhood, or to provide for their elderly parents. In these instances, renaming a value as "security" or "recognition" or "respect" or "family" is appropriate. Just be sure that you don't dilute your real dreams.

MAKING TIME FOR VALUES

*M*any "experts" will tell you that once you've articulated the big values, like spiritual development, the rest of your life will fall in line behind them. But letting go of the daily choices that don't reflect our values is much harder than that. It's so easy to fall into the habit of doing what we've always done, out of the unexamined belief that it is "right." One reason articulating your values is so useful is that it can help you carve out more time for what really matters to you.

In the daily grind, things like comparison shopping for household purchases or driving your kids to every after-school activity become so automatic that it's hard to evaluate whether your reasons for doing them even make sense. As Dorothy Lehmkul, author of *Organizing for the Creative Person*, points out, "If you're saying something is important in your life but you aren't spending time on it, then you need to change either what you say your values are, or the way you spend your time." Checking your schedule for activities that aren't truly important to you is one way to clear out space for the things that do matter.

Here's a way to discover whether you are currently putting your daily choices where your mouth is. The work below asks you to step out of the worlds of abstract thought and make-believe and into the nitty-gritty of your daily life. The following two exercises force you to ask: Do my current activities reflect my values—or someone else's? Do I want to go on living according to these values? If so, what is their appeal to me?

MINE/THEIRS EXERCISE, PART I

Take a blank piece of paper and rule off three columns. Head the first column "I. Activity," the second "II. Justification for This Activity," and the third "III. Does This Reflect My Values or 'Theirs'? (M or T)."

First, list in Column I all the "directions" you are currently running in: those piano lessons you're taking, your garden projects, driving Jill to soccer practices/games, your job, and all the delightful, if overwhelming, et ceteras that make up your life.

Second, look at each activity and ask yourself: "How do I justify spending my time doing this?" and write the answer in Column II. You may write that the reason for driving Jill to soccer practice is that "the only time Jill talks is in the car." Or you may drive Jill because "Mothers are supposed to drive their kids to every sports practice."

Third, examine your reasons for performing each activity. Look at each one to determine if it reflects a true value of *yours*, not your mother's, not your partner's, not your father's, not your ex's, not your housemate's, not your boss's, not your old college chum's. Are your reasons congruent with something you truly value, or do they represent a borrowed system of beliefs? If the trips to soccer practice represent your desire to have conversations with Jill, write a big *M* (for "Mine") beside it in Column III. If the rationale represents someone else's values, such as your parents' belief that mothers ought to drive their children everywhere, mark a big *T* (for "Theirs").

Here's how one person filled out the Mine/Theirs list.

MINE/THEIRS EXAMPLE, PART I

I. ACTIVITY	II. JUSTIFICATION FOR THIS ACTIVITY	III. DOES THIS REFLECT MY VALUES OR "THEIRS"? (M OR T)
Saturday morning housecleaning.	It's what I've always done: vacuum, dust, bathrooms, etc.	Theirs: my mom's specifically. Neither John nor I care if the house is that immaculate every week.
Watercolor lessons.	Artists need to have a wide repertoire of skills.	Mine: I love learning new painting techniques!
Grocery shopping to find best bargains.	The best way to get the best deals is to read the ads for all three stores and then make lists and go to all three. Also check ads for coupons and see which place may be giving double or triple coupons that week.	Theirs: My father made my mother account for every penny of household money, but in my family's current situation, my time is more valuable than the money I save shopping this way.
Giving our amazing holiday parties.	We're known for giving the parties. Everyone talks about them and prays they'll get an invite.	Theirs: My husband thinks this is a great way to network for his business, but in fact, by the time the party actually happens, he's so wiped out, he tends to stay down in the den watching sports with some of his old school buddies—not much networking going on.
Going to the gym five mornings a week.	Everyone says exercising on a regular basis improves our health.	Mine: Now that I have a trainer who keeps me improving, I feel so much better!

| Going to church on Sunday and being on the flower arrangement committee. | It is important to take time out from doing to focus on spiritual things, and when you belong to our church, you have to be on a committee. | **M**ine and **T**heirs: I be**l**ieve in focusing on spiri:ual things, but don't really do it in church—I'm more just standing/sitting there doing what I'm told (sing this, read that, listen now . . .). |

Once you've identified the activities that don't really reflect your current value system—these are the ones marked with the *T*s—concentrate on getting rid of them. You'll get help doing that in the Mine/Theirs Exercise, Part II.

MINE/THEIRS EXERCISE, PART II

Take a blank piece of paper and rule off two columns. Head the first column "I. 'Their' Activities" and the second column "II. How to Eliminate 'Their' Activities." In Column I, write down once again all the activities you listed as "Theirs" in Part I of this exercise. In Column II, list a step or steps you can take toward eliminating this activity from your schedule. This way, you'll practice keeping your attention focused on what really matters. If driving Jill fits your mother's value system more than it fits yours, could you join a car pool? Could your friend Nancy drive Jill in exchange for a weekly helping of your homegrown tomatoes? Is this a topic of discussion to have with your ex?

Some of you may bump up against some very big, very old messages here, the kind that say "You're a husband and father now—you don't get to do what you want!" or "People in our family *always* do such-and-such!"

It's hard to eliminate activities prompted by such potent messages. If this happens to you, feel free to jump ahead to Chapter Twelve, "If It's *Still* Hard to Get Going . . .," for help minimizing their effect on your choices.

Now let's see how the same person filled out the second table.

MINE/THEIRS EXAMPLE, PART II

I. "THEIR" ACTIVITIES	II. HOW TO ELIMINATE "THEIR" ACTIVITIES
Saturday morning housecleaning.	Get one of those books on efficient housecleaning and only do things that *really* bother *us*! Make a list of cleaning chores that can be done biweekly or even monthly.
Grocery shopping to find best bargains.	Just stop. Use my in-store card for the sales it covers and forget the rest.
Giving our amazing holiday parties.	Have a frank talk with husband. If we decide to continue throwing the event, plan it for a Sunday and have him do prep on Saturday, so he will stay upstairs for networking during the actual party. Also, keep it simple! Maybe an outdoor 4th of July party with pizza and paper plates!
Going to church on Sunday and being on the flower arrangement committee.	Attend the Sunday morning meditation session at the community center instead. Look into doing longer meditations on Thursday evenings when I used to have to deal with flower arrangements.

It's not hard to imagine that this person, having implemented the changes suggested by the Mine/Theirs work, now finds life simpler and more rewarding. Human beings—not just Renaissance Souls, but everyone—experience the most productivity, creativity, and joy when they tap into the wellspring of their most deeply held values. And honest priorities are especially important for those of us who often feel overwhelmed or guilty.

Now it's on to the centerpiece of the Renaissance Soul strategy: Renaisance Focal Points.

Here I am in college—with all this time to learn whatever I want. But how do I choose? My parents say to pick something that really appeals to me, but when I look through the course catalog there's hardly anything that doesn't appeal! Last semester I signed up for so many classes I ended up running around like a chicken with my head cut off. This semester I can't decide what to take, and I've already missed out on some classes because they closed before I went to sign up.

—Charlotte, nineteen

s a Renaissance Soul, you're full of ideas. But do you have trouble following through on them? Many of my workshop participants laugh with recognition when I quote Jeanine, a sixty-four-year-old client of mine, describing her predicament: "I don't have the slightest trouble coming up with ideas, believe me. Just ask my husband. It drives him

crazy how many things excite me—for a short time. But when it comes down to zeroing in and really following through, that can be a different story entirely."

In this chapter I'll help you break out of this behavior pattern and the unhelpful self-deprecation that so often comes with it. You'll see how it's possible to engage in a variety of interests while attracting the considerable rewards of focus and clarity into your life.

I'd like you to start by taking out a sheet of paper and listing all the interests that currently excite you, in no particular order. What would you like to be doing? What fascinates you? Which subjects call out to you? You may have just one strong calling at the moment, or you may have dozens. Either way, please know that this list isn't meant to last into eternity or even to the beginning of next month. It's just a description of your *current* interests. You may return to it anytime you like to make additions or deletions.

When you're done, ask yourself: What keeps you from following all these interests?

"Are you *serious*, Margaret?" you might ask. "Did you *see* my list? How am I going to get a PhD in archaeology and train for a triathlon and perfect the art of flaky pastry? There isn't time in *anyone's* life for all those interests, let alone mine. I've got to narrow down my choices. I know that I can't have it all."

Fair enough, but here's another question: So what keeps you from making a choice? "You've got to be kidding! How can I commit to studying archaeology when I know that means leaving behind my dream of opening my own pastry shop?"

And there's the rub. Most of us wouldn't have any trouble managing our many interests if we weren't, well, mortal. If there were no time constraints—if we didn't have to pick up the kids by two p.m., if we didn't need to devote fifty hours a week to bringing home the bacon, if we didn't have to spend all that wasted time sleeping, if we could live forever—then we wouldn't have to choose between one lively pursuit and another.

My goal here is to help you satisfy your soul here on planet Earth, where most of us do have obligations and bills and those enjoyable but time-consuming biological drives to eat and sleep. I find it interesting that in a world full of books and courses about how to manage time, improve performance, and make money, there are few pieces of advice that apply to the Renaissance Soul. What we Renaissance Souls need is a different set of tools, ones that will lend shape to our lives without fencing us in. Our style cries out for a brand-new way of thinking about life design. Let's start that new life in one of the happiest places on the planet: an ice-cream store.

THE ICE-CREAM SAMPLER

For most of our lives, choosing has meant losing. That's why I propose that you try *focusing* instead. To help you see what I mean by "focus," I'd like you to imagine for a moment that you are in an ice-cream store. This is a very fancy ice-cream shop, one that sells an amazing variety of ice creams, frozen yogurts, sorbets, sherbets, and Italian ices. If the owner asked you to choose just one flavor and only one flavor to eat today and forever after, the store would probably close around you as you tried to make the "right" decision—and you'd still be hungry.

Now what if the owner insisted that you eat *every* flavor in the store, all the thirty-plus ice creams and all the sugar-free frozen yogurts and all the fat-free frozen yogurts and all the sherbets, sorbets, soft-serve ice creams, and Italian ices—not reducing your choices by even one flavor. That, too, would stop you in your tracks, right?

It isn't too hard to see the parallel between this predicament and that of the Renaissance Soul. When we have to choose just one thing, we refuse. If we think we need to choke down everything, we're overwhelmed and confused. Either way, we're left unsatisfied.

But suppose the owner of the ice-cream store offered you another option. She smiles at you with a knowing look. "You don't have to choose between one thing and *every*thing," she says. "How about trying my famous 'four-flavor sampler?'"

The idea is simple: you can choose a platter of four flavors to enjoy during your visit. The servings aren't as large as single-flavor servings, but they're big enough to satisfy your cravings.

"Sounds nice," you say. "But hmmm . . . there are hundreds of flavors in the store. I'm not sure I could narrow my choices down to just four. How do I know if I'm picking the best ones?"

"No problem," the owner says. "The next time you're in the store, you can try a different four-flavor sampler. You can use flavors you've chosen and liked during this visit, or you can pick an entirely new combination. It's up to you. And if you come back a third time, you can use what you've learned from the first two samplers to try yet another combination."

So you might choose a chocolate flavor you love to be in all three samplers; mango might be bumped out by coconut in the second sampler; and by the third try you'd know whether the white chocolate cheesecake or the raspberry swirl was a more delicious accompaniment to the chunky cookie dough you just discovered.

You just might find the perfect set of flavors and contentedly order them time after time. But being a Renaissance

Soul, you probably wouldn't settle on just *one* sampler to satisfy your sweet tooth for all eternity. That's fine, because you
could continue to swap out flavors at each visit. Most important, you wouldn't just be standing in front of the display case,
as frozen as the ice cream itself. You'd actually be having
something to eat!

In other words, by focusing on four flavors you can more
easily make a decision and nourish yourself. *Focusing brings
more, not less.* Amid a world of possibilities, focusing offers variety but also clarity and concentration.

HOW TO FOCUS:
THE RENAISSANCE FOCAL POINT STRATEGY

I'd like you to think about your own activities and choices in
terms of this sampler metaphor. I use the phrase "Renaissance
Focal Points" to describe the "flavors" in your sampler. Just as
you might focus on four flavors during one trip to the ice-
cream store, the Renaissance Focal Point strategy asks you to
come up with four (or so) key interests that you feel strongly
about and wish to focus on *for now.* So at this stage of your life
you might choose teaching high-school economics, baking,
running, and delivering meals to shut-ins. The list of current
interests you made earlier in this chapter can be helpful in
picking your four. Later, you may change your Focal Points to
reflect a different set of interests.

The Focal Points approach is a good fit with the Renaissance Soul style of work and play. For one, it frees us from
indecision. Instead of spending so much time just thinking
about what to do next, we can actually move into meaningful
action. That in itself can be a great relief. It's also true that
by maintaining a reasonable number of interests at one time,

we can satisfy our sense of possibility and our craving for variety. Energy that we once frantically devoted to keeping *all* our options open can now be channeled into doing at least four of the things we love to do. And that happy energy becomes self-replicating. We get a high from one activity that carries us into another. Our days move along in a real hum of excitement that has nothing to do with frenzied overstimulation.

Let me show you how the Renaissance Focal Point strategy allowed one young man to dig his way out of a particularly deep funk of indecision and inactivity. When it came to paid work, Emory, who clerked in a record store, knew what he wanted: to manage a nightclub. But he seemed to expect this new career to settle down on him like a mantle instead of his having to go out and make things happen for himself. At the same time, he had so many interests outside of his job that he never received satisfaction from any of them. His guitar sat in the corner calling to him, and his new marriage was wilting from inattention. Even though he loved how his body felt after exercising, he never latched on to a regular schedule and often skipped his workouts for weeks at a time. His friends grew tired of hearing about his big dream to live in Italy for three months and write a series of comic plays. Yes, and what about his friends? He wasn't seeing enough of them, either. . . .

One reason Emory stands out in my mind is his strongly physical response to the idea of Renaissance Focal Points. When we went over this approach he let out a sigh of relief that could be heard down the hall. He was thrilled to realize that he didn't have to spend the rest of his life trapped between picking one interest or having to face dozens.

Which didn't mean he narrowed his long list of interests down to four Focal Points in an instant. (As you'll see, not everyone chooses exactly four Focal Points, but like many people, Emory found it a manageable number.) But as he brainstormed about possible Focal Points, he found several that would work well together in his first sampler. His first Focal Point was to spend more time with his wife. In addition, he decided to strengthen his career credentials by taking an introductory management course at the adult-education center. He also committed to writing a short comic play. Finally, he decided to power walk for an hour five mornings a week.

As Emory dedicated his energies to these four Focal Points, there were some interesting developments. As he and his wife spent more time talking after work, cooking and just hanging out together, she became an enthusiastic supporter of his playwriting efforts. As the script developed, she suggested that they stage an informal production. Emory and his wife found themselves painting scenery together and scouring tag sales for props. The experience was so satisfying that the two of them are now planning to develop other short plays that they can offer to perform at high schools and senior centers. Who knows where *that* will lead?

The management course showed Emory that managing a nightclub with dozens of employees would require grueling hours—not just the predictable late nights but early mornings and long afternoons as well. But the class got him thinking about managing a retail store instead, with its more predictable schedule. He talked to his own manager at the record store, who gave him a list of contacts to check out.

Power walking turned out to be satisfying for Emory because he was doing it frequently enough to see results—but he realized he didn't need to do it full bore. He cut back to a schedule of shorter and less frequent walks and made room in his sampler to learn Italian, often listening to language tapes when he walked. His sampler still contained four activities but now looked slightly different: writing more plays, spending time with his wife, pursuing his retail-management contacts, and learning Italian.

So, no, Emory didn't become a nightclub manager, he wasn't bound for Italy (yet), and his guitar still gathered dust in the corner. But six months after he was introduced to the Focal Point approach, he had the satisfaction of several in-depth experiences and was looking forward to new ones.

I can't emphasize enough what a powerful difference it makes in a Renaissance Soul's life to feel free to focus on three or four or five things for now, and let others wait until later. We simply can't juggle dozens of interests at once. And yet there is a kind of abundance that flows from establishing a tighter focus. If Emory had been trying to pursue every one of his interests, he never would have had time to say yes to the new opportunities that arose.

Your Renaissance Focal Points may not look anything like Emory's. (Although you're probably thinking... *hmmm...* *one-act comedies? studying Italian? I've got to try those one day!*) That's perfectly fine. To show you the diversity among sets of Focal Points, here are some examples from other Renaissance Souls.

Denise's Renaissance Focal Points

Attending business school

Filming documentaries

Traveling

Richard's Renaissance Focal Points

Being a present, more reliable father

Sticking with the flute

Collecting farm implements

Doing fix-it projects

Ed's Renaissance Focal Points
Facilitating meaningful activities for the elderly
Developing a meditation practice
Golfing
Doing pottery

Amy's Renaissance Focal Points
Competing in archery tournaments
Spending quality time with her family
Developing new advertising material at work

Catherine's Renaissance Focal Points
Finding new ways to promote her gift shop
Scouting out unique merchandise
Creating shop displays
Training shop employees

Coming up with your first sampler of Focal Points is a dynamic process, one that I hope will bring you joy. It's also a serious endeavor that will require some deep thought and a willingness to tinker with your combination so that it best reflects your current needs. Here are a few guidelines for selecting Focal Points:

Most people choose to maintain four Focal Points at once. When it comes to Focal Points, four seems to be a lucky number for Renaissance Souls. Having four simultaneous interests seems to strike a balance between our love of variety and our need for concentration. But ultimately, you must choose the number that is best for you. As we've seen, a few Renaissance Souls enjoy committing themselves fully to just one interest at a time. Some rotate their interests with the seasons. Others will prefer to engage in two or three or even five Focal Points at any given time. When I meet very ambitious Renaissance Souls, I remind them that the purpose of Focal Points is to set boundaries. Any more than five Focal Points, and it's likely that you will once again experience paralysis or indecision.

Don't let practical concerns shoulder out your dreams. Later, I'll show you how to integrate your Focal Points with practical matters such as pulling down a good income and taking care of the kids. But for now, I don't want you to worry about how you'll get the housework done if you're in the backyard all afternoon building a shed or who will look after Mom while you're volunteering at the state-history museum. This is your time to create dreams that are interesting, exciting, and satisfying for *you.* There will be plenty of time for the real world soon.

Include paid work as a Focal Point only if you love your job. Renaissance Souls can be so enthusiastic about their work that they list it as a Focal Point. (You can see that in Catherine's and Amy's lists.) But for Renaissance Souls, the intersection of passion and income is frequently in flux. If following your interests means shedding your current career for another, or if you think you might want to let a day job finance your four-flavor sampler, then leave paid work off your list of Focal Points for now. At this stage of the process, the main thing is not to let yourself stall out on the problem of money. I want you to concentrate on approximately four areas that you find so engaging that you'd happily shine your energies in their direction even if they didn't pay a penny.

Likewise, list unpaid work only if you love it (or if you're cultivating a special interest). Caretaking for elderly relatives, doing the laundry, getting dinner on the table—all are important tasks. But unless these duties constitute your heart's work, leave them off your Focal Points list. Someone who regularly volunteers at a food pantry may certainly include that activity as a Focal Point—as long as that activity holds real meaning for her. Richard, a divorced dad whose Focal Points were listed earlier, felt that he had been spending only "business" time with his son, going through the harried motions of dropping him off at school or making sandwiches for lunch. He wanted to devote time to special activities, such as playing hide-and-seek together. So Richard decided to include these special activities— but not the daily must-dos of parenting—in a Focal Point.

Don't worry about whether your Focal Points are markedly different from one another—or closely related. Richard, Denise, and Ed, whose Focal Points were listed earlier, are all examples of Renaissance Souls who maintain a balance among divergent passions. But what about Catherine? She sees her gift-shop business as one of those umbrellas I've mentioned before. Each of her four Focal Points is directed toward one umbrella (her store) while satisfying her interests in design (by creating enticing displays), sharing her knowledge (by conducting employee seminars), working with artists (by hunting down merchandise in their workshops), and basking in the spotlight (by handling her own publicity).

Don't feel pressured to make each Focal Point action-oriented. One of the most frequent questions clients ask me is, "If I start following four Renaissance Focal Points, will I have to be rushing around all the time?" There is absolutely nothing about being a Renaissance Soul that requires you to go, go, go all the time—unless you *want* to. Your sampler could consist of nothing but reflective pursuits. It did for one of my clients, whose sampler was devoted to daily meditation, studying religious texts, and spending time in a rural abbey.

You may find that over time, the pace and intensity of your samplers balance out. When one Renaissance Soul opened his new consulting business, he had a sampler of lively, active Focal Points that included securing bank loans and wooing clients over power lunches. Now that he's decided to turn the business over to one of his employees, the Focal Points on his current sampler are far more restful. In fact, one of his current Renaissance Soul goals is to have more hours in the day than things to do. But he is not tied to this slower pace for that infamous "rest of his life." The contents of his next sampler may again have him on the go.

Remember: This is not your last sampler. Yes, you should take care in considering each set of Focal Points that you create. But don't let yourself get bogged down in choosing the *perfect* sampler. You can always change your Focal Points later. As time passes, you can add and subtract interests, thereby experiencing a lifetime of fascinating combinations. My friend Gregor put it well: "This really means the end of 'The End,' doesn't it? One thing will always lead to another. Being a Renaissance Soul means I can pursue the infinity of interconnections."

GETTING FOCAL POINTS "RIGHT"

Many of my clients—no matter what their age—are haunted by the feeling that time is running out for them. If they don't create the perfect set of Focal Points right now, their tense faces say, all will be lost! If you find yourself hung up on "getting it right this time," try the Give Me Time! exercise on pages 40–43.

***Know that Focal Points can last for a long time—if you so
choose.*** You may have experienced a rush of pleasure upon learning the distinction between focusing and choosing, only to find
that your joy soon turned to anxiety. Do you look down the road
a few years and picture yourself frantically juggling ever-
changing interests, always in flux, never feeling calm and settled?

In response, I say: Life with Focal Points is much steadier
than life without them. The Focal Points in your sampler can
last for significant periods of time. Take my nephew, who recently left his job as an editorial assistant at a prestigious publishing house to attend a demanding massage-therapy school
full-time. My guess is that massage will serve him as a focal
point for several years. Currently he is complementing his interest in massage therapy with black-and-white photography
as well as traveling throughout the United States and France.
His life five or ten years from now may well look much the
same as this year, even if parenting may replace traveling, at
least while the children are very young. Even those of us who
hang out on Ben Franklin's extreme end of the interests continuum may go for long stretches of time with a calming consistency to our lives.

THE RENAISSANCE FOCAL POINT SAMPLER

I've designed the following exercise as a means to create a
safe place for you to sort through ideas for your first Renaissance
Focal Point sampler. You need not feel pinned down by anything
you write. Feel free to jot down and explore any possible Focal
Points that are already coming to you and to play with them as
you continue reading. Eventually, you'll find that three, or four,
or five seem best for you at the moment—and remember, you
can always change your sampler later.

CREATING YOUR FIRST FOCAL POINT SAMPLER

You can use the five blank squares (there's an extra square in case you want to pursue more than four Focal Points at once) below for jotting down ideas in very erasable pencil, or you may want to use Post-it notes that you can pull off and replace at will. That way you'll know these particular choices aren't cast in stone! You may want to turn back to your list of current interests from page 87 for inspiration.

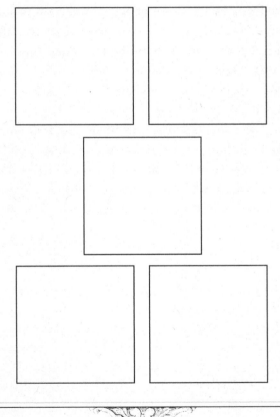

So far, I've asked you to set aside practical issues as you dream up your first four Focal Points. This dream work is hard work, so take a break to savor how much you've accomplished. Consider putting this book down for a while, whether it's for a few days or just long enough to pour a cup of coffee. You'll come back to these Focal Points later in the book, but feel free to tinker with your choices as you continue to read and learn about your Renaissance Soul.

When you're ready, we'll look at an issue I've asked you to set aside up until now: money. None but the independently wealthy can afford to buy into a life-design concept that doesn't address the problems of income and education. Many Renaissance Souls hold themselves back from the life-design process until they've considered certain questions: How do I earn a living? And how can I get training to pursue all these interests? In the next section (Part III), I'll tackle these matters.

Once you've experienced the liberation that comes with understanding those practical issues, you can begin designing your new life (or lives) without reservation. In Part IV, I'll describe Renaissance Soul life design in depth. There, we'll talk about making commitments, managing your time, and keeping your momentum going.

Part III

Practical Realities:

Career Design for Pursuing Your Passions

FIVE

Your J-O-B: No More Day Jobs

My brother and I are both Renaissance Souls, yet we ended up with such different life designs. My four Focal Points are quite varied, so I have used a variety of part-time jobs to move them forward and put money in my pocket. Eliot, on the other hand, needs a full-time, well-paying job while he saves to open his own coffee shop. He's kept his current position as a regional manager of a grocery chain while taking advantage of the company's free classes in staff management and customer engagement—skills that will come in handy when he runs his own place.

—*Luke, forty-five*

*T*ake a look at the diagram that follows. It consists of two circles. One contains your Focal Points. The other surrounds your source of income. Most Renaissance Souls initially find that these two circles are completely separate; their work and their "real lives" are miles apart.

Focal Points/Income Circles

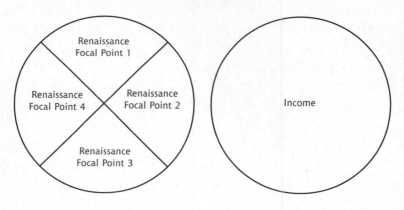

For most of us, the ideal circumstance is that these two circles start to move closer and closer, until eventually they overlap. At that point, your passions are the source of your paycheck. In this chapter, I'll show you ways to bring those circles together.

WHY A J-O-B IS BETTER THAN A DAY JOB

*S*andra worked as a publicist for a demanding, irritable socialite. But she wanted to earn a living as an R & B singer. She had been taking voice lessons and had started to pick up some work on the weekends. But it would take time before she could rely on her income from singing gigs to pay the bills. In the meantime, was she stuck with a job she hated? For Sandra, did it all boil down to that old cliché, "Don't quit your day job"?

Not at all! We all know that a day job is something you do just for the money while you look to the rest of your life for satisfaction. Unfortunately, many Renaissance Souls design their lives this way: they look in the classified section or on the

Internet for a paying position they feel they are "qualified" to
do. Once those forty (or fifty, or sixty) hours per week are
squared away, they then try to fit the rest of their interests
around the edges. Initially they are optimistic and full of energy. But what happens? The pressures, politics, and personalities of that job use them up. By the end of the workweek,
they have little energy left for the real passions they'd hoped
to engage, often feeling demoralized and depressed.

What I suggest instead is something I call a J-O-B. I spell
the word out to remind Renaissance Souls that it is both *only*
a job and *more than* a job. A J-O-B is a smart way to hitch your
goals to a revenue source. It pulls the double duty of bringing
in money while moving you closer to a Focal Point. Even if
you're aching to launch your dream career right this minute,
by the end of this chapter you may feel much more positive
about a J-O-B than you can now imagine. Why? For two key
reasons: because you will have learned how to pick a J-O-B,
and what that J-O-B says about who you are.

HOW TO PICK YOUR J-O-B

*H*ere's an idea. Instead of toiling away at a job that drains
away every ounce of your vital life force, why not pick a J-O-B
that carries one or more of your Renaissance Focal Points forward?

Say, for example, that a young high school graduate trav-
els with her family the summer after her high school graduation to an exotic country . . . let's call it Lower Slobovia.
During the trip, she becomes fascinated with the old women
there who weave baskets. Many are well past ninety, even one
hundred years old. In typical Renaissance Soul fashion, our
teenager is dying to photograph these women's amazing faces,

write their life stories before their culture dies out, and also understand more about why, after decades of weaving baskets made of a local fiber, their hands have no wrinkles or liver spots.

This young woman returns to the States with a vow to follow through on these ideas. But she doesn't have the funds to book a return trip, nor does she know how to work professional photography equipment. Without a certain amount of money tucked away, she won't be able to pursue her interest.

Needless to say, when this young woman peruses the classified ads, she's not going to find lots of positions available for someone interested in Lower Slobovian basket weavers! To make things even more challenging, let's also say that this high school kid's only marketable skill is rudimentary database entry. She needs to work, but what can she do?

Well, she can perform database entry for an airline, so that she can get reduced rates on her trips to Lower Slobovia. Or she can do the same for a photography company, so she can have access to the best equipment available for her portraits— at a discount. Or she can take her data-entry skills to a magazine like *National Geographic* or the *Smithsonian*, where her fellow employees will understand and nurture her passion for Lower Slobovian basket weavers. Not only can these J-O-Bs move her a little closer to her Focal Points, they will contribute to her energy level, not dry it up. Can you imagine how much more purposeful and enlivening any of these positions would feel compared to one that she picked out at random in the classifieds, such as entering data for a local insurance company or a doctor's office?

I've had J-O-Bs myself. When I first opened my coaching business, needless to say I didn't have enough clients on day one to meet my financial obligations. This is true for most businesses: It takes a while to get the word out and to build up a steady base of repeat clients. Since I needed money, I cast about for a J-O-B. What did I choose? I taught the Commercial Drivers License Class at a local college.

This class required—actually, it demanded—the least creative kind of teaching known to humankind. I was instructed to teach exactly what was in the manual and then administer sample tests to my students. These requirements ignored the fact that the men in front of me had been driving the big rigs for twenty years and I've never even sat inside one. And there were plenty of other disadvantages as well. The class was held in the basement of the college's physical plant. It was cold, damp, and windowless. Half the time the door was locked when I arrived and I'd have to track down a janitor with a key. I've been—among other things—a teacher at one of the country's premier reading institutes, and there I was teaching by rote and freezing to boot.

So why did I take this J-O-B? Well, at this stage of my business I needed to do several things. I wanted to bone up on the latest career research. For the workshop handouts I was creating, I needed access to a professional-grade copy machine, the kind that collates and staples and bakes blueberry muffins. Most important, I wanted to network with the career-center professionals who provided training and development workshops for the school's faculty and staff. This J-O-B not only freed up my brain for all my other tasks; it allowed me to sit and read career-related materials for hours at a time while I administered sample tests. I received the all clear from my boss to use the school's copiers, as long as I brought my own paper. And as a staff member, I received an important perk: networking opportunities during free career-development classes. I wasn't just making a few bucks to keep my family from dipping into savings as I moved into a new business. Instead of letting a job use me, *I* was using this J-O-B to make my new business profitable more quickly.

FIVE CRITERIA FOR A J-O-B

A J-O-B should provide at least one of the following benefits; a really great one will give you two or three.

1. *Income or benefits.* By definition, a J-O-B always provides income. But the size of that income depends on your needs. Some people need freely flowing sources of cash, but others can draw upon their savings until at least one Focal Point becomes profitable. In the meantime, they may need just a few extra dollars or health-insurance benefits to keep themselves or their family on steady fiscal ground.

Discounts are another useful benefit. What do you need to move your Focal Points forward? Airline tickets? Professional clothes? Athletic equipment? I often think of a client, a high school Latin teacher who looked every inch the stereotypical scholar: tweed jacket, suede patches on each elbow, never owned a television. Yet one of his Focal Points was writing an elaborate history of Greek thought. For that, pencil and paper no longer seemed suitable. He wanted a computer to help him work more efficiently. And so for a period of time during one summer, maybe six or eight weeks, you could find this academic working Tuesday and Thursday mornings at Circuit City. He'd deliberately asked for the slowest hours of the week, when he'd have time to learn about the computers for sale and which software was the best for his project. He stayed just long enough to earn money for a new computer—and to benefit from his employee discount.

2. *Energy.* A J-O-B can help you conserve your energy, so that in your off-hours you have plenty of bounce to pursue your Focal Points. It's a less obvious point that a J-O-B can also *balance* your energy. For example, I had a client who told me early in our first session that he worked in insurance but what he really wanted to do was write a novel. As our discussions proceeded, he decided to keep his high-paying insurance career as his J-O-B but to commit significant time after hours to his writing. On the Friday of that first week, he called in something of a panic. "I don't know what's going on," he said. "I sat down to write last night, but I ended up going bowling with a friend of mine instead. And I don't even *like* to bowl!"

When I asked a few more questions, it turned out that my client's J-O-B was not selling insurance, as I had assumed. He was an actuary who sat by himself in his cubicle all day, using a computer to work out life-expectancy tables. Naturally, the prospect of sitting home alone in front of a computer in his off-work hours was unappealing. When a friend called to see if he'd fill in for a missing team member on the bowling team, off he went. This client needed a more social J-O-B that would balance out the solitude of writing. He talked to the human resources department at his company and moved into a position where there was more person-to-person interaction.

The opposite may be true for Renaissance Souls whose Focal Points involve compassionate, caregiving work that focuses on the needs of others. They may find their patience quickly tapped out if their J-O-Bs demand similar qualities. It's a good idea for these people to avoid J-O-Bs in hospitals, human resources departments, or other places where they are expected to focus on other peoples' problems.

3. *Time.* A J-O-B may save you time if you're allowed to read, make phone calls, or work on the computer while at your desk. Or maybe a J-O-B offers an easy commute that frees up an extra hour or two each day. Sometimes, successful pursuit of your Focal Points will require you to be available at a certain time of the year or day. One client of mine, a bored junior-high-school art teacher, wanted to volunteer with dying children as one of her Focal Points. But the times that the children most needed her—weekday mornings, when their parents were at work and the kids were full of energy—were also times when she was occupied. So she searched for a J-O-B that would free up her mornings.

The next time I saw this client, she cupped her palm and extended her hand toward me, as if she were offering me a precious jewel. In her hand was a classified advertisement for a personal care attendant. Now, if I'd told this woman when I first met her that she might want to spend her days as a personal care attendant, she would have dismissed me as a kook. But when she spotted an ad for this J-O-B she was thrilled. That's because caring for two elderly and wealthy sisters paid as much as her current day job, and the hours were perfect: from 7:30 Sunday morning until 7:30 Tuesday morning. She would even be paid for sleeping at the house. She was hired, thanks to the enthusiasm that distinguished her from ninety other applicants, and she spent mornings Tuesday through Friday volunteering for a hospice program.

4. *Training and equipment.* Don't sniff at the opportunity to get training on expensive equipment or to polish skills that you'll need for your Focal Point. Your current so-so day job might just become an excellent J-O-B if it offers access to language labs or sophisticated libraries, free computer classes, networking seminars, or other workshops. I had one client who took an entry-level J-O-B with a corporation that made vents and ducts for large industrial buildings. He wasn't at all

interested in vents and ducts—but he did have his eyes
trained on the company's computers and design software. His
boss appreciated his sharp attention to the work he was hired
to do, so he agreed to let my client attend company classes on
computer-aided design.

5. *Networking and publicity opportunities.* Offer your
skills to a place filled with people who really get you and who
can talk your talk. One of my favorite examples is a middle-
aged widow who needed to reenter the workplace. She had
some secretarial experience, but she really loved art. Without
more formal training, we agreed it would be difficult to break
into an arts career right away. But she could perform basic administrative work at a nearby art museum. There, she could
talk to curators and volunteers about her favorite subject. A
couple of months into this J-O-B, flyers arrived to promote a
new exhibit. My client asked if she could use a nearby blank
wall to create a publicity display for the exhibit, using the flyers and other material. Over the weekend, the artist in her
went to town, and she arrived on Monday morning with an
eye-catching display. When it was time for the exhibit to leave
and for the display to come down, everyone agreed that the
once again blank wall looked sadly empty. So they asked her
to create another display. And so it went. As each new exhibit
was announced, she'd have long conversations with the staff
members most closely associated with it. These collaborations
continued until someone mentioned that another museum
was hiring a display artist. With their blessing and recommendations, she applied for the job—and soon this woman, with
no specialized graphics degree, was earning a much higher income at a prestigious art museum.

A FEW GOOD J-O-BS

Here are some sample J-O-Bs and their benefits:

- Adjunct college instructor: use of the pottery wheel in the art building
- Parking lot attendant or box-office attendant: plenty of undisturbed reading time
- Receptionist in a hair salon: a great place to let people know about your new massage business
- Assistant in a well-baby clinic: opportunities to pass out brochures for your line of sportswear for nursing mothers
- Marketing representative for a small community cable station: exposure to the studio area and the technical side of television production
- Professional organizer for successful and busy women: opportunities to establish a client base for your future interior design firm
- Sales representative for an established hotel chain: chances to build connections in the event-planning business
- Manager of an American Youth Hostel property: experience in the hospitality industry and good references for your future bed-and-breakfast, cleaning, or catering business
- Human resources position at a large corporation: experience and contacts for an outsourcing center

BUT WHAT IF I HAVE A "REAL" JOB, NOT JUST A DAY JOB?

*P*erhaps you do not have a day job, but a "real" job, one that you've trained for and paid your dues in and pursued to a level of success. Yet when your passions lie elsewhere, even a prestigious career can come to seem like merely a day job, one that drains away the energy you have for pursuing new challenges and interests. If this describes your situation, the J-O-B paradigm can work for you, too. Begin by holding your job up to the J-O-B criteria listed starting on page 108. Does it meet the standard of two or three of the five criteria for a J-O-B? If not, the next step is to ask if your job could be made to do so with a little creative effort. Could you take advantage of equipment available at your office if you repurposed your lunch hour? Could you cultivate contacts in other departments who might have skills that would further one of your Focal Points? Could you arrive at work an hour later and stay an hour later to take advantage of your fresh morning energy each day to pursue your passions?

Many Renaissance Souls end up in the offices of career counselors because they *hate, despise, absolutely cannot take* their current jobs for one minute longer. But often when they realize their identity rests with their Focal Points, they decide to stay on at their current position. As a job, it stinks. As a J-O-B, it gives them more money per hour than they might be able to make elsewhere. Or it frees their mind to focus on their Focal Points because they've been there so long they can practically perform their tasks in their sleep. It's the *opposite* of golden handcuffs. The personalities and politics of the place become amusing rather than consuming, and they tend to suffer less from workaholism—all because their identity has moved elsewhere.

HOW TO ANSWER THE QUESTION
"AND WHAT DO YOU DO?"

Every one of us has been asked, "What do you do?" at parties. Our habitual response reflects the idea that our identity is somehow equivalent to how we earn money. This equation works—*if* you happen to love what you receive your W-2 for doing. If you're a real estate agent who adores connecting people with places they love, you'll glow as you talk about your work, and your fellow guests will leave the party with a positive mental picture of you. But if you're passionate about Lower Slobovia, but totally misplaced in a day job entering data for an insurance company, you'll probably say, with a resigned tone and body language, "Oh, I'm doing office work at Clayborne and Clayborne." Each time you say this, you'll feel a little more like a failure. And we, the questioners, will never get the chance to say, "Oh, you should talk with my brother-in-law—he's a professor of Lower Slobovian studies! He's looking for a research assistant!" So here are two things to keep in mind for successfully integrating your interests and your income:

+ Your identity must live in the Focal Points circle, not in the J-O-B circle! You are *not* someone who cranks out legal paperwork all day; you're a snowboarder training for the X Games. And you're *not* an assistant to a real estate appraiser; you're a mapmaker plotting out Civil War battlefields.

+ You must always answer any ritual questions regarding what you "do" in terms of one or more of your Focal Points, not your J-O-B.

When I went home for Thanksgiving the year I taught the Commercial Drivers License Class, nearly a dozen relatives asked me what I was "up to these days." I did *not* produce puzzled boredom by saying, "Whoopee! I get to teach experienced truck drivers how to pass a stupid, meaningless test." Instead, I talked about the challenge of creating a brochure for my new business. I got lively responses, including, "Oh, well, you know I do graphic design! Why don't you e-mail me your questions?"

When you put the focus on your Focal Points, a strange thing happens. The pressure that comes from confusing your identity and your J-O-B lifts. Life at work becomes lighter, more energizing. Again, consider my situation. There I was in a dank, dark basement. I was teaching a ridiculous class to a bunch of people who knew more about the subject than I did. Had my identity been wrapped up in this work, all of the injustices I was suffering would probably have eaten at me. I would have become involved in all the petty politics of the place, trying to get decent heating and a room key and a promotion. Had my identity been dependent on commanding respect as the Commercial Drivers License Class teacher, I probably would have tried to convince the truckers to take everything the manual said and the whole test process very seriously—and I would have been frustrated by their resistance.

Instead, because I knew that I was using this J-O-B to get what I wanted, and because I knew this work had nothing to do with my identity, I didn't take the politics and locked doors personally. The fact that I laughed with the truckers instead of struggling against them meant that at the end of the class, they gave me a standing ovation and a gift certificate to the local mall. This was unheard of at the college—and soon I had an even better J-O-B teaching their staff-development classes!

PUTTING THE PIECES TOGETHER

*L*ooking again at the Focal Points/Income Circles diagram, most of my clients start out with the two circles wide apart. They need to hold down a J-O-B to make money and to help move one or more of their Focal Points forward, and they are not initially paid for any activities relating to their Focal Points. They network, stash away some extra money, take classes, volunteer or intern, and acquire new skills. Slowly, as they start taking on landscape-design clients or bringing in funding for their new magazine, they move themselves toward a place where one or more of their Focal Points are income producing. And eventually they earn enough to reduce their J-O-B hours or drop their J-O-B altogether.

It's also important to recognize that some people choose *never* to bring their income and passion circles together. There are Renaissance Souls who prefer holding down one steady J-O-B as they rotate through hobbies, not careers. Others find that their interests are tainted once they are required to be a source of income. I once worked with a potter who said vehemently in our first session, "Margaret, I never, ever want to have to make little piggies when little piggies are in, and little ponies when little ponies are in. I don't want to sit at my wheel and think, 'Now what are the galleries buying this year?'" Similarly, I have clients whose interests nearly always include nonpaying activities such as meditating or spending time with their young children. No one should ever feel that their Focal Points are somehow less serious or legitimate if they don't produce money.

For those who wish to bring the circles together, the next chapter offers strategies for getting paid for your passions.

I used to have a humdrum job that took me away from the things
that interested me most. Now I have a career scheduling
entertainment events for football and baseball games, which allows
me to integrate all my Focal Points—love of music, entertaining,
and organizing anything—into a single profession.

—Genna, thirty

I know how other people get paid for the same combinations of
skills I have: they develop a life-coaching practice. But if I pursue that
dream, I know I'll fail. I just don't think it's in me to go around tooting
my own horn the way I'd need to to get a business off the ground.

—Griffin, thirty-five

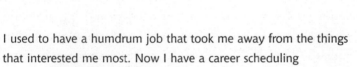o people who love change have to start at the bottom
over and over again every time they switch careers?
The answer is no, for a variety of reasons.

For some, tackling a series of new careers or J-O-Bs can be a brilliant adventure. Renaissance Souls often don't set out with a particular career in mind. Before settling (if ever) on a job, they pursue their interests and passions in the spirit of a great quest. Lee Kravitz, for example, didn't hold down a "real" job until he was thirty-three; instead, after graduating from Yale, he bought a Land Rover with friends and traveled for two years through Turkey, Iran, Pakistan, India, Nepal, and Afghanistan. He lived in London, Paris, and on a kibbutz in Israel. After returning "flat broke" to his native Cleveland, he moonlighted for years as a bartender while freelancing as a magazine journalist and photographer. "I never followed a career path," he says. "What I followed was my inner need to explore the world and share what I learned with others." Kravitz did some of that sharing by taking a job at Scholastic, where he channeled his energy and experience into creating magazines for teenagers. Not a bad background for someone who is now editor-in-chief of *Parade*, the largest-circulation magazine in the world. In this position Kravitz continues to be driven by a desire to learn new things and tell stories that enrich people's lives.

Still, many of us have dreary images of entry-level positions. You enter a new field, with the most basic responsibilities and pay. While your ex-colleagues are making partner and buying vacation homes, you're fetching coffee for your new boss (whenever she sets you free from the fax machine, that is). But there's no reason you can't transition from one line of work into another without plummeting down to the bottom of the office food chain. A J-O-B, discussed in the previous chapter, is one option for keeping your income flowing as you educate yourself in a new interest. But when you're prepared to get paid for your Focal Points, you may have more to offer the working world than you realize. Here I'll show you how to

translate your skills so that you—and your potential employers—see the potential in your Renaissance resume. We'll also
return to the subject of "umbrella" careers, which may cover
several of the interests that excite you the most.

One way of starting over without starting at the bottom is
to launch your own business or freelance career. Lots of people have the knowledge to produce goods or serve clients, but
many fear the sales and publicity activity that free agenting
requires. This chapter also presents the experiences of several
Renaissance Souls who learned to set up their own businesses
despite their distaste for "selling themselves."

GETTING THE JOB WITHOUT CLIMBING THE LADDER

*A*s Renaissance Souls follow tempting new lines of work,
we accumulate a variety of experiences along the way. These
experiences build skill capital we can cash in on when we
swap out one career for another.

One Renaissance Soul I know, Earnest Urvater, used his
skill capital to make a radical career transformation. Earnest
began his professional life at a national laboratory, where he
researched elementary particles. From there he moved on to a
university, where he developed another skill by teaching for
ten years. So what has he been doing recently? Exactly what
you would expect from a Renaissance Soul: independently
producing documentaries about such diverse topics as the effects of plastic waste on the earth's ocean waters and pedagogical techniques for piano.

Did Earnest go out and start over, paying to take classes at
a film school and then serving the usual apprenticeship as a
production assistant? Not exactly. While he was teaching, the
university acquired a television studio. Earnest's Renaissance

Soul couldn't resist. He became involved with the studio, creating instructional videos for his science students and gaining hands-on experience as a producer. By the time he'd decided to make a full career switch, he'd already learned how to edit video, write scripts, and successfully solicit grant money from the state. And instead of going into each new project cold, he could draw on his existing base of scientific and pedagogical knowledge *and* his wide range of academic contacts.

Rebecca Southwick usually prefers to be self-employed, whether as a therapist, alternative healer, home remodeler, or writer. But when she decided to apply for a position in a community program to rehabilitate run-down houses, she found that her varied background helped her stand out among other applicants: "I got the job specifically because I'd been a carpenter *and* I had a therapy background. They had a lot of problems in this program and needed someone who could understand and work with both the contractors and the homeowners. They were very clear that the negotiation skills I'd developed as a therapist and healer were a real plus."

Then there's Heather Colson, who trained as a florist, electrician, massage therapist, and farmer before turning to sculpture. Heather has taken only one art class, but she earns enough from her art to support herself and the beautiful farm she owns. She feels that her previous work as a massage therapist was a form of art education: "A lot of times when I try to actually think about how a particular bone, say an ankle, works, or how it connects to other bones, it doesn't end up looking right. But if I turn my brain off and just let my hands do it, it comes out right." Did *she* start all over when changing careers? No.

Sometimes our experiences are more useful than we realize. My client Julie finally made a decision that was a long time coming: she had outgrown her banking career and had her eyes trained on a fund-raising position. Despite the clarity of her goal, she felt handcuffed by her lack of experience. As a single mother with a young daughter to support, she couldn't afford to take on an entry-level position or to enroll in a master's program in managing not-for-profits.

Instead of dwelling on these obstacles, I asked Julie to imagine herself as the head of a nonprofit organization, someone who needed to hire a fund-raiser. What qualities would that person want in a new employee?

"Cold-calling experience," Julie offered. I was surprised at how quickly and confidently she responded. It turned out that Julie had put herself through college as a telemarketer—and she actually *enjoyed* the work. So she did in fact have two things: cold-calling experience *and* a passion for a task most of us—even many fund-raisers—find distasteful.

Julie also recalled an experience with a raffle at her daughter's school. On the morning of the raffle, Julie learned that nearly twenty tickets remained unsold. She asked if she could try her hand at selling them. "Don't even bother," the school secretary groaned. "It took most of the parents on the raffle committee two full weeks just to sell ten tickets apiece. Besides, it's too late anyway." But with the secretary's permission, Julie took the tickets with her—and sold all of them by lunchtime. Another feather in her cap. I suggested she make the most of these two experiences by securing recommendations from both the school and the telemarketing agency.

We also discussed that a not-for-profit organization would appreciate the skills she'd cultivated in her current position at the bank. She knew about money, she was responsible, she knew how to dress, and she knew how to talk to people who hold the purse strings.

After just one session Julie had a whole new view of her existing skills. The gap between her current experience and her dream job had narrowed considerably. She wasn't going to become a professional fund-raiser overnight, but she could confidently move closer to her goal.

Or consider Marian. She was a young, vivacious Southern Californian who dressed like a model and danced like a pro. But when she came to me, she was bored. Not with her personal life—she'd just bought an amazing new home with her partner, still hadn't finished her album of photos from a trip to Bali, and had such a large network of friends that she said, "I could be answering Instant Messages all day."

But work was another matter. "Whenever I've been out of work, I just stumble into something else. You know, I meet a friend of a friend at a great party and when they hear I'm looking for a job, they tell me about *X*. And because I love new experiences, I say, 'Sure,' and I do it for a while, and then it gets old or the company gets bought up or I get downsized— you know the story. And then I meet someone else, and go to work somewhere else. . . . But after the initial novelty wears off, none of these things really excites me, you know. And I'm not good at hiding my disinterest."

Picking up on that last statement, I asked Marian to think about what interests she thought might hold her attention, not for "forever," but well after the first blush of novelty had faded. She thought and then said, "Animals and travel." She gave me an impassioned speech about how the same people who were devoted to health foods didn't notice what they fed their pets. The few who did had to drive long distances to find wholesome organic pet food. "And that's a crime!" Marian said. "Healthy food for animals is just as important as healthy food for people!"

"What do you think it would take to make healthy pet

food easily accessible?" I asked. We did some brainstorming and then Marian summarized: "Someone would have to make it, someone would have to convince stores to carry it, and enough people would have to want to buy it to make the stores keep ordering."

Marian had articulated a great combination of activities for herself. To earn money (after all, she did have to help pay the mortgage on that new house), she would represent companies that produced lines of healthy animal food, selling their products to grocery stores around California. "That will feed my travel bug a bit without keeping me from home too long," Marian noted. At the same time, she would use her passion and her effervescent personality to educate animal owners about the importance of healthful pet foods. "I could go on talk shows and set up booths at pet stores and write articles and do a column for newspapers!" she said. This she envisioned as a hobby that could lead to paid speaking or consulting gigs in the future.

How would Marian make this happen? I asked Marian to list all the jobs she'd "stumbled" into since graduation. She was right: it was an odd assortment of positions, and none of them had anything to do with animals or travel. But Marian *had* been a receptionist; and she *had* written informational packets for an insurance firm; and she *had* trained customer-relations employees for a telephone company; and she *had* spent almost a year selling school sweatshirts, hats, and other accessories to college sports departments. She could compose her work history to emphasize her persuasive abilities and sales experience; clearly she'd be a dynamite interview. Likewise, after doing the appropriate research, she could effectively use her writing skills and all her creative energy to inform pet owners about the values of nutritious food for their animals. A few months ago, I received this postcard from Marian:

> Can you believe it? Not only do I make a hefty five-figure income from my commissions selling organic dog food and cat food, but I got all my expenses paid to *come to Hawaii!* I'm addressing a dog breeders' conference here on the latest research in nutritional needs for large dogs. And I've been asked to write about it for a national publication when I get home! Talk about not being bored. . . .

If you find it hard to see how your skills, abilities, and personality traits can translate from one arena to another, try out the skill translation exercise that follows. Use a notebook if you prefer.

TRANSLATING YOUR SKILLS INTO A NEW POSITION

Picture the position you want in your new area of interest and describe it:

....

....

....

....

Imagine that you are the person in charge of hiring for this position. What abilities, skills, and personality traits would you want your ideal employee to have? Fill in your answers below. (If you aren't sure, do some research and return to this exercise.)

SKILLS

_____

_____

ABILITIES

PERSONALITY TRAITS

Now list the positions you've held in the world of work, both paid and un-paid.

Look at each position you've held and think about the relevant abilities, skills, or personality traits it may have encompassed, even if you weren't thinking of the job in that way at the time. Now go back to the columns and put a star next to each requirement you satisfy. Then write your cover letters and resume, framing your past experiences in the light of the starred abilities, skills, and personality traits. Where possible, get in touch with the people who saw you exhibiting the desired qualities and get them to write letters of reference highlighting those elements of your performance.

If you are missing several important abilities or other qualities, consider taking on a J-O-B, part-time volunteer work, apprenticeships, or internships (see Chapter Seven, "But I Don't Want to Go Back to School!" for more information) that would strengthen you in these areas.

PRESENTING YOURSELF TO POTENTIAL EMPLOYERS

Employers don't care whether you're a Renaissance Soul or a specialist. They just want to know if you can get the job done. But because resume readers and employers are busy people, you'll need to present yourself in such a way that your relevant skills are crystal clear, both in your resume and during interviews. For the tips that follow, I'd like to thank Jane Sommer, associate director of the Career Development Office at Smith College, and Jane Celwyn, director of career development at Barnard College.

Learn the tribal customs. Sommer points out that Renaissance Souls need to understand that each different type of work has its own subculture, and, within that, its own tribe. "When you want to join from the outside, learn how the tribe dresses and talks," she says. To gain this knowledge, don't send out resumes right away—first, spend time talking with people in the tribe. Ask them: "What makes someone successful at what you do? What are the challenges in your field?" Their answers will tell you much about the profession's values and the skills it requires. Listen to the words they use and make a note of the lingo. Do they speak of customers—or clients? Do they talk about "core competencies"—or "basic skills"? Then, says Sommer, "Compare those words to what you know about yourself. If it's a good fit, take the words and use them."

Translate your resume into tribal language. After you've interviewed several members of the tribe and have concluded that you want to join up, apply what you've learned to your resume. Sommer refers to a client who'd been in arts marketing and wanted to move into paralegal work. She sent in a draft cover letter for a law firm in Beijing. Although she met a lot of their criteria, says Sommer, "she wrote as if she were applying for another marketing position: potent, punchy, using sales terms, lots of bullets, and with repeated references to her success with 'customers.' She needed to think about the law culture and tribe, and refer to 'clients,' cut the hard sell—essentially, she needed to pay close attention to her tone and terminology."

Avoid "skill resumes." The skill resume is a format in which you categorize your experience according to different skills, not by chronological work experiences. This type of resume became popular several years ago, and Renaissance Souls often see it as a way to camouflage their unusual job history. But, says Celwyn, that's exactly the problem: "Skill resumes get thrown in the garbage. Employers see them as a disguise." Instead, use your cover letter to describe your relevant skills and take control of how an employer sees you.

Identify common denominators. Identify the common denominators between your background and the job you desire.
Show, right up front in your cover letter, that you have the
skills that your prospective employer needs. Sommer suggests
writing, "I've had a great many different positions in my life,
and the common denominators have been . . ." Don't expect a
swamped executive to go hunting for that information in your
resume.

Don't apologize. Avoid sounding defensive about your desire
to switch careers. Beware of phrases such as "Although I'm
presently an attorney . . ." or "Even though I've worked in several fields already . . ."

*Mention skills that may not be mentioned in the job descrip-
tion.* Of course, during an interview you'll want to highlight
your most relevant experience first. But Celwyn points out
that as a Renaissance Soul, you've probably picked up other
skills that an employer can use. Can you speak another language? Operate video equipment or graphic design programs?
Have you acquired understanding of other cultures while
traveling or studying abroad? Have you shown a capacity for
teamwork or leadership on a sports team? These qualities may
not be listed in the job description, but look for an appropriate
moment to mention them and be sure to include them in your
resume. Something you mention may just give you an edge
over the competition.

*Be prepared to interview with someone younger than you
are.* If you are past the age of thirty, you may find yourself
sitting across the table from a prospective employer who is
younger than you are, especially if you are in a technical or
creative field that attracts young people. Sommer notes that

the employer may be wondering: Will this person take supervision from me? She tells her clients to address this issue head-
on with a comment such as, "If I were in your shoes, one of
the things that might concern me is whether a person my age
will be comfortable taking supervision. I want you to know
that I have enormous respect for your expertise, and I'm looking forward to what I'm going to learn, as well as contribute,
in this field." The employer may also wonder whether
you have the appropriate computer skills. If your position demands familiarity with a specialized program, learn it. And
note your ability on your resume.

OPTION ONE: AN UMBRELLA JOB DESIGNED TO FEED
MORE THAN ONE INTEREST

For people who like to integrate their interests into one paying position, the umbrella provides a cool, shady haven. You
may remember that an umbrella covers a multitude of activities at once, but it looks like a traditional job or hobby to the
outside world. Depending on the specifics, umbrellas can include careers like journalism, business management, teaching,
litigation, consulting, entrepreneurial work, event planning,
and many others. Some umbrellas fit for life; some don't.
Because an umbrella so neatly meets the need for several simultaneous interests *and* provides the cover of a "legitimate"
job title, it's worth investigating whether there is an umbrella
out there that shelters *your* current combination of Focal
Points.

Of course, almost any job involves performing several
tasks. A highway toll collector handles several responsibilities: handing out change, getting along with supervisors,
keeping accurate time sheets, and giving directions to lost

VARIATIONS ON A THEME:
ONE WRITER'S UMBRELLA CAREER

An umbrella career isn't *always* protection from external criticism. Patricia Horan knows this firsthand. As a writer, she certainly has a clear, "acceptable" answer to the question, "And what do you do?" She can say simply, "I'm a writer," or "Yes, I still write." No concerned glances. No offers to help her find a "real" job.

But look at the range of interests Patricia has hung from her umbrella career: She's written a home-improvement book for women; an award-winning poem that will be turned into a play; a children's book; articles for labor journals; and scripts for Broadway stars such as Nell Carter and Colleen Dewhurst. When we spoke, Patricia was at work on books about time management and feng shui.

Despite her easily identifiable career, Patricia often receives criticism for not zeroing in on one type of writing. Sometimes she chooses not to tell people about everything she's working on in a given moment. "If I did," she says, "I'd probably have to wear a sandwich board!"

In the end, what other people say doesn't matter all that much. "Unfortunately, I can be pretty good at buying into other people's criticisms of me," Patricia muses. "But my impulse to move on when what I'm writing about no longer intrigues me is so strong, it's one of the few things about myself I *don't* condemn. I just can't argue with the excruciating boredom that would otherwise come up!"

---

drivers. Yet umbrella careers encompass more than just tasks. They offer the chance for you to practice what you're passionate about. Unless making change and giving directions are among your Focal Points, collecting highway tolls does not count as an umbrella.

That doesn't mean an umbrella job will never include boring tasks or distasteful moments. A journalism career, for example, can satisfy passions for writing, and travel, and talking to fascinating people. But it can also involve tasks you might not find so thrilling, such as making interview appointments, standing in the security line at the airport, and even filling out those employee time sheets. You can love journalism as an umbrella career without loving the need to find a pet sitter every time you dash off for another exciting assignment.

If you have a family member or partner who is anxious about your future, your identifying an umbrella—a single, familiar "job title" they recognize—may be a great relief to them. They may feel you have finally found the career that will last you "forever," and they will support you with enthusiasm. This can be helpful for some Renaissance Souls, but be careful: If your loved ones believe you will consequently soon be happily climbing that one career ladder to inevitable fame and fortune, they will be even harder on you than usual if you tire of that umbrella and want to move on to something else. Try not to use umbrella careers as a way of avoiding honest talk about your Renaissance Soul with the people you care about.

Umbrellas can be sorted into two main types. The first involves a repeated activity or set of skills that is applied in a broad variety of ways. My revered editor, Kris Puopolo, follows one basic process for each book she edits. She reads the manuscript or proposal; negotiates to buy it; consults with the author; edits the material; and works with the art, marketing, and publicity departments to develop a title, cover, and marketing plan. There's a logic to the sequence of these steps, so Kris usually performs them in the same order each time. Yet when she talks about her career, it's clear that Kris is a Renaissance Soul who works under a wide, multicolored umbrella:

> I love editing different books because they give me lots of chances to check out new ideas. For example, I recently took on a book project about crafts. Now, I'm not that much of a crafts person, but while I edited the manuscript I came to appreciate the politics behind crafting—creating instead of consuming. You might call me an "armchair" crafts enthusiast. Another time I edited a book about yoga and depression. I related to it initially due to my interest in psychology; I knew little about yoga. But I was paid to delve into that manuscript, and now I practice yoga myself on a regular basis—and have convinced my mom to try it as well. So, yes, each book goes through a similar process, but as a Renaissance Soul, I love the bouncing around from one thing to another that book editing involves.

Documentary filmmaking is an umbrella, too. Consider the award-winning documentary filmmaker Ken Burns. Even though he is totally identified with one profession, there's no question Burns is a Renaissance Soul. In our interview I had no sooner described the nature of umbrella passions than he said, "You've come to the right man! By deciding to become a documentary filmmaker, I chose a career that educated all of my parts." He then went on to list some of those "parts": writer, small businessman, collaborator, and editor. And Burns was quick to point out that wasn't all. This umbrella also incorporates his good physical conditioning ("You have to be in good shape to work fifteen-hour days"), his editing skills ("I get to kill 'the little darlings'"), his passion for thinking in nonlinear ways, and his ability to understand the nuances of music, sound production, and the spoken word. "And of course

I also get to be a bit of an evangelist because, to me, what's significant about what I'm doing is sharing the meaning I see behind the films." Yet despite all the variety documentary filmmaking can provide, Burns agreed that this process can become formulaic for some. He deliberately creates ways to keep the process as fresh as possible for himself. "For example, I love inviting young people to work with us on the documentaries. They haven't yet learned 'the right way' to do things, so they come in with wide-open creativity. Their mistakes become our challenges, our lessons. . . . Every step of the production is both familiar and startlingly new."

Another umbrella career that involves the application of one process to a variety of subjects is teaching. There is a process—communicating information and instructions, creating assignments, maintaining discipline, encouraging curiosity and learning—but each year brings a fresh set of faces and personalities. Elementary school teachers have the additional fun of applying their teaching skills not just to one subject but to five or even more, including reading, math, writing, science, and social studies. An elementary school teacher's passion is teaching, not necessarily third-grade math or phonics. It is the variety of subjects he gets to teach—and the challenge of teaching each subject effectively—that keeps his Renaissance Soul happy.

Writing can also be a fulfilling umbrella profession. Consider Pulitzer Prize winner Tracy Kidder. His nonfiction books mostly follow a pattern: He becomes an almost-invisible fly on the wall of a given setting and describes what he learns. However, the walls change dramatically. He has immersed himself in the world of a fast-paced computer company (*The Soul of a New Machine*), an inner-city school (*Among Schoolchildren*), the evolution of a town (*Home Town*), a nursing home (*Old Friends*), the building of one home (*House*), and the world of a rural Haitian medical clinic (*Mountains Beyond*

Mountains). His day-to-day experiences, the people he met with, the things he needed to understand all varied dramatically from book to book. As Kidder said when I interviewed him, "It's wonderful to be paid to indulge my curiosity." He went on to share a typical Renaissance Soul sentiment: "It's true that, after I'd written *The Soul of a Machine,* I probably could have made an excellent living just writing more about the computer age. But I didn't want to do that. In fact, the very idea of going on and on writing about computers horrified me!"

The second type of umbrella career allows you to pursue one main interest while wearing many hats. Take Rob, who works for Conner Prairie, one of the nation's premiere living history museums. For several years, Rob's guiding interest has been museums that represent rural and farm life. When he began working at Conner Prairie, his job was to research and supply the museum with livestock that would best re-create the animals owned by an Indiana farm family in 1886. To figure out which animals were appropriate, he had to perform scholarly research. But he also had to help restore an old barn; pitch his project to fund-raisers at wine-and-cheese parties; track down owners of rare breeds of pigs, sheep, and chickens; and even rent a trailer to pick up a Jersey cow. Of his career, Rob says, "I picked this because it's dynamic and forever changing."

Or take my daughter, Lori Lobenstine, who once headed up the teen leadership program for Girls Inc. in a heavily Puerto Rican city. At Girls Inc., teen girls built their leadership skills while participating in mentoring, health workshops, outdoor leadership challenges, and other activities. While she held this job, Lori would have described herself as a youth worker, because she has a passion for stimulating and cooperating with teens so they can have more influence over the factors that affect their lives. In this position, Lori did not apply a "youth work" skill to one interest after another in the

way that an editor applies editorial skills to diverse book projects. Instead, she applied a variety of skills toward her over-
arching goal of helping teens.

On any given day you might have found Lori writing a
grant proposal, climbing a ropes course with a group of girls,
painting the teen center, training other workers, or even learning to cook Puerto Rican dishes as part of a research project
with teens and their mothers. She held a recognizable job title
and received a regular paycheck, but that was all that was
"regular" about her work. Likewise, while a Renaissance Soul's
current main interest may be massage, she might well get so
bored sitting in one room of a spa attending to one customer
after another that the spa owner sees fit to send her on her way.
However, creating her own massage business and employing
all the different faculties that entrepreneurship requires may
keep her involved in this particular passion a lot longer.

YOU AND YOUR UMBRELLA

Below is an alphabetical list of twenty umbrella careers. Just for fun, try selecting the four you find most appealing and see how many of your Focal
Points might fit underneath each umbrella. To help you along, I've included
a few of the various interests and skills that each umbrella covers—but you
may certainly think of others.

1. Athletics director/manager (public relations, fund-raising,
personnel management, sports)

2. Book editor or critic (one basic editorial process applied to a
variety of subjects and projects)

3. Camp director (events planning, child psychology, outdoor skills,
land and building maintenance)

4. Chamber of Commerce president (community history, small business advocacy, outreach, fund-raising)

5. Community activist (inspirational speaking, politics, negotiating, fund-raising)

6. Foreign Service officer (diplomacy, negotiation, economic and/or foreign policy development, usually applied to a variety of cultures)

7. Home restorer (working knowledge of architecture, history, building/contracting, communication)

8. Import-export business owner (one set of skills applied to products purchased from a variety of countries and sold to different customer bases)

9. Innkeeper (hospitality skills, gardening, decorating, cooking)

10. Mayor/town manager (strategic planning, politics, budgeting, public speaking)

11. Minister (theology, inspirational speaking, social work, building maintenance)

12. Outward Bound leader (outdoor skills, planning, psychology, working with youths)

13. Personal assistant (organizing, psychology, travel planning)

14. Retreat center manager (fund-raising, budgeting, organizing, hosting)

15. Restaurateur (cooking, personnel management, budgeting, decorating)

16. Talk-show host (interviewing and research skills applied to a variety of guests)

17. Teacher, especially elementary school or in a broad field, such as American studies (one process applied to different subjects and students)

18. Tour planner (one set of organizational, research, and people skills applied to different countries and groups of clients)

19. Writer (same skill applied to different subjects)

20. Zoo director (zoology, personnel management, fund-raising, strategic planning)

OPTION TWO: THE TWO-FOR-ONE APPROACH

*A*nother way to incorporate various interests under recognizable career labels is the Two-for-One Approach. This approach is especially appealing to Renaissance Souls who find themselves very close to the middle of the continuum of interests, without quite as many changing interests as a Ben Franklin but without the single-subject mind-set of a Mozart. The essence of the Two-for-One Approach is having *two* careers (or unpaid interests) that combine to make *one* Renaissance Soul life. Two-for-Ones might include careers as a banker *and* a journalist; stay-at-home mom *and* activist; or musician *and* yoga instructor.

A benefit of the Two-for-One Approach is that the rest of the world doesn't have much difficulty understanding people who split their time between two careers. And if you can find two careers that completely satisfy your curiosity, that's terrific. But it's not a good idea to adopt the Two-for-One Approach merely as a lifelong hedge against criticism. Most Renaissance Souls will still feel restricted by having only two careers—and then the rest of the world will get judgmental again. As I've said before, it's best to proudly display your nature rather than hide it.

It is, however, quite possible for Renaissance Souls to use this approach if one of the two careers is an umbrella. My client Florence, for example, thrives on running her Web design business, because of the variety of activities she can choose from on any given day. She is also a passionate gardener of the small plot behind her condo. "I've moved past the hobby stage," she told me with evident pleasure. "My garden has been selected for several garden tours and I have won significant prizes at the New England Flower Show."

"If your financial condition allowed, would you want to give up your business and give more time to your garden?" I asked her. Florence looked startled. "Oh no," she responded immediately, "I couldn't let go of my business. I'd do it even if I won the lottery." She clearly enjoys the two main tracks she's chosen. When I asked her if she participated in any other activities, such as playing an instrument or taking up photography, her answer said it all. "Why would I want to do that? I *couldn't* do that—at least not this year." One umbrella passion, one additional focus, and that's it for now: Florence is definitely a Two-for-One Renaissance Soul.

Another version of the Two-for-One is the combination of one career that remains constant with another career that changes regularly. This is the route most often taken by Renaissance Souls who have one passion that requires constant practice to give satisfaction. Staying proficient in a foreign language, maintaining the physical skills necessary to play a particular sport, staying current with all the latest square dance routines, or pursuing some form of musical expression are examples of this type of passion. My client Frank has played the violin since he was six. Sounds a bit like Mozart, doesn't he? Given that he recently turned fifty, that is a pretty long haul. Frank specializes in playing old favorites for seniors, and local retirement centers line up to hire him. So where's the Renaissance Soul in all this? Check out Frank's "other" passion in his Two-for-One Approach: It has changed far more frequently than most of his friends can understand. Frank has been a biologist, an Episcopal priest, a macrobiotic chef, a staff member of the American Friends Service Committee, a classical singer, a shiatsu massage therapist, a Peace Corps volunteer, a world traveler, a pianist, and an advocate for fair-trade coffee. Clearly, playing his violin has been the only constant in Frank's first half century of living. He definitely "qualifies" as a Two-for-One Renaissance Soul.

OPTION THREE: CASTING LOOSE

Some Renaissance Souls will never truly thrive in a corporate setting, especially if their preferred working mode is to manage a host of challenges simultaneously. These folks are often more energized when they become free agents, whether freelancers, consultants, or entrepreneurs. Why? Because running an independent business is the perfect opportunity to wear many hats.

Free agents can carve out niches that are as wide or as narrow as they like. There are plenty of responsibilities, but they're the kinds that suit the adventurous minds of many Renaissance Souls. In addition to providing their product or service, free agents are often (but not necessarily) their own publicists, generating the next assignment or sale. They can nurture their creativity, learning to develop a Web site and brainstorming for a clever name for their business. They can broaden their expertise in business and financial areas, learning how to handle accounts (or at least how to hire a good accountant) and pay their self-employment tax. Many Renaissance Souls are *wired* for successfully running a business. They are in seventh heaven when they can move from one new project to another (as good outside consultants do) and when they get to think about many different aspects of a project (as good entrepreneurs must). It's what they thrive on. Thus energized, they are more likely to generate excellence in the products and services they offer. These Renaissance Souls shine with an inner light that attracts clients and economic opportunity.

But I Hate to Sell!

This brings us to an assumption that stops many Renaissance Souls and would-be entrepreneurs in their tracks: that they'd have to take on the personality of a used-car salesman in order to survive financially. Here's where I get the most stricken looks from many of my workshop participants. "I get that I'd be good at running my own business because I *do* like wearing lots of different hats, but I just know it would never work," they tell me. If I ask for an explanation, I hear the same one over and over again: "I'm just not any good at selling myself! I can't get out there with those brochures and blow my own horn."

Sometimes a person's fear factor is under control until we begin to talk about writing press releases, speaking to local groups to highlight their service, or approaching their local paper for some free publicity. Then panic sets in. "I just can't do that, Margaret!" they say to me, half-angry, half-begging me to understand. "I just can't talk about myself like that! It would be like bragging."

So does that mean you should give up on your dreams and sit with your hands quietly folded in your lap? Or persist, and become an obnoxious, pushy braggart? Fortunately, the answer to this dilemma lies outside it. For while the fear of change and risk is built into the human psyche, *this* fear is based primarily on the false assumption that to bring your dreams to fruition you must go out and bore the world by talking about yourself.

Wrong!

Sure, it seems obvious that if your Renaissance strengths lead you to become a free agent of some sort, you're going to have to let the world know about your talents. But I am not talking about being pushy here. What I *am* talking about is the necessity of passing on needed information about an important gift you have to offer others.

I once worked with a woman, Roberta, who lived in California. One of her Renaissance Focal Points was to become a therapist specializing in helping people get over phobias. Roberta had a reading disability, so this dream took her years to accomplish. Finally, however, she finished all the course work and passed the demanding licensing test. With pride and significant financial investment, Roberta leased office space, ordered business stationery, installed her own business phone, and was ready to go. She sent out her business card to people in a position to refer clients, placed small ads in the local papers, and e-mailed her friends to let them know she was finally "official."

What happened? Very little. Roberta conferred with her peers. They told her she had to go out and really market herself. She had to get herself written up in newspapers and give talks to medical associations, and . . . Roberta heard no more. She just froze. All that work, all those years, and she sat in her office absolutely paralyzed.

Fortunately she got in touch with me, and the story has a happy ending. Why? Because I was some sort of magician who could drop clients onto her doorstep? Of course not. All I did was tell her a story. I had her imagine that a young woman who lived in Marin County, at the northern end of the famed Golden Gate Bridge, gave birth to a very sick baby. And I had her imagine that the little baby's grandmother lived in San Francisco, at the southern end of the same bridge. I told her that this grandmother, who wanted so much, of course, to help her daughter with this ill child, had a phobia about bridges. This meant that if the young mother were to get any help at all, she would have to bundle her sick child up and take it all the way into the city. All because no one had taken the trouble to inform the grandmother there was an easy cure for her phobia, a cure that took no more than one or two sessions of therapy!

I then challenged Roberta. Was she willing to get that information into the hands of the grandmother's doctor and into the paper the grandmother reads at her breakfast table? Her response was instantaneous: "Of course!" And Roberta saw that the focus of any newspaper article about her business would be about the *gift* she had to offer (the release from phobias through hypnosis), not about her. We weren't talking about "Look at ME" articles or lectures, but about sharing important information. Being generous enough to share is a quality we all can be comfortable with; it has little to do with bragging and tooting one's own horn.

Success Without "Selling Yourself"

If you want to become an entrepreneur but are uncomfortable with the hard sell, here are a few soft-but-successful ideas:

Distribute guinea-pig gift certificates. When I began my coaching business, I didn't want my first clients to feel like the guinea pigs on whom I tested my skills. But I needed people to see that I could help them with their problems and spread the word. So I printed up gift certificates for my service and handed them out to folks I knew, asking them to pass my gift certificates along to anyone who might need a life coach. I targeted people who were in a position to know others in need: an acupuncturist, a hair stylist, and a newspaper columnist. They gave out my certificates as gifts; the recipients assumed that their friends had paid for the session. When they came to my office, they could devote their attention to my service, not obsess about being one of my first clients.

Create your own national organization. Kitty Axelson-Berry, who began a memoir-writing business for corporate executives, needed to get publicity and establish her credibility in the field. So she founded the National Organization for Memoir Writers. She held meetings that were written up in the papers, which brought her free publicity. When she met with new clients, her title as director of this organization made them feel more comfortable.

Supply a gift. Paid advertising costs a great deal of money but yields unpredictable results. Putting their name out there can also be uncomfortable for people who don't like "selling themselves." Joan Setkevitch, an artist skilled in drawing homes and landscapes, heard that her local historical society was creating a large quilt to raise funds, and offered to provide a rendering of the historical society building for the quilt's center. Whenever the historical society landed a piece about the quilt on the news or in the papers, Joan's gift was mentioned, bringing her publicity.

Combine your passions to set yourself apart. In my town there are several massage therapists competing for business. One enterprising Renaissance Soul, Cheryl Summa, who has an interest in Hawaii, gardening, and physical therapy, has set herself apart with her Spirit of Aloha service. It features a Hawaiian massage technique, a hot-stone treatment, and a client room filled with orchids and the sounds of birds singing. The theme attracts the many people who love massage *and* who'd like to visit Hawaii, especially during the long, cold Massachusetts winters.

Set up multiple locations. When I began my business, I wanted people to understand that I was a serious, capable professional. So I set up three offices in three different towns. I had my own office, of course, and I also borrowed the offices of two friends for use in the evenings. On my business cards and everywhere else I advertised, I could state: "Offices in Amherst, Belchertown, and Northampton." Now I'm too busy to travel to my clients—they have to come to me!

Your Gift Is Bigger Than You Are

"But Margaret," someone in my workshops usually pipes up here, "that's all very well and good for people offering therapy or selling brilliant new technology or for people who have other clear gifts to share, but what about those of us who want to do something for ourselves? I want to *leave* psychology and do theater. . . ."

The content of what we offer does not matter. What matters is that we are motivated by something bigger than ourselves. It can be a conceptual issue, such as peace. Or it can be a specific group of people whose needs or desires we are filling: widows, fellow immigrants, parents, theater audiences, clients, music lovers, patients, readers, Renaissance Souls, or phobic grandmothers. Regardless of the form our cause takes, we have a gift to share, not a horn to toot or a miracle gizmo to sell. Thinking about our gift gives us the energy to move forward and do things that, if we thought of them as "sales" or "marketing," might well be beyond us. We gain freeing energy when we understand that our passions can have a positive effect on others.

Let's look at Mozart again, this time with a different purpose. Mozart lived between 1756 and 1791, a time when Europe was still a largely agrarian society. The nobility, which accounted for only 2 percent of the population, owned (depending on the country) from 15 to 40 percent of the continent's most critical resource: land. Consequently a large part of the population lived with extreme hunger as a daily fact of life. Did Mozart spend his time doling out food to the hungry or crusading for change? Obviously not. What was he doing? Being paid to write minuets for the nobility, so they could dance to the very best. Yet, because Mozart was willing to share his gift, innumerable social workers, emergency room staff, teachers, personal care attendants, and others doing stressful jobs can, even today, relax themselves with his melodies going to and from work. Mozart's gift from two hundred and fifty years back helps them continue giving gifts of their own!

If we allow ourselves to pursue the things our Renaissance souls want to pursue, someone else will get what his or her soul needs as well. Which does not mean that we are back at the old "sacrifice yourself, take care of the rest of the world" solution. We all have a place at this banquet. There is no "either them or us" choice here. So we can forget about being terrified of tooting our own particular horn and instead throw all our positive Renaissance Soul energy into the orchestra of human exchange.

How to Find Another Person to Sell Your Dream

"I don't know all that much about Mozart, but if he were alive today, he'd have to be out there hustling just to get a shot at 'sharing' his gift," a workshop participant once challenged me. "And I'm *not* outgoing. *I'm* your classic introvert, and I'm just too plain shy to do that!" And that may well be true. Even if you'd be tickled to have your gifts shared around the world, you may simply not have the daring or the skills to make that sharing happen. But who says that *you* are the one who has to handle matters such as publicity and marketing? Dr. Barbara Reinhold, author of *Free to Succeed: Designing Your Life in the*

New Free Agent Economy, counsels people who are interested in pursuing their passions as free agents rather than nine-to-five employees. Time and time again she stresses the advantages of having a partner who can do for your dream what you cannot. For some this may be a financial backer; for others, a detail-oriented, keep-everything-organized administrative assistant. For shy Renaissance Souls it may mean considering working with volunteers, interns, or paid staff who understand the gift you're trying to share *and* whose own gift involves "getting out there" for things they believe in.

If you are a truly introverted Renaissance Soul and need one of these talented "big mouths," I would encourage you to start the process in a nonthreatening way: by going through Rolodexes, e-mail address books, and even holiday-card lists, noting everyone who is outgoing and comfortable in the spotlight—*regardless* of whether you think the person would be remotely interested in sharing your dream. From there you can decide whether to place phone calls, send an e-mail, or drop a note (for shy folks, using the written word is often easier) to the most approachable people on the list, describing the volunteer or paid position and *why* you need such a person. The conversation or note ends with a request to spread the word. Some contacts will try; others won't. But eventually, the shy swan will link up with one or two extroverts who just love the challenge of helping someone else solve a problem. Yes, there will be false leads and dead ends. But you don't need a hundred people to sell your dream; one skilled person will do just fine!

PREPARING FOR CHANGE

In this chapter you've learned different styles of working that will help you get paid for your passions. You've learned, too, that acknowledging your Renaissance Soul grants you the capacity for more honest self-assessment. You'll know when you're getting ready to make a change, and you can prepare for that change by saving money toward a specific goal and building up new skills needed to transition to a different position. The following chapter will help you find the resources you need to make this transition.

I love the idea of being a Renaissance Soul, and I have no trouble coming up with Focal Points. But it hasn't been all that long since I paid off my student loans for my BA in criminal justice, and now I want to be involved in finding ways for elephants and poor farmers to coexist in rural Thailand! How do I get training for that? And what's it going to cost me?

—*Randy, twenty-eight*

*Y*ou may frequently find yourself with Focal Points for which you have few, if any, credentials. Unlike those who come up through the ranks of a single field, Renaissance Souls often jump headfirst into new areas.

Back in 1978, when I got it into my head to run a bed-and-breakfast, what was my domestic claim to fame? The D– I got on the apron I made in an eighth-grade home economics class? More recently, I had been living with my family in a two-bedroom ranch in northern California, working for the U.S. Postal Service in their downtown Oakland office. Owning a large Victorian bed-and-breakfast in a small New England town, meeting the needs of happy vacationers, was as different as could be from my circumstances at the time. Most of my friends couldn't imagine why I would want to make such a drastic change. I couldn't imagine why I *wouldn't* want to.

Given our love of the unknown, Renaissance Souls may also gravitate toward subjects in which no formal training has yet been established. This certainly was true for Randy, determined to help Thai elephants and farmers coexist more peacefully. There was no book I could hand him, no government guidelines to offer. And certainly his local college did not offer a degree program designed to help him maneuver his way through the new cultural experiences he'd face as a mediator for the elephants and farmers of a country so different from the one in which he grew up.

One of the trying features of life as a Renaissance Soul is that you can fall in love with subjects that you don't understand very well. That passion can leave you standing atop the infamous Square One, feeling like a rank beginner even when you're in your twenties, forties, sixties, or eighties. Often, it isn't realistic to take a conventional approach to your goal, stepping from Square One to Square Two, then laboring away until you can reach Square Three, and so on. Since you change interests frequently, it may not always be advisable to invest time and money in long-term schooling, entry-level jobs, or expensive equipment, assuming such things even exist for your Focal Points.

But if you keep fussing about a lack of relevant diplomas or knowledge, you risk getting stuck on Square One forever. When you're wondering how you can ever find your way toward a new Focal Point, remind yourself of Ben Franklin.

Even in today's world of interdisciplinary studies, what academic program could possibly credential him for all his professions and hobbies? This in no way negates either the Renaissance Soul's love of learning (we're often teased about being perennial students) or the need for credentials in some very specific fields. But most Renaissance Souls need to develop nontraditional ways to get where we want to go. (Randy, for example, found direction from an Internet resource, www.allforelephants.org, that specifically addresses the dangers facing elephants in Thailand.) This chapter contains strategies that can help.

The suggestions in this chapter can also be useful if you're struggling to put a finger on your very first set of Focal Points. It's possible that you have unconsciously left delicious possibilities off your plate, assuming that you'd have to spend endless years in a classroom to "learn enough," or that you cannot make a Focal Point fit your fiscal or family situation. By showing you creative ways to get started, the follwing strategies can strengthen your belief in your own potential.

HOW YOU GET FROM THERE TO HERE: THE REVERSE FLOWCHART

Flowcharts are the darling of manufacturers, who depend on them for the efficient assembly of everything from ballpoint pens to airplanes. They work like this: you name your goal—say, assembling a ballpoint pen. Then you identify the first step (acquiring the supplies—a plastic shell, the spring that goes inside, the ink cartridge, and the cap) and peg an estimated time of completion; then the second step (inserting the ink cartridge into the plastic shell) with its own target completion time; and so on, until the pen is complete. And it's not only manufacturers who love flowcharts: In my experience nearly everyone does. Caterers use them to keep a lid on pre-party chaos; business owners have flowchart analyses of their quarterly financial goals tacked over their desks; and lots and lots of individuals use them to slice their biggest dreams into a series of bite-sized actions. But this conventional business tool doesn't always help when what you're trying to assemble is a brand-new, as-yet-unknown, experience. How can you identify a task you may not even know exists or determine how long something will take you when you've never done it before?

This is what Joy, a client of mine, discovered when she fell in love with handmade sweaters on a trip with her husband through Europe. She became excited about opening a store devoted to top-of-the-line sweaters in the resort community where she lived. But she'd never run her own business or worked in retail before. How was she to know whether to draw up a business plan first and use it to attract backers, or get the financing lined up first and *then* lay out her business plan according to how much money she raised? And how could she figure out whether she'd need to trademark her store's name, when she was totally new to this endeavor, or take a course in employment law? What about family obligations? How would she manage those while running a business?

At this stage of the process, a better tool for Joy was the *reverse* flowchart. Introduced by Barbara Sher in *Wishcraft: How to Get What You Really Want*, it's like a treasure hunt in which you find the treasure right off the bat. So your first step is to identify your goal. Joy's goal was to have her own imported-sweater shop, fully stocked and open for business.

The next step is to ask: What are three steps you *know* you'll need to take before you find your treasure? Even if you're a novice to your new activity, you can probably take a stab at the answers. Joy came up with these three steps: (1) secure financial backing, (2) set up accounts with suppliers, and (3) learn the legal requirements for small businesses.

Then Joy asked herself: "What do I need to do before I can get financial backing?" Although Joy knew almost nothing about corporate financing, she could say: "I need to know more about who offers this kind of backing." She knew that banks lend money, and that sometimes business owners raise capital by bringing investors on board. But, Joy said, "How do people find investors? And are there other sources of money?"

The process had yielded a specific question. Joy knew that there were books on the topic, so she decided to visit the library the next day and ask for help finding the appropriate resources. Okay, now she was cooking: Here was one task she could do *immediately*. But she also wondered if the government offered some kind of assistance for small-business start-ups. Joy placed a question mark next to this item.

And what did she need to do before setting up accounts with suppliers? She needed to figure out which suppliers offered the kind of high-end sweaters she wanted to sell. While Joy had made good connections for suppliers of European sweaters on her trip, she was also eager to learn about sources of beautiful sweaters from other parts of the world. How could she do that? Could another retailer provide some suggestions? Joy decided to look up other sweater stores on the Internet. In addition, perhaps someone she knew had a contact with a retailer. Joy decided to hold a brainstorming extravaganza to find out. (I'll discuss brainstorming extravaganzas in just a moment.)

Joy also needed to understand just what the law asks of small-business owners. What would she have to do to learn everything she needed to know? She had several options, including hiring a lawyer, but Joy decided she'd like to take a

Wednesday-night class she knew was offered at the local community college. What would she need to do before she could take the class? Clear out her schedule on Wednesday nights. On Wednesday nights she usually took a hot dinner to her Uncle Bob, who was housebound and couldn't work his kitchen appliances very well. Joy decided to call her sister Trudy, who usually took dinner to Uncle Bob on Mondays, and see if they could switch days.

At this stage, Joy was no longer tempted to stew over her lack of experience, sitting around the house and mumbling, *Guess I'm not experienced enough to run a business...Maybe I need to get an MBA.* Instead, she'd pinpointed *exactly* what she didn't know, which is a kind of wisdom in itself, and then identified the resources she'd need for educating herself as a new business owner. This process helped her come up with reassuringly small steps that would move her closer to her Focal Point.

Joy's Reverse Flowchart

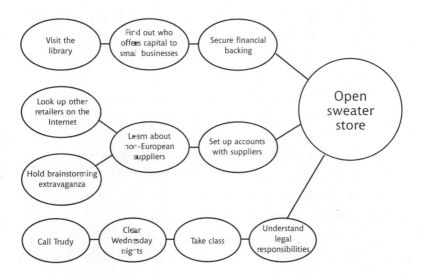

BRAINSTORMING TRICKS

*W*hen your reverse flow chart asks you to fill in missing pieces of knowledge, inspiration, or equipment, it helps to bring together a group of people and pool their intellectual and imaginative resources on your behalf. I call this strategy the "brainstorming extravaganza."

To hold a brainstorming extravaganza, invite a dozen or so friends, relatives, or colleagues over. They don't need to know you particularly well. They don't have to understand much about your areas of interests. Nor do they need to give a hoot about Renaissance Souls. But they should love coming up with new ideas and thinking quickly on their feet. (Most people are delighted when you ask them for help brainstorming. However, providing food for your extravaganza never hurts.)

At her brainstorming extravaganza, Joy asked: "Does anyone have a personal contact with an upscale sweater retailer?" Other Renaissance Souls might questions such as "How can I take art classes when my schedule and budget are already so stretched?" "I've spent a lot of money on my brochure but I'm not sure how to distribute it. Do you have any ideas?" "Does anyone know where I can find other people interested in developing nutrition education programs for the public?"

When everyone is ready, gather them in one room and follow these steps:

1. Be sure participants' phones are turned off.

2. Have a blackboard, easel, flip chart, computer, or note pad available for taking notes. If you have difficulty taking notes quickly, ask a friend to serve as secretary.

3. Pose your question to the group.

4. Ask participants to call out any and all ideas that pop into their heads. Remind them that the goal here is quantity, not quality.

5. Do not allow ideas to be evaluated at this time—no praising, criticizing, or other forms of commentary!

6. When people have run out of steam, ask for clarification of any suggestions you don't understand. Refrain from arguing or objecting (nothing shuts down the creative process faster than "But I already tried that!" or "With *my* husband, that'll never work." .

If the group seems a little stiff and tentative at first, try having people write their ideas down on a piece of paper rather than calling them out. You can also ask them to push things to the outer limits, writing down three absolutely crazy ways they might solve this problem if they didn't have to worry about any moralities or legalities. This often gets the group loose and laughing.

Once you have run through steps one through six, you might try what I call *opposite brainstorming*. Pose your question in reverse: "How can I be absolutely sure that I'll be too busy and too poor to take my art class?" Ideas that pop out might include: "Go out and buy yourself a lot of high-end items you really don't need" or "Say 'yes' to every charitable organization that asks you to do volunteer work for them." While many of the responses will be silly, a gem or two usually can be culled from the lot. In the example here, you may have already recognized the need to budget carefully—but haven't thought about honing your ability to say no to competing time commitments.

Another approach is to challenge the group to answer your question in the most ridiculous manner possible. I call this *loony tunes brainstorming*: "Buy up all the lottery tickets to be sure you won and then money for art classes would be no issue." "Get a doctor's note saying you had to take art classes for medical reasons so your employer would have to give you time off from work." "Have an affair with the instructor so you won't get charged for the class."

Once you have a good, long loony tunes list, ask your brainstorming pals to help you fashion each idea into a more realistic suggestion. The lottery-ticket idea might produce the question: Might there be sources of money I haven't even thought of—an upcoming birthday check? an old Treasury bond? The doctor's-note idea might yield: "Is there any way I might get something similar through work?" "Could I take art classes during my scheduled vacation time?" The affair idea could get you wondering: "Is there a barter arrangement I could work out with the school or instructor that would lead to a reduction in costs?"

When your brainstorming extravaganza is over, sort through the ideas, picking out the ones that make sense to you. You can follow up over the coming days and weeks. In the meantime, you may experience an additional benefit of brainstorming: the forward motion created when you get a group of people involved in your Focal Points and pulling for your success.

The Big Brainstormer: Help with Your Focal Point Sampler

If you like, you can apply brainstorming to the really big question: Which among all of your possible interests should you select as your current Focal Points? Your friends can help you brainstorm ten, twenty, fifty possible Focal Points—and even suggest new interests you might enjoy. You can then ask the group to choose the set of Focal Points *they* think best fit your present situation and mind-set. Their responses and yours can be revealing, sometimes unintentionally. If you find yourself wishing the group had chosen golfing, swimming, and quiet time instead of entertaining, taking wine-tasting classes, and growing bonsai trees, then you've got an important piece of information in your hands.

Hosting a Resource Party to Locate Equipment and Other Resources You Need

Brainstorming extravaganzas are lively, fast-paced, energizing, and usually give everyone involved a great time. But they require a whole group to focus on *your* issue, *your* question, *your* Renaissance Focal Points. If that makes you uncomfortable, you can hold your own version of what Barbara Sher in her book *Wishcraft* has designated a "resource party." At a resource party, everyone invited—not just the host—receives help finding equipment, materials, useful information, and contacts. Here's what to do:

1. Invite a diverse group of people to your party. Ten or so is a good number.

2. Instruct participants to bring three very specific wishes to the party. (To help clarify, I usually give a few examples, saying something along the lines of, "Maybe you need to borrow an amp, or you want the use of a canoe in October, or you wonder if anyone knows a good house sitter/pet feeder for when you take your weeklong writing workshop.")

3. Before the party, take three-by-five-inch index cards (one for each person at the party, including you) and number them, starting with one. Make the numbers large enough so that they can be seen easily from across the room. As guests arrive, hand each a number. The final card is for you.

4. The person with card number 1 shares a wish first. This person might ask about the amp, for example.

5. Anyone who is able to help with this wish holds up a card. If guest number 3 and guest number 7 both have an amp they'd be willing to lend, and you know someone who doesn't use his anymore, you will each signal by holding up your cards, and the person making the request will jot down your numbers and the word "amp." At this point, none of these cardholders should speak and bore the room with the fine print of their offer.

6. Should no one hold up a card in response to the amp wish, the person asking has the opportunity to state a second wish.

7. Once everyone has received responses to one wish, the party takes a break. During this time, people can seek out those with the numbers they have written down and exchange whatever information is appropriate.

8. Proceed with as many rounds of resource sharing as folks have energy for.

At the first resource party I held, one woman brought brochures for her candle business and asked people to suggest good display spots. Before the evening was over, all her brochures had been eagerly taken by participants to share with friends or put out somewhere. At another party, a high-school student who shared a bedroom with two brothers asked about a quiet place to read up on colleges offering interdisciplinary studies. He ended up studying his brochures and guidebooks in a beautifully landscaped, bird-filled garden.

WHAT IF YOU STILL NEED INFORMATION?

But what if, after making up a reverse flow chart and brainstorming, there's still information that you just don't have? For example, Joy wasn't sure how to find out about possible government assistance for small businesses. Your chart may tell you to learn about careers that will take you outdoors—but if you and your friends have spent your working lives trapped in cubicles, where do you get that information?

Fortunately for Renaissance Souls, there are fast and nearly stress-free ways to learn what you need to know. Thousands of individuals, organizations, and other resources are just waiting to be of service.

If you're thinking of opening a small business, for example, who better to turn to than the Small Business Administration? It has offices around the country that offer seminars, workshops, and written material containing a wealth of practical, up-to-date information for the prospective entrepreneur. It also boasts a counseling service (known as SCORE, or Service Corps of Retired Executives) staffed by volunteers who are happy to share their experiences. Another often overlooked professional organization is your local Chamber of Commerce. Yours probably offers minicourses on marketing and creating business plans. Business associations and local community development organizations also stand at the ready, awaiting your questions. Women's groups and minority associations, if they are relevant, can help with new ventures as well.

You'd rather find funding for your artistic endeavors, you say? Your state's arts council or commission on arts can help. Frequently such agencies sponsor artist-in-residence programs that fund talented people. The National Network for Artist Placement (NNAP), based in Los Angeles, and the Ford, Guggenheim, and Rockefeller Foundations all offer grants as well. And on a smaller scale, local artists' alliances and cooperatives serve up information and assistance.

Many times when I have been stumped, a reference librarian

has turned me on to a resource I didn't even know existed. If you are seeking the unusual, or the unusually precise, run your query by one of these professionals. They've spent years familiarizing themselves with the vast array of reference books and online material available and also have access to vast, expensive databases. When you're still on Square One, a librarian (or a seasoned bookstore clerk) might help you find the broad overview you're looking for. For budding entrepreneurs, I love *199 Great Home Businesses You Can Start (and Succeed In) for Under $1000* by Tyler Hicks. Books can also provide the blow-by-blow on a highly targeted subject, from *Make Your Own Model Dinosaurs* by Danny A. Downs and Tom Knight to *How to Write a Children's Book and Get It Published* by Barbara Seuling. Keep in mind that books offer information about other topics near and dear to the Renaissance Soul. Is "getting close to nature" one of your Focal Points? Then you could look into *Sunshine Jobs: Career Opportunities Working Outdoors* by Tom Stienstra or *Outdoor Careers* by Ellen Shenk. Do you want to work abroad? There are books chock-full of details on the subject, such as *Work Your Way Around the World: The Globetrotter's Bible* by Susan Griffith. Are you a student who's itching to see the world? Try *Planning Your Gap Year* by Nick Vandome. Fortunately, even the most highly focused of these titles are often available at your local library.

Whatever your subject, a resource is out there somewhere. Browse the Internet for journals, websites, blogs, discussion forums, and chat rooms related to your topic. Don't let not knowing keep you from getting going!

VOLUNTEERING DOESN'T HAVE TO MEAN
LICKING STAMPS

*A*lthough brainstorming and research are crucial, Renaissance Souls who are casting off an old life and lighting out for new territory also need relevant experience. And if we are not working our way up through traditional channels, a key way to gain this experience is to volunteer within the field. You can often find opportunities that are offered on a part-time basis, or outside working hours.

"Oh, but I've tried doing that, Margaret," protested Karen, a Renaissance Soul workshop participant. "I volunteered at the art gallery and ended up licking stamps in a back office. What good was *that* going to do me?"

Karen's mistake was to limit herself to formalized volunteering opportunities, the kind that you get when you call up the volunteer hotline at a museum, historical society, or symphony hall. These opportunities are usually restricted to traditional volunteer roles such as fund-raiser, docent, or gift-shop clerk. If you *want* experience in fund-raising, guiding tours, or clerking, that's great. For most of us, however, this is not the way to get the hard-core, hands-on experience that can serve as training for our Focal Points.

Renaissance Souls will fare better if they think of volunteering as a kind of bartering arrangement. You give a service to a person or organization, and in return you get exactly the training or experience you need. Opportunities like this are rarely listed in volunteer newsletters. You'll probably need to create them yourself.

My client Fern volunteered to create window box arrangements for her dentist's office, so that his patients would have something pretty to look at. All he paid for were the boxes and plants, and all she asked in return was the chance to photograph her work, and a letter of reference from him if people liked what she did. Fern did the work over the weekend, with such positive results that soon other dentists in the building wanted her to do the same for them. A local paper picked up on the story and by the time all was said and done, Fern had publicity, photos, and letters of reference to help launch her dream of an indoor gardening business.

Al, who wanted to move out of management and into computer training, also created a volunteer position that proved critical to his progress. A quiet, soft-spoken man who felt that people were more afraid of computers than they needed to be, Al offered to teach beginning computer classes at the local senior citizens center and his town's library. In exchange, Al would practice his skills and gain exposure. He developed creative materials using easy-to-remember analogies to explain how e-mail and the Internet worked. One elderly gentleman was so thrilled with Al's slow, patient way of teaching that he raved about him to his son. The son remembered this praise when his biotech business decided to become more computerized. Guess who got the big contract for training all the firm's employees on the new system?

Two Questions for Volunteers

When you're looking for experience that will expose you to paid professionals and hands-on work, you need to make contact with the right person. Asking the wrong one can quickly lead to dead ends, or a parched pucker from licking all those stamps. Before you pick up the phone, ask yourself two questions:

Will I, or will I not, be in direct competition with this person or organization when my Focal Point is up and running? Let's say that one of my Focal Points is helping women with financial planning. I am particularly interested in working with novices, so I decide I'd like to offer a Financial Planning 101 workshop for women at the local adult learning center. But I am also a novice to the adult-ed teaching format. Looking over the catalog, I notice that Ed Jones, a financial planner, runs a course on investments there each semester. So, hoping I can see what Ed does and how he does it, I ask him if he'd let me assist him during one of his courses. But would Ed want to help me? In many cases, no. He would view me as direct competition. Why should he pass all his hard-earned tricks of the trade on to me, just so I can compete with him in the adult-ed catalog? If I want to learn from someone with Ed's experience, usually I would be better off asking someone who teaches in another town.

But under certain circumstances, Ed may be a perfect first "boss." If Ed specializes in retirement planning and has been in business for so long that he actually turns clients away, he might respond positively to my offer. He might see me as sufficiently out of his league as to be no threat whatsoever. Or he might suggest we divide the territory, with my eventual workshops directed at the newcomer to investing and his directed at the more financially sophisticated client. In this case, the competition issue is moot. And we may both benefit by homing in on our clients' precise needs.

Does this individual have any control over my field of interest? Karen, our art lover, probably found herself licking stamps in the back room because she did not know to ask herself this pivotal question. She probably called the local museum and pressed the number indicated for volunteer information. Her call goes to Mrs. Bryce, the board member in charge of volunteers. Mrs. Bryce fusses over Karen, tells her how desperately they need people like her, especially during this major fund-raising drive, and before Karen knows it, the only pictures she gets to see are those on stamps! Even if Karen had tried to tell Mrs. Bryce about her true interest—she wanted to understand the museum's techniques for hanging large canvases so she could display her own wall-sized fabric collages in the lobby of a nearby hospital—it probably wouldn't have made much difference. Mrs. Bryce works with volunteers, not with canvases.

Karen needs to talk to someone directly involved in displays. This may take some footwork on her part. She might call a few university art departments and find out the recognized title for people whose duties include hanging large canvases. Thus armed, she could call the museum and ask for the appropriate person or department.

Framing Your Request Effectively

Once you reach the right person, it's important to be able to present your volunteering idea effectively. How you frame your request can directly affect whether you hobnob with the bigwigs or sit alone making fund-raising calls.

The Four Frames method allows you to ask for a directed opportunity to get the experience or information you need without feeling you are imposing. It is structured to give people a chance to help you follow your Renaissance Focal Points while gaining something positive for themselves.

First Frame: The Big Picture. In the first frame you share what it is you are trying to accomplish.

Second Frame: Why Them? It's important to explain why you'd like to work with this particular person or organization. You'll need to be specific and do your homework. Research the field well enough so that you can explain your choice

Four Frames

Applying the Example of Joy's Sweater Store in Text

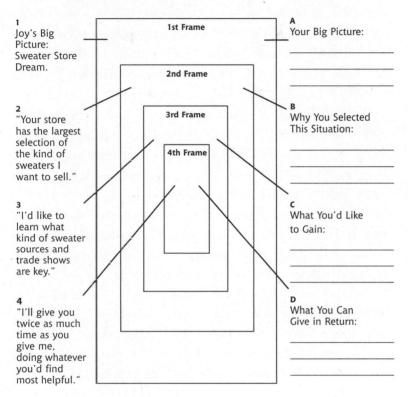

1
Joy's Big
Picture:
Sweater Store
Dream.

2
"Your store
has the largest
selection of
the kind of
sweaters I
want to sell."

3
"I'd like to
learn what
kind of sweater
sources and
trade shows
are key."

4
"I'll give you
twice as much
time as you
give me,
doing whatever
you'd find
most helpful."

1st Frame

2nd Frame

3rd Frame

4th Frame

A
Your Big Picture:

B
Why You Selected
This Situation:

C
What You'd Like
to Gain:

D
What You Can
Give in Return:

convincingly. And be sure your reason rings true. Coming at a stranger with glib, false flattery can only backfire.

Third Frame: Why You Want to Volunteer. Now describe *exactly what* you want to get out of this volunteer experience.

Fourth Frame: What's in It for Them? Tell the person what you are willing to give back in exchange for the experience you seek.

Let's take a look at Joy, the Renaissance Soul who wanted to open her own sweater shop. She used the Four Frames method to land the perfect volunteer opportunity with Cassandra, the owner of an upscale women's clothing store located in a similarly affluent tourist destination in another part of the state. Notice that she didn't choose a nearby retailer who might perceive Joy as potential competition.

Joy shared with Cassandra her special love of masterfully crafted and beautifully designed sweaters and how her trip had given her the idea of opening a store specializing only in sweaters (Frame 1). She then explained that she'd decided to speak with Cassandra because she had seen more sweaters she loved in Cassandra's shop than anywhere else in the area (Frame 2). This statement rang true for Cassandra, who knew she devoted a larger-than-normal square footage to sweaters. She felt pleased by Joy's sincere attentiveness.

Joy then went on to Frame 3, spelling out exactly what she wanted from Cassandra: "I wondered if you would be willing to sit down with me for three hours and talk to me about sweater suppliers—how to find them, how to evaluate them, how to deal with them effectively." She coupled this request with Frame Four: "In exchange, I would be willing to give you six hours of my time to do whatever task(s) would be most helpful to you." Because Joy did not have any expertise in retail and so could not offer an equivalent service to Cassandra, she offered a two-for-one time exchange. Cassandra happily agreed to spend three hours on an upcoming Sunday evening with Joy in exchange for six hours of Joy's time. Joy ended up driving a departing relative to the airport (about a six-hour round-trip) on an afternoon while Cassandra was at the store. When Joy last wrote to me she said her store would never have succeeded the way it did had she not initiated that successful

Four Frames exchange with Cassandra. And she was able to acquire the information she needed without being an imposition on anyone—or licking a single stamp.

FOR EXPERIENCED ADVICE, FIND A MENTOR

*T*he Four Frames method allowed Joy to gain very specific information in a limited amount of time. Renaissance Souls can also find it helpful to work on an ongoing basis with a mentor or a life coach.

For people who choose just one path in life—especially if they choose it early on—mentors are often presented to them by their schools or industries. Consider Rachel, who is a Mozart in the world of biochemistry. Even before she went on her first date, Rachel was in love with organic compounds and processes. In high school, she was recruited by a mentorship group that paired promising girls with women professionals in the hard sciences. Rachel's mentor helped her decide where to apply to college and even wrote her a recommendation to her own alma mater. Several years and three degrees later, Rachel walked into the human resources department her first day on the job at a pharmaceutical firm. There she was given an electronic ID, a health-care-provider directory—and a mentor, one of the firm's senior chemists. He took Rachel out for coffee once a month. Over the years, he helped Rachel handle a notoriously difficult boss and steered her toward research on selective serotonin reuptake inhibitors before anyone had heard of Prozac. Without the mentors assigned to her at various stages of her life, Rachel would probably still have become a chemist. But she might not have found herself on the fast track toward the elite coterie of whizzes who develop the cutting-edge psychoactive drugs.

Renaissance Souls deserve mentors, too. But mentoring has lately become so institutionalized—usually as part of organized programs in schools and companies—that Renaissance Souls may forget that mentorship has traditionally been a less formal affair, open to everyone. The word "mentor" goes back to Homer's *Odyssey*, in which Odysseus asks Mentor, his elderly advisor, to look after his son Telemachus while Odysseus sails off to fight the Trojan War. That's it. There was no structured program, no organization that brought Mentor together with his young charge. I like to imagine Mentor taking young Telemachus out for tea and olives, teaching him how to manage a household, choose a wife, comport himself in war, and do all the other things required of young Greek men at the time.

Today a mentor is still a lot like Mentor—someone who has already done whatever it is that you would like to be doing. Mentors know more about the reality of a particular field of endeavor than you do. Mentors can be your entrée to the old-boy (or old-girl) network, or they can provide models for standing courageously outside these networks. They are sources of the kind of information and connections that come only from experience. For Renaissance Souls trying to break into a new area, mentors are indispensable.

Mentors can provide answers, sometimes to questions you don't yet know to ask. That's what happened to Ira, a dynamic go-getter in his late twenties. Two of his interests were home schooling (which he hoped to eventually pursue with his bright two-year-old twins) and the class and ethnic bias in standardized education assessments. As a result of our work together, Ira decided to start an e-zine for homeschooling parents worried about college admissions tests for their kids. At this point in the process, Ira knew little about e-zines except that he subscribed to several. Through a chat room, he found Harry, who published two e-zines of his own.

"If you hadn't suggested I find a mentor, I would have lost a lot of valuable time reinventing the wheel," Ira told me. "Harry shared with me so many tricks of the trade it made reaching my readership easier and more efficient. He got me set up with links, taught me about being an affiliate, and showed me how to make my e-zine known by participating in key chat rooms. If it hadn't been for him, I wouldn't have known that I needed my street address on my e-zine home page or that it could be legally classified as advertising and subject to spam laws. You know me; I'm into so many things that an important detail like that might have passed right under my radar screen."

A mentor can also be a great help if you feel stuck. My neighbor Sara told me how she found that out. "I had tried everything I could think of to get a cooperative organic farm off the ground," she said,

but I just couldn't get the financial pieces to all fall into place at the same time. Oh yes, my friends and I had brainstormed about the problem. But none of them was rooted in the world of community agriculture. Only when my cousin happened to mention how much she liked the mentoring program at her company did I get the idea of looking for someone within the organic farm community to be *my* mentor. I found a woman who had worked in various phases of alternative agriculture most of her adult life. One of the things she did was connect me with a pair of local entrepreneurs. Their goal was to back an educational organic farm that could serve as a role model for farmers interested in branching out into more organic farming. With their finances and my farming experience, the banks finally listened.

Thanks to her mentor, Sara moved from feeling totally stuck to feeling part of a win-win situation. "I couldn't have ever gotten there without her!"

How do you find a mentor? In some fields, it's easy. If you want to start a business, you can get in touch with one of those retired executives at SCORE, available through the Small Business Administration. When you want to change fields within a single industry, you can draw upon connections you've already established. Rick Jarow, author of *Creating the Work You Love: Courage, Commitment, and Career*, believes that mentors come to those who earnestly pursue their true interests. "By aligning yourself with the particular field and your own authenticity, you will be drawn to a mentor who is suited to your own growth and who needs your kind of stimulation," he says. Sometimes you may in fact find that when you put yourself in the path of like-minded people—going to networking groups, attending trade conferences, boldly talking up your new idea—a mentor will appear. You start by chatting excitedly with another person in front of a restaurant-supply display. You discover that this person owns a chain of bakeries, and soon you're talking regularly about how to distribute your line of desserts.

But you can also approach someone you admire and just *ask* this person to be a mentor. Pick up the phone. Say, "I love your work," and explain why. Ask: "Can I buy you lunch and learn more about what you do?" Most people find this kind of request irresistible, not irritating. Although mentors do not look for a concrete exchange of services with you, you don't need to feel as if you're begging. True professionals realize that someone with your charm and chutzpah could eventually make a valuable business ally.

In a pinch, your mentor does not have to be a living person or one you know personally. In her book *Creating a Life Worth Living*, Carol Lloyd interviews inventor Lynn Gordon, who confesses to using "invisible mentors," bright and interesting people whose careers she's followed in the newspapers.

When I first dreamed up my consulting service, the term "life coach" hadn't made it into the mainstream lexicon yet. So I took Gordon's advice and looked to famous experts on career design (the closest topic to my own subject). I noted where they held lectures and workshops, whether they sold products in addition to their services, whether their audiotapes were distributed independently of their books—all from afar.

My client Juanita also used this approach as she pursued her cutting-edge Focal Point: cataloging farming methods of indigenous people in arid regions, so their techniques can be adapted by other areas of the world where water is becoming scarce. Juanita turned to Margaret Mead's writing whenever she needed tips on approaching a new culture, and she used her late uncle's detailed archaeological notebooks as models for her record keeping. Juanita also confessed to me that whenever she was tempted to succumb to the nagging voice that said, *How can a city girl like you understand farming?* she would call up another voice, one that belonged to her fifth-grade Girl Scout leader, Mrs. Abigail: "Don't ever forget: You girls can do whatever you put your minds to!"

"And you know who my mentor is for breaking into this esoteric field that's only become a Focal Point for me in my forties?" Juanita asked, laughing. "My college alumni directory! Whenever I need a contact in a new country, I just find a fellow alum who has connections there."

THE LIFE COACH: YOUR IMPARTIAL ADVISOR

*A*s you wend your way toward a Renaissance life, you may need an advisor who won't mislead you by blowing your gifts and talents out of proportion (as some parents and spouses are likely to do) or by minimizing them (as some parents and spouses are likely to do). Some friends, possibly jealous of your choices, may be unnecessarily negative. Others, living vicariously through your new adventure or "escape" to freedom, may push you farther and faster than it's right for you to go.

That's where a life coach can step in. You may not have heard of life coaches, but these folks are members of a rapidly growing profession. According to the journal *New and Emerging Occupations*, there are currently about ten thousand executive and life coaches in the United States. Don't confuse coaches with therapists, who often dive deeply into your past to locate the sources of emotional pain. Life coaches are not mentors; they are not proficient in your field. Nor are they traditional career counselors, who administer standardized tests, connect you with headhunters, and tell you which businesses in your field are hiring. Rather, life coaches are experts in critical thinking and problem solving. In both personal and professional matters, they act as neutral, clear-sighted advisors who can help you evaluate your problems and offer impartial feedback. They can have the motivating power of a sports coach or the gentle but knowing wisdom of a grandmother who won't let you kid yourself. A life coach can lend a hand when you slip into an old habit of making negative generalizations, and help you identify whether positive "rewards" or challenging "punishments" inspire you to greater success. A good life coach can also help you stay accountable if you use your sessions together as helpful deadlines.

Life coaches can be especially useful when you'd like to bounce ideas off someone who is not in any way vested in *which* set of Focal Points you choose or *when* you choose to pursue them. Unfortunately, the need for this level of detachment tends to rule out using someone you hold near and dear as your life coach: The spouse facing a move or lifestyle change given what you're suggesting; the business partner who may have to buy you out; the coworker who won't be able to stand work without you there; or the friend who will sorely miss you if you decide the perfect place to combine your current Focal Points is not where you currently live but three thousand miles away—these members of your inner circle can hardly be expected to maintain complete neutrality, no matter how hard they try.

Most cities and towns boast several life coaches, but you can also work long-distance with the many coaches who will counsel you over the telephone or via e-mail. And when you choose a coach, remember that Renaissance Souls don't need ducks for coaches, we need swans! Look up a potential coach's Web site, or ask for promotional material. Read the testimonials from previous clients; do any of them sound like thriving Renaissance Souls? Then call the coach on the phone. Say, "I'm the kind of person who has a lot of interests. Can you help me figure out how to move forward?" Listen carefully to the coach's response. Does he fall into the singular, talking about helping you follow your *bliss* or guiding you toward your *path?* Or does she say something along the lines of, "I'm delighted to hear you say you have lots of interests! I'd love to help you feel fulfilled rather than overwhelmed." In the words of Iris Marchaj, associate director of Smith College's Executive Education for Women program, "If you can't figure out how to put it all together, get a coach who knows about

Renaissance Souls." This means finding a life coach who can demonstrate experience thinking creatively about the economic, personal, and practical implications of pursuing multiple passions.

$\mathscr{I}$ hope I've convinced you that there are ways to get the ideas, information, ongoing support, and guidance that will nourish your dreams, even if you don't want to start at the very bottom of a new field. In the next chapter, I'll focus on issues particular to younger Renaissance Souls. If you're not in that category, you can skip to Part IV, "Successful Life Design for Renaissance Souls." There, I'll provide you with concrete steps for making sure your follow-through isn't subverted by distractions, obstacles, or planning methods that aren't designed for Renaissance Souls.

EIGHT

What If I've Got My Whole Life Ahead of Me?: Renaissance Soul Strategies for Young People

So far, most of the people I've heard about were adults when they discovered they were Renaissance Souls. They'd at least been to college or had jobs already. What I want to know is: can this stuff help me figure out how to do "Life After High School" as a Renaissance Soul?

—*Alice, seventeen*

*I*n this chapter I'm going to look at the unique options open to those of you who have identified yourselves as Renaissance Souls early in life, perhaps in high school or college. For your self-awareness and maturity in recognizing your Renaissance qualities, congratulations. By understanding your personality traits so soon, you can set the stage for a lifetime of maximum flexibility and satisfaction.

There are many options open to all young people, not just

Renaissance Souls, including college, paid work, homemaking, parenting, or taking a year off. Each of these paths offers unique opportunities and challenges for Renaissance Souls—and, of course, you don't have to choose just one. Let's take a look at each option through the Renaissance Soul filter.

COLLEGE: WHICH SCHOOL WILL YOU ATTEND?

If adults have to parry the eternal question "And what do you do?" college-bound kids are besieged by grown-ups who inquire, "And where do you want to go to college?" Of course, your high school grades, test scores, and financial status may limit your choices, but even then there are usually hundreds of colleges that remain possibilities. For some Renaissance Souls, selecting a college is like choosing just one ice-cream flavor: nearly impossible. Under the pressure, some young Renaissance Souls let parents or guidance counselors make the choice for them—an abdication of responsibility that simply makes other life decisions even tougher. I've known a few Renaissance Souls who have simply walked away from the problem, sabotaging the application process out of a fear of being tied down to one college . . . and then one major . . . and then one career. If you know you love to learn and would enjoy continuing your education, don't throw the proverbial baby out with the bathwater. Instead, try using some creative limitation to make the decision easier. Below are a few criteria that will help you find a school that allows for the full exercise of your Renaissance Soul. If a school doesn't meet these standards, cross it off your list. Once you're down to four or five schools, stop leafing through all those thick college guides and make your selection from what you've got.

1. *Does the school offer a broad range of courses?* Large state universities allow students to choose from classes in everything from the history of witchcraft to advanced astrophysics. Smaller liberal arts colleges, especially those in remote locations, often cannot support the kind of staff required to teach such a wide variety of subjects. But if you prefer the atmosphere of a smaller college, you can inquire whether the school has a cooperative arrangement with other colleges to expand and share offerings. For example, my client Joel was shy and had been homeschooled for much of his life. Intimidated by the thought of going from studying in his living room to attending a huge university, he very much wanted to go to a small college. At the same time, he also hoped (among other things) to perform specialized scientific research one day—he'd done an internship in biology the previous summer and loved it. At first Joel assumed that meant he'd be forced to go to a large university. Imagine how pleased he was to discover that Amherst College, just the kind of small school he'd love, has a partnership arrangement with the University of Massachusetts, Amherst. So Joel could study the cello and classical languages at Amherst College while taking advantage of the University's offerings in applied genetics.

2. *Does the school have an interdisciplinary majors program?* Interdisciplinary programs (also sometimes known as multidisciplinary programs) allow students to combine two or three interests into one major. Under such a setup, students can take advanced courses that might normally be open only to students who had already met all the requirements in a particular area of study. For example, a student who is interested in the archaeology of ancient civilizations might develop an interdisciplinary major encompassing high-level courses in geology, languages, and history, but it would not be necessary for that student to have taken a dozen preliminary classes in each of those fields before being allowed in. Often the school offers a list of suggested interdisciplinary majors, but it may also be possible to create your own in what is called an independently designed major. It's always possible to take a double or even triple major instead, but in that case you'll have to complete the full credit requirements in each field, which may require additional semesters or years of school.

Even if you do not plan to pursue an interdisciplinary or independently designed major, it's a good idea to consider only those colleges that offer these options. As a Renaissance Soul, you want a school that is friendly to students with multiple interests, rather than a place where everyone is expected to focus in on one specific, traditional major. One easy way to locate schools with interdisciplinary programs is to visit the Web site www.petersons.com and run a search for colleges that meet the criteria for what the site calls "multi/interdisciplinary studies." You and your parents may be pleasantly surprised at the variety of schools that allow you to break away from the traditional core curriculum, including tiny private schools, large state universities, and Ivy League institutions. Even that bastion of traditional education, Harvard University, is creating a more flexible set of requirements that places a higher priority on interdisciplinary approaches.

3. *Are there enough extracurricular activities to meet your needs? Are extracurricular programs open to most students?* In all likelihood your Renaissance Soul interests extend beyond the academic. Therefore you also want to make a point of checking out the extracurricular activities that are offered. In addition to investigating areas that already interest you, be sure to see if there is a wide enough range of new possibilities as well.

One of my brightest clients, Erin, had her pick of the best schools in the country. She chose Wesleyan in Connecticut in part because the catalog listed quite a few unusual things she'd never heard of before, such as the Indonesian gamelan, a type of orchestra made up largely of percussion instruments, including gongs, drums, and xylophones. Even as a young Renaissance Soul, she knew she'd probably tire of some of her current interests before her college years were over, and wanted to keep her options wide open. Another student, Martin, chose a school in Florida in part because there he could pursue baseball all year round, but it was the fact that the school offered intriguing extracurricular activities such as working with dolphins and spending weekends studying coral reefs that really clinched his decision to attend.

If you are athletically inclined, be sure that the schools on your list have a strong intramural sports program in addition to NCAA teams. Plenty of Renaissance Souls manage competitive sports along with a challenging academic load and other extracurriculars. But some students discover that the time and travel commitment required for playing at the NCAA level leaves too little time for their other interests. To balance out your time commitment you may well choose to enjoy a sport (or two) in a more relaxed situation.

Also, do some research—perhaps by visiting the school—to find out how limited or competitive the extracurricular activities are. Dedie, a high school senior, was a member of the debate team and hoped to keep up this activity in college. As she visited prospective schools, she was amazed to find that on some campuses the debate team was so competitive it was limited to only those students who committed to the team for all four years. Even these students had to slowly "work their way up" year by year before they were allowed to represent the school at national tournaments. Dedie disliked the idea of

---

RENAISSANCE SOUL UP A TREE

In the photo I have of him, Adam Campbell-Strauss sits high in the branches of a tree, sporting a "One People, One Planet" T-shirt and beating away on African drums. This is the photo Pomona College chose for a brochure to attract future applicants.

Yet when I met Adam, he was certain that no college would ever take him seriously. His interests were scattered—almost literally—to the four corners of the Earth. He loved drumming. He played with several bands and toured as percussion accompanist with a chorale selected by Trinidad's steel-band expert Jessel Murray. But Adam also had a passion for camping and the Survival Living course at his high school. Not to mention that he volunteered in the after-school program at the local elementary school, or that he helped build his family's house. He'd also taken a year off after high school to volunteer with an environmental group in Oregon and teach ecology.

Adam was surprised to learn that colleges seek out this kind of passion in their students. Now a Phi Beta Kappa at Pomona, he's thinking of studying public-health issues. Renaissance Soul Adam now understands he'll never have to pick just one thing to do for his entire life. He is no longer "up a tree."

such a long commitment, so she eliminated those schools, happily paring down her list of possibilities. She ended up choosing a school where the debate team was open to anyone, and people were chosen to represent the school based on their passion and skill level, not the number of years they'd been a member of the team.

4. Do the academic requirements allow enough time for all your interests? Take some time to think about which matters more to you: the academic reputation of your school or the number of activities you can successfully pursue while there. You may find academic rigor and expert professors absolute essentials for a satisfying college experience, and a resume featuring a big-name school can help you manage the career transitions you are likely to make later on in life. But some Renaissance Souls are frustrated to find that an intense academic environment does not allow them to play sports, spend hours creatively submerged in Photoshop, take weekends with the outdoor adventure club, and clean up polluted streams. There is no right answer to this question, only *your* answer.

ANSWERS TO "SO WHAT'S YOUR MAJOR?"

*A*lthough most colleges don't require their students to declare a major until the end of sophomore year, friends and family can and often do expect you to have an answer to the question "So what's your major?" even earlier than that. This is true whether you're still in high school or well into your first years of college. As a Renaissance Soul you may well be drawn to many subject areas. If you haven't decided on a field of concentration, try not to let this question put you on the defensive. Here are a few diplomatic responses that will showcase your maturity and thoughtfulness:

+ "Each of my college applications included a box that undecided students could check off. In fact, the catalogs indicate that students should avoid rushing into this decision until they are more confident about it."
+ "Did you know that my school doesn't require me to declare a major until the end of my sophomore year?

I plan to use the first two years to explore a variety of interests and will narrow my choices later."

✦ With some particularly pushy people, it sometimes is easier to randomly pick just one of your present interests and give that as your answer: "I'll study French. It's a great interest of mine." And then you can turn the subject toward your love of French and light up the conversation with your passion. Note, though, that this strategy works best on people who aren't part of your inner circle. With good friends and close family, discuss your approach to college with greater forthrightness. That way you won't set them up for puzzlement or even feelings of betrayal later on.

YOUR MAJOR: APPLYING THE FOCAL POINTS STRATEGIES

Ah, the first two years of college, when Renaissance Souls get to spend hours poring over course catalogs and experimenting with classes across the academic spectrum. Do take this time to explore! Sign up for courses in the topics you love, but also block out some time each year to leave your comfort zone and venture into new subjects or activities simply because they seem forbidding (linguistics? theater?) or frightening (creative writing? economics?). After all, Renaissance Souls thrive on learning new things.

Yes, have fun checking out what you can during these first two exploratory years, but don't let the hundreds of choices bring you to your knees. The decisions will be easier if you apply the exercises in Chapter Three, "Panning for Golden Values." Once you've clarified your values, use the Renaissance Focal

Points strategy to stave off paralysis. Let's say a student, Brianna, has identified four Focal Points: spiritual growth, staying in shape, political action, graduating with distinction. Brianna plans to keep fit by playing Ultimate Frisbee outside her academic schedule. She also joins a grassroots political organization. So when Brianna opens her course catalog, she looks for classes that will move her other two Focal Points forward. She selects an honors course, another in Bible history. That leaves her with room on her schedule to either fulfill core requirements or explore other subjects.

Although college offers a uniquely bountiful platter of possibilities, I'm here to testify that life doesn't fade to a dull gray upon graduation. If you follow the advice in this book, your future will be filled with new delights and unmarked paths. Do not turn yourself into a pretzel in the belief that every course selection you make as an undergraduate must be the absolutely perfect choice.

Eventually the time will come for you to settle on a major (or two). Although this can be an unnerving prospect for Renaissance Souls, it doesn't have to be. Instead of seeing this decision as a lifelong choice imposed by grim-faced administrators, look upon it as a chance to experience the benefits of *focus*. No, you won't have as much time as you'd like to pick up every course that looks exciting, but you will discover the satisfaction of delving more deeply into several interests. And by then, if you have checked out several subjects in your first years, you'll have gained knowledge about yourself. Are you attracted to an umbrella career, such as journalism? In this case, you'll have little trouble deciding on a major that will get you writing about an array of fascinating topics. Or, by your sophomore or junior year, you might well have discovered an eagerness to learn absolutely everything there is to learn about fifteenth-century China. If so, you may be the kind of Renaissance Soul who follows a sequential pattern of interests. Great! Don't resist the call to study China or anything else out of fear that it might not hold your interest for the rest of your life. Remember that by following your current interest with gusto, you're more likely to make a successful transition into *another* interest later in life. (For more on the subject of passion and power, see Chapter Two, "Yes, but . . . : Common Doubts of the Renaissance Soul.")

If, by your junior year, you do not feel strongly pulled toward a single subject, don't despair. You may be one of those fortunate people who thrive on handling three or four or five subjects at a time. For you, the best major is usually a broad one that encompasses several fields at once—a kind of umbrella major. Interdisciplinary studies programs are full of appealing choices, though traditional majors can sometimes allow for a surprising amount of breadth. Take a look at the testimonies of these happy students:

David (Oberlin): "I love history, philosophy, religious studies, comparative sociology, ritual, and politics. So I chose a multidisciplinary major in comparative religions. This major involves enough disciplines to include everything I'm interested in plus leaves room for new subjects."

Aaron (Macalester): "My folks were surprised when I decided to do an independent study with English courses at the heart of it. They thought back to English majors when they were in school and assumed a fairly narrow focus. But at Macalester, even the standard English major includes topics like British and American literature from a variety of historical periods, plus African-American literature, Native American literature, and African literature. When I read writing from so many different times, peoples, and cultures, I feed a lot of my different interests. That works in perfectly with the research I hope to do on language in indigenous cultures and the cross-cultural role of psychological archetypes."

Hester (Brown University): "I didn't exactly do an interdisciplinary major or independent study. Instead, I declared a major right out of the course catalog: women's studies. How can you go wrong with that? You can learn about the women of any country, any culture, any religion, any time period, and study everything and anything they are or have been involved in. We're talking fifty-three percent of the population here, after all."

Jake (Indiana University): "Writing has always been my main interest, so I'm very comfortable with a major in English with a focus on composition. I also have two minors, one in philosophy and the other in Spanish. Having two minors and a major has meant that I can't take many extra electives, but I like having to have *some* restrictions when I select courses for the semester."

WORK-STUDY J-O-BS

If you work to put yourself through school, look for a J-O-B instead of an ordinary job. That is, try to find paid work that satisfies one of your Focal Points, perhaps by allowing you to read on the job or letting you rub shoulders with experts in a favorite subject. (See Chapter Five, "Your J-O-B: No More Day Jobs," for more on how to choose a job that advances your passions.)

MAKING YOUR STUDIES MORE "PRACTICAL"
(BUT STILL RENAISSANCE-SOUL-FRIENDLY)

*P*arents and guidance counselors may urge you to "be practical" in picking or designing your major. This is especially likely if they themselves were brought up by people who believed the "cradle-to-grave, climb-that-one-career-ladder" approach was the only way to financial success. You and I know better; perhaps more important, your college's career center will likely also understand that today's environment can be downright inhospitable to people married to just one job field. If someone wants you to study a subject you don't love, talk to a career counselor who understands your point of view. The counselor may be willing to get in touch with whoever is applying the pressure.

You can often enhance your future marketability and placate worried parents with some relatively painless steps.

1. Take your Renaissance Soul love of learning and apply it to taking and maintaining fluency in foreign languages. Doing so not only will open doors to other countries and cultures but will be a plus on a future resume as well.

2. Because entry-level positions often require familiarity with office software programs, learn them now—perhaps in a J-O-B. Later you just might cinch a fashion or publishing internship because you can manage spreadsheet or graphics software.

3. In addition to learning how to use particular software, you can use your Renaissance Soul passion for understanding new things to tackle at least one computer science class. That way you'll be knowledgeable about the building blocks of software as new programs come and go.

4. Ride one or more of your Renaissance Soul passions into a position of leadership, whether that means being captain of a sports team, your college's representative to a community group, editor of your college newspaper, and/or an officer in student government, a service club, or a sorority or fraternity.

All of these things will be attractive to future employers—or useful in an entrepreneurial career—and help your Renaissance Soul move from one career to another with greater ease.

Another way to enhance the practicality of your Renaissance Soul education is to pay attention to the number of courses you take in any given field of interest. Consider the words of my client Ann, who followed her heart by majoring in comparative literature with a minor in history: "In addition to my comp lit and history classes, my transcript was filled with courses in German, political science, and piano performance. I had a great time in college, but now I realize that with just a few more credits or slightly different course selections, I could have declared a second minor in any of these subjects. It seems like a waste to have studied so hard and not have anything official to show for it."

Another practical approach that plays on your Renaissance strengths is to deliberately seek out unusual combinations of majors or minors that reflect your passions. If, for example, Ann had matched up her English major with a major or minor in piano performance, eventually she could not only consider teaching piano, but also her chances of writing music reviews would dramatically increase. An architecture major might intend to launch a Stateside practice after graduation. But if he is also interested in other cultures, a major or minor in Arabic could one day help land him a job designing buildings in the Middle East—a handy and remunerative option if the travel bug should strike later in life.

GRADUATE SCHOOL?

Somewhere in the fall semester of your senior year in college, you are likely to experience a feeling of déjà vu. Questions about your future start coming at you just as they did in high school, only now people want to know what you plan to do when you *leave* college. Mozart types have no problem answering this question: They have had their eyes set on medical school or joining the FBI for years. But for Renaissance Souls, answering this question for themselves, let alone for others, can once again prove a challenge.

This is another great time to make use of the "Panning for Golden Values" strategy. You need to know, for example, which you value more: well-planned-for financial security or spontaneity. Adventurous types may eagerly accept their roommate's "Come backpacking through Europe with me!" invitation. But if you place a higher value on security, *your* choice may be different. Instead of traveling now, you may decide instead to apply for advanced-degree programs that are likely to open up several careers in the future. Because such programs increase your chances of being qualified for a good job no matter where your interests may turn, this plan may be a better match for your current values. You might even be surprised at how versatile an advanced degree can be. For example, you probably know that an MBA is useful for careers in management, finance, or entrepreneurship. But it can also help you land positions in nongovernmental organizations in developing nations—handy if you ever become fascinated with Armenia or Uganda. Government organizations such as the Small Business Administration will also see an MBA as a plus, as will many large nonprofit organizations, such as the Red Cross. If you hope for the security and benefits of a federal civil service job, an MBA can be helpful in obtaining a management position there as well. Other areas of study that can open many doors include any degree that lends itself to world travel, such as international relations or world economics, or any line of work that takes you into many surprising and frequently unique situations, such as detective work, emergency relief work, or investigative reporting.

When you're thinking about graduate school, keep in mind that just because you *can* do something, doesn't mean you *should* do it. Yes, you may be bright enough to go to law school or medical school or gifted enough to be accepted by a top-notch MFA program. But do not spend precious years of your life and incur huge financial debts pursuing something that you can't truly, delightedly claim as one of your Focal Point passions! My heart breaks to see Renaissance Souls who have invested so much money and time in graduate studies that they feel imprisoned by their vocation, instead of energized and open to their changing interests. In this regard, be aware that professors who appreciate your love of learning may press you to follow in their footsteps and acquire an advanced degree in their field. Their encouragement can be very affirming (and even go to your head!), but try to take it as that and nothing more. This is *your* life you are going to live, not theirs, and the tightly focused niches of academia may be more enjoyable for them than for you.

THE CORPORATE WORLD?

For the Renaissance Soul who thrived on the flexibility of the college years, a first job in the corporate world can be quite a shock. After all, at least in your last years of college you had considerable control over your schedule. You could take classes only three days a week, for example; and as long as you got your assignments done, nobody cared whether you took time off during the day to pursue your passion for bird identification and took up your schoolwork after the sun went down.

Now you're spending eight or more hours a day in the same building, at the same desk in the same cubicle, working for the same boss, five days a week, fifty weeks a year. What's more, many of the people around you seem to experience no horror at the thought of doing this year in and year out for the rest of their working lives!

Of course, you will be learning a lot in your first months and years, and perhaps experiencing the rewards of a deeper understanding of your work, approval, raises, and promotions. But sooner or later, and often sooner, the unwary Renaissance Soul will come up against the very crisis that this book is about.

But what if you are a *wary* Renaissance Soul? How can you accept a first job out of school when you are aware in advance that you are not a Mozart, that you're not likely to thrive in a corporate environment designed to reward those willing to pay their dues and make a years-long climb up the ladder to success? When your role switches from student to employee, how do your Focal Points survive the dramatic change of culture?

Below are some tips for those of you struggling with these questions.

Learn not to overdo. Your first months at a corporate job may find you pulling late nights and weekends as you haul your way up the steepest part of the learning curve. And what little free time you have may well be lost to the mechanics of learning your way around the adult world: furnishing an apartment, exploring a new city or town, or perhaps learning to cook for yourself. As a Renaissance Soul, you're likely to find these experiences invigorating. But you may be disappointed when you don't have the time to pursue Focal Points that aren't covered by your job.

Accept that you'll need some time to adjust to a new life. Soon you'll have your new home set up, and as you become accustomed to your work environment, you can begin to make a more accurate assessment of what your work does and does not truly require of you. Rakesh Satyal, one of the brightest young Renaissance Souls I know, makes a useful comparison to his first year at Princeton, when he tried to read absolutely everything on the reading list. After he'd been at college awhile, he learned what he could skim or even cut out completely while still mastering the subject. "When I started life in corporate America, I was the same way," he says now. "It took me a while to learn the boundaries and rhythms of the job. I needed to learn why higher-ups would say to me, 'What are you still doing here? Go home!' Eventually, I figured out what every Renaissance Soul should know from the get-go: after the initial time spent getting grounded at work, you have to start taking more time for yourself. When key interests are ignored for too long, there's the terrible risk of losing touch with them altogether."

When you first start out, it can definitely be tempting to model yourself after your coworkers, many of whom throw their entire lives into their work. And it's certainly fine to do so if you're a *sequential* Renaissance Soul whose work *is* your current Focal Point. However, if you are trying to juggle three or four Focal Points at once, be careful. Young people often develop habits that can stick with them for life. For Renaissance Souls, staying in touch with Focal Points should be nonnegotiable.

Use your nonwork time wisely. Time management is a persistent challenge for the Renaissance Soul, so I've drawn up a series of strategies that are discussed in Chapter Ten, "Time-Management Magic for Renaissance Souls." These strategies are meant for you as well as for older Renaissance Souls. It's also smart to steel yourself against the specific distractions facing young Renaissance Souls fresh out of college.

Instead of falling into a wake-up-work-eat-watch-television-sleep routine, use your nonwork time as consciously as possible. Maybe you'll need to go to bed earlier and wake up earlier than you did in college so that you can pursue Focal Points before work saps your energy. Maybe you'll decide not to include a television in your purchases for your new home. And when your schedule and budget allow for a night out, you might choose activities such as concerts or poetry readings that feed your passions.

Know why you're there. When all that's available to you is an entry-level job, the kind that'll have you booking appointments and fetching coffee as you learn the business, you may ask yourself: *What's the point? By the time I work my way up to doing something relevant, I'll probably have lost interest and be off to something totally different!*

It's a good question. But having a variety of changing interests does not mean you can't stick around a job for a meaningful period of time. This is especially true for sequential Renaissance Souls, who often give all their energy to one Focal Point for a decade or more before moving on to another, and for those with an "umbrella" that lasts them for dozens of years. And the true Renaissance Soul changes Focal Points only when he or she has reached a level of mastery and becomes bored. Being a Renaissance Soul is not the same thing as being a "Change Junkie," to use Po Bronson's vivid term from his book *What Should I Do with My Life?* For example, many Renaissance Souls enjoy learning new languages—and few quit after the beginner's work of memorizing verb tenses and vowel sounds is done. They know that the real fun of learning to converse in Arabic or Russian has just begun. The same is true for corporate work. Knowing that your opportunities for mastery of the field lie just around the bend—after the necessary entry-level work is done—can sustain your energy and interest for longer than you think. Working in an environment full of people who share your interests will help, too.

So, yes, you may find yourself filing papers or taking minutes at meetings at first. But if you decide to learn everything you can, as fast as you can, you may progress out of the proverbial typing pool faster than most. Remember Marilyn Tam, former president of the Reebok Apparel and Retail Products Group and onetime vice president of Nike, Inc., who laid the foundation for her success by eagerly asking questions of people across every department? Or perhaps you'll thoroughly enjoy the journey up several rungs of the corporate ladder but recognize that you just don't want to make the sacrifices necessary to reach the tip-top. That's fine, too. You will have accumulated plenty of experiences that will take you into different careers and interests.

In the meantime, if the corporate position you have chosen overlaps with one of your Focal Points, you can use your entry-level work as a kind of J-O-B, not necessarily as an end in itself but as a means toward your Focal Point. If you're an office assistant who organizes corporate conferences, for example, you may actually have more face time with company hotshots than your midlevel counterparts do. Take advantage of this opportunity to learn from great minds or to subtly network. If your corporation offers classes that can advance one of your Focal Points, take them or get permission to use special equipment you can't easily find anywhere else. Then you can use your free time to pursue additional interests.

Don't become a slave to your paycheck. My friend Rakesh is fortunate that his first job aligned directly with a couple of his interests. But some of you will choose to take J-O-Bs instead. That's great, as long as the work moves you closer to one of your Focal Points, offering you access to computers or great minds or health insurance. But when a J-O-B's primary allure is a big paycheck—especially if it's in a time-consuming field, such as a finance or law—be sure that it doesn't blot out the rest of your life. As I've mentioned, if your coworkers are one-track specialists who eat, sleep, and breathe their careers, this attitude can be dangerously infectious. For a specialist, a race to the top of the career ladder can be thrilling and even fulfilling. But for a Renaissance Soul, finding a way to keep your own dreams afloat is critical. Remember that you are in this career for a different reason from that of the people around you: You're here to satisfy a particular financial goal, not stay for life.

To underscore this fact, some of my clients literally set up separate banking accounts, to see their dream funds grow and remind themselves that their identity does *not* reside within the income circle. Take Reese, a college grad whose first full-time J-O-B was as a manager with a phone company. He needed his comparatively high salary to pay off his student loans, but his real dream was to pilot a plane. So he arranged for his paycheck to be deposited directly into his checking account. Once it was in there, he went to the bank, used the ATM machine by the front door, and withdrew his weekly "pilot training" money in cash. "I loved seeing all those twenties in my hand each week before I re-deposited them into my

Focal Point account. Each bill that came out of the machine was like a little sign. It was like it said, 'Yes, Reese, you're really using your corporate gig to get where you want to go!'"

J-O-BS FOR HIGH SCHOOL GRADUATES

*M*any of you want to go to work as soon as you are out of school. How does being a Renaissance Soul affect the decisions you make as you enter the working world?

It gives you a real plus!

Why? Because you will be coming at your first experience with full-time paid employment with a very different perspective from that of most of your peers. Whereas others might feel crushed by the pressure of finding a lifelong career, or demoralized by the difficulty of finding interesting work straight out of school, *you* will know that your true identity lies with your Focal Points, not with whatever job you start out in. And many of you will be looking for a J-O-B that you can use to move one or more of your Focal Points forward—which means that the time you spend at your J-O-B will be more purposeful.

Recently when I shared some of this with a parent of a Renaissance Soul high school graduate, he looked at me as if I were crazy. "Do you know what kind of jobs are out there for kids right out of high school? Low-paying, dead-end jobs at the mall, or being a super-low-level-preschool aide or janitorial worker, that's what. How can a kid apply all that fancy Focal Point stuff to jobs like that?"

Am I crazy? Let's take a look at some real-life situations. I'll start with Andrew. What was the first job he landed out of high school? A minimum-wage job at a fast-food place near his old high school. When I met him Andrew was bored, frustrated, and hating every minute of it. He hated telling people he worked at "that stupid place" and had already had a few run-ins with his supervisor due to his "lack of enthusiasm." Not surprising for a Renaissance Soul who shared with me his love of vintage airplanes, his passion for working on his old Mustang, and the kick he got out of organizing *everything*. "I'm so good at it my mom even let me organize her kitchen after it got remodeled," he told me.

As Andrew came to see that what he needed was not just any old job but a J-O-B that could help him enjoy one or more of these passions, he realized his days at the fast-food place were numbered. But where could he go instead? His grades were poor and he had no marketable skills. Low-level restaurant or retail jobs looked like his destiny.

So what was wrong with starting with low-level retail? At this stage of his young life, absolutely nothing, as long as the store had a connection to at least one of his interests. What J-O-B did Andrew decide upon? He became a stock boy at a shop near the airport that sold plane parts. How did he *use* that J-O-B? First of all, he happily threw his organizational muscle into creating a more efficient system for shelving and locating stock. More important, he let customers and fellow employees know of his knowledge of older planes. Soon, plane owners with a question about an obscure propeller or engine were seeking him out. As he moved up to the store's front desk, he became part of the mini-universe of the local airport and even was offered the chance to fly during his off-hours with some of the plane owners he met.

Eventually Andrew attended aircraft maintenance trade shows on behalf of his employers. There, in addition to looking for products for the store, he rubbed shoulders with people who owned the old World War I planes that absolutely fascinated him. He struck up a conversation with an older man who told Andrew he'd consider hiring him to help maintain and expand his plane collection. When this man contacted Andrew's boss at the airport store, did Andrew get a glowing reference? You bet. The last I heard, Andrew was happily accompanying the older man's antique planes to shows around the country, and his vocational classes in airplane technology were paid for by his employer.

Consuela also used her Renaissance Soul life-design techniques to make her first job out of high school a J-O-B. Married to her high school sweetheart and pregnant with their first child, Consuela was not in a financial position to even consider college. Instead, she applied for every housekeeping and food-service job available at the local city college. Given the high turnover in these areas, it didn't take Consuela long to land a housekeeping job. Consuela would be the first to tell you that cleaning dorm bathrooms is hardly a thrill a minute. So why did someone who loved learning new things take this dull job? Because it gave her significantly reduced tuition at the university. Plus, she gained access to employee benefits such as career/life-skill training and leadership development workshops. Her supervisor was even required to let her attend them on the clock.

Clearly, it's possible to take a minimum-wage, entry-level job and turn it into something that feeds your Focal Points. But these jobs aren't the only things out there if you think creatively about your passions. My client Bonnie is a great example. She loved working with older people and had taken short-term volunteer positions in nursing homes and senior centers during high school. She'd also maxed out her high school's offerings in French and hoped to continue her studies in college. In fact, Bonnie received a scholarship, but some unexpected family medical bills left no additional funds for books, student fees, travel, and miscellaneous living expenses. Under the circumstances, Bonnie delayed admission for a year and used the brainstorming techniques in Chapter Seven to come up with a fabulous alternative to a day job: she became a traveling companion to prosperous but lonely widows who wanted to visit France. Bonnie used the networking contacts she'd made during her volunteer work to line up clients, and got to travel with the type of people she enjoyed most to her favorite part of the world six times in nine months, all expenses paid. What did she do with her salary? Stashed it away in the bank until she had enough to complement the scholarship money. What did she do with the glowing reference letters she received? Stashed them away too—who knew when they'd come in handy as she continued her Renaissance Soul journey?

As your J-O-B gives you a first taste of money, whether a little or a lot, enjoy it. But remember, as a Renaissance Soul you are going to want the freedom to live a life of many changes. So be extra careful not to rack up credit card debt on frivolous items or take on overly ambitious payments for a new car. Remember, you're planning for a lifetime of flexibility. Heavy debt, especially for things you don't really need, will make it harder to follow new interests.

LEARNING WHILE EARNING

Even if you don't plan to get a college degree right after high school, you can still find opportunities to learn. There are plenty of jobs that pay you to learn the skills involved. Consider union apprenticeships: You won't be making as much money as full union members do, but you won't have to choose between learning and earning either. Many potters develop their skills by working as a potter's assistant, and many actors will tell you they learned more by working in small community or off-off-Broadway plays than they could ever have learned in a classroom. If you love connecting people with homes and neighborhoods, you can often take just one class to prepare for your state's real estate exam; the rest you'll learn by doing. Similarly, my client Susan recently was trained to be a radiation technologist, entirely on the clock.

Larry, another high school graduate, did not have to hit the pavement the way most teenagers do. His dad *built* pavement with his own paving business; as each of his sons finished high school they were expected to come work for the company. *Forever.* Larry's two older brothers, neither of whom were Renaissance Souls, counted themselves lucky. In fact, some Renaissance Souls are also tempted to work for their families straight out of high school, not because they love the industry but because it's familiar and easier than making their way in the outside world. They tell themselves they certainly won't stay the expected "forever," not realizing just how hard leaving will be once they've put down roots in such a cozy work environment. But Larry didn't fall into this trap. He dreaded joining his family's business. Why would he want to still be paving streets at seventy-three like his dad? However, when Larry tried to think of an alternate career, he realized he didn't know exactly what his interests were. He just knew he didn't want to do one thing all day. Running a tar truck until retirement sounded worse than prison.

When Larry learned more about his Renaissance Soul nature and needs, he realized he'd like to start his own business. He wasn't yet sure what kind of business he'd like to operate, but he loved the idea of being in charge and carrying a multitude of responsibilities. Suddenly, working in the family business looked quite different. Larry gratefully turned working at the paving company into a J-O-B. Holding on to his dream of starting his own company, Larry made a point of working in as many different parts of the business as he could. The fact that his father started all his sons in low-level positions was fine with him: he was eager to see how all the pieces worked and fit together. A smart Renaissance Soul, he also made a point of being his family's representative at the local university's Family Business Center.

When he felt ready, Larry talked with his father about wanting to go to business school and eventually start his own company. His father was stunned at first but, much to Larry's surprise, turned out to be the one who set him on his path. "If you're going to go out there and have your own company, son, why don't you run one that makes a decent street-paving machine? These old ones weren't designed for the wear and tear roads get nowadays." Who knows if Larry will end up doing exactly that (and for how long!), but the suggestion definitely gave him a highly focused topic to discuss in his application essay for business school.

YOUR WORKING STYLE

As you search for a J-O-B, you will need to pinpoint the best style of work for you. Older Renaissance Souls, with more life and career experience, have a leg up on you here: They can review their previous jobs to discover when they flourished and when they didn't. They have considerable background data for answering such questions as "Are you better at working for someone else or on your own?" "Are you better at working four long days and having three days off or do those long days just kill you?" It's important to find the right working style—and know whether you want to be independent, on the clock, or in the fresh air—because a mismatch between you and your work environment can lead to self-doubt and frustration, which is especially perilous for Renaissance Souls, already criticized enough for being "flaky" or "wishy-washy."

Here's an exercise that can clarify your best working style: Ask yourself the following questions and write down your answers *to the extent that you know them right now.* Then ask anyone and everyone *who knows you well* (ideally at least half a dozen people) the same questions.

1. Will I do well working *for* someone, or do I need to be my own boss?
2. Can I handle the uneven cash flow of self-employment, or do I need to have a regular paycheck?
3. Am I good at doing what is asked of me? Do I follow through? Do I finish on time?
4. Am I good at getting myself started on projects? Sticking to them when things get a little rough?
5. Can I admit my mistakes and learn from them?
6. Can I admit when I don't know something and ask for help?
7. Do I need to work outside and get physical exercise, or can I work more effectively in an office?
8. Do I work better with other people or by myself?

Armed with the answers, you can evaluate the extent to which jobs you are considering for J-O-Bs are a good fit for your preferred work style.

THE UNPAID CAREERS: HOMEMAKING AND PARENTING

One of my favorite bumper stickers reads, EVERY MOTHER IS A WORKING MOTHER! Making a home or becoming a parent isn't remunerated with a paycheck, but it is a valid choice made by many young people (most often women) who choose doing that over attending college or seeking paid work. You don't hear a lot of folks glamorizing motherhood or home-making these days, but provided you've explored all your op-tions and have an external source of income, this option provides a host of advantages for the Renaissance Soul.

For one, there's impressive potential for variety. Life at home lets you change the menu frequently, whether it's a lit-eral menu for lunch or dinner or a series of choices about in-terior design or children's activities. This variety, so sustaining to the Renaissance Soul, can be had on even the tightest of budgets. I know one financially stretched mother who made cooking more fun by making a huge pot of rice every Sunday and then creating a different accompaniment for it each day, perhaps Indian curry on Monday, tomato sauce on Tuesday, a vegetable and tofu mix on Wednesday, and so forth. A Renaissance Soul client I saw years ago gave herself the same type of pleasure by taking her three active young boys to a dif-ferent state park, forest, or waterfall each Saturday afternoon, weather permitting. She never knew what bird they would see, what beautiful stone would catch their eye, what fascinat-ing observation one of her young ones would make as they jumped over rotting logs or skipped stones across a newly dis-covered stream. All this, and no costly movie tickets, no for-tune for theater popcorn and sodas.

Homemakers and parents work hard, but they can often control what kind of work they do at any given time. That means you'll have more fluid time than Renaissance folks who work in an office. When you're at home, if you feel like doing something physical, you can wash windows, race your kids up a hill, or clean out a closet. When you feel like sitting still, you can read to a young one, balance the checkbook, or quietly fold laundry while the kids are listening to a tape.

There are some dangers to watch out for, however. Many young Renaissance Souls who become parents right after high school can find their other choices limited for many years to come, not just by the time involved in parenting but because of the financial obligations that come with supporting a family. Also, even the most creative parent and homemaker faces a daunting set of repetitive tasks. It's easy for a Renaissance Soul to feel resentful in this role. So make a concerted effort to connect with at least one Focal Point interest that takes your mind, if not your body, out of the home. Then use the resources at your disposal—the Internet? the telephone? the library?—to connect with a mentor or brainstorm with a friend. Perhaps you'll learn how to set up a home business that will reflect one of your outside Focal Points and maintain your connection to the (paid) working world. After all, given your Renaissance Soul nature, the odds are pretty good you won't be staying home "forever."

TAKING A YEAR OFF

No matter what your future plans, you may want to take a year off after high school or college. Perhaps you need a break between formal education and whatever comes next. Maybe you want time to further explore your values and Focal Points. You may even decide that you want some additional "growing up" time before taking life's next step.

If this is a path you are considering, here are several points to keep in mind:

+ You're in good company: Many successful people took time out when they were younger. When Ralph Waldo Emerson expressed surprise that the great poet Walt Whitman hadn't published books earlier in life, Whitman's response was, "I've been simmering."

+ Just because you are taking a year "off" doesn't mean you can't improve your resume at the same time. Speaking two or three languages, understanding other cultures, and operating specialized equipment are all seen as pluses by college admissions directors and employers. So you might decide to postpone hiking the Appalachian Trail for now. Instead, consider hiking in another country, preferably one in which you can practice a language you've studied, and take along video equipment to capture your experiences. When you return, you may have an edge over a competing applicant for college or a job.

+ Taking a year off from academic or employment pressures doesn't mean you need to take a year off from your Renaissance Focal Points. If you are interested in archaeology, for example, check out books like *Archaeo-Volunteers: The World Guide to Archaelogical and Heritage Volunteering*, edited by Eric McCloskey. Or if you are drawn to both helping other people *and* seeing the world, you could look at a book like *The 100 Best Volunteer Vacations to Enrich Your Life* by Pam Grout.

+ Look into the Americorps VISTA program. Americorps VISTA seeks out young people ages eighteen to twenty-four who are willing to spend a year performing a variety of projects, including clearing trails, tutoring children, and aiding disaster victims. A willingness to travel is a must. Should this program serve one or more of your Focal Points, you would receive room, board, living expenses, and some additional funding to help you begin college when you're done.

WHAT IF YOU CAN'T DECIDE AMONG COLLEGE, WORK, AND OTHER PATHS?

*B*eing a Renaissance Soul, you might well see advantages in all the options I've described here: college, work, homemaking and parenthood, and time off. So one key question is likely to pop up here "But how do I choose which of *those* paths I should take?" Happily, you have plenty of time to do all these things in your lifetime. But you will probably need to choose one (or maybe two) for starters. If you really don't know which you want to do, you might want some assistance from a wise family member, guidance counselor, or life coach. You may also carefully review your current Focal Points and use them as a guide. With your list of Focal Points in hand, ask yourself these questions:

+ Which of the options will move one or more of my Focal Points forward?
+ Which is the least restrictive?
+ Which am I most drawn to?

Take the time to think about these issues. Coming up with serious, honest answers to these questions will greatly help you arrive at an option that works well for you, at least for *this* stage of life.

Now let's look at concrete tips for making Renaissance dreams—even for those of us who start out practically penniless and with few connections—come true.

Part IV

Successful Life Design for Renaissance Souls

NINE

Committing Yourself to Action
the Renaissance Soul Way

Yes, I've got my four Focal Points figured out, and it sure makes
my empty-nest years seem a lot more exciting. But how do I know
I've picked the right ones? I don't want to put a lot of time and
energy into developing these just to find out I was off base
somewhere.

—*Catherine, forty-eight*

ow you are ready to construct the current phase of
your life around your first set of Focal Points. The
Renaissance life design begins with a goal-setting process that's
specifically geared to accommodate your patterns of thought
and action. You may have long ago discarded traditional goal-
setting tools like the five-year plan, with its assumptions of a
long-term commitment and lockstep progression (no distractions allowed). But that doesn't mean that you *can't* or *shouldn't*
take advantage of other planning strategies. Time after time,

studies have shown that people who say, "Oh, I'll do *X* when I get around to it," or "I'll pursue my goal of *Y some*day," rarely ever see their dreams take shape.

As a Renaissance Soul, goal setting can't work until you feel safe enough to make some commitments. So let me introduce you to one of the most reassuring items in the Renaissance tool kit: the PRISM test.

COMMITMENT GETS SAFER: THE PRISM TEST

The PRISM test puts your current set of Focal Points through a rigorous evaluation. Just as light bursts into color as it passes through a prism, this test allows you to examine your Focal Points from new angles, thereby clarifying and confirming your eventual selections.

Why is the PRISM test so important to Renaissance Souls? It goes back to that old problem of doubting your choices because your earlier ones didn't last forever, and you now see the danger of being tempted away by another intriguing interest that may call to you tomorrow. Once you have put a Focal Point through the PRISM test, however, you are far less likely to second-guess yourself, and far more likely to stick with something long enough to get satisfaction from it.

You don't need to evaluate all of your Focal Points at one sitting. Many people like to introduce one Focal Point into their lives at a time, until they have reached a number they feel comfortable with. If you're not yet sure which Focal Points you'd like to try first, you can always come back to this section when you're ready.

Up to this point, I've encouraged you to think of your Focal Points in somewhat general terms. "Writing," one person might list for a Focal Point. "Being a good dad," another might say. This openness is a great jumping-off position, because it allows for maximum possibility as you mull it over, brainstorm, or think about how to integrate it with a paycheck. But before you begin the PRISM test, you'll need a clearer sense of what it is you're testing. Take a moment to revise each of your Focal Points in the form of a more precise statement. The writer might jot down, "I want to write a · novel and get it published." The father might write, "I'll take an active role in more of my son's activities."

Once you have identified this more precise Focal Point statement, you're ready to view it through the PRISM test, checking out its five elements: Price, Reality, Integrity, Specificity, and Measurability.

P: Price. What will it cost you to get to your Focal Point? Here "price" refers not just to dollar amounts but also to other kinds of costs, including time, emotional stress, and sacrifices from your loved ones. Amy's archery decision is a perfect example. Since daylong workouts were too high a price to pay for winning the Northeast Archery Championships, she aimed for *eligibility* in the contest instead.

Sometimes it takes some soul-searching to retain the essence of what you want to do with a Focal Point while cutting its price. Take Vicki, a client of mine who was "just dying" to go to France. To finance the trip, she was working two jobs and ignoring the yoga and poetry writing that usually kept her calm and steady. After a few months, she was exhausted and frazzled but still determined to make her dream come true. So we looked at what Vicki really wanted from her trip to France. It quickly became clear that she loved being surrounded by French-speaking people. To dramatically reduce the financial and emotional strain of reaching this goal, Vicki went for the essence of her Focal Point by replacing the expensive trip abroad (and the required second job to fund it) with a trip to French-speaking Quebec, Canada.

R: Reality. Time for a reality check. What will the day-to-day, nitty-gritty of engaging in this Focal Point really involve? Lots of people decide they want to manage retreat centers because they love going to them. But attending retreats and running them are quite different things. As you look into your Focal Point, ask yourself not just *how* you will get there but whether you'll enjoy the reality once you've arrived.

Suzy, a client who'd had medical school on her mind, decided that today's kind of doctoring, with its pressure to pack the patients into the waiting room and then zip through a fifteen-minute consultation, was not the best daily reality for her. To this Renaissance Soul, the essence of being a doctor was restoring health. Since she was also strongly attracted to traditional Chinese medicine, she decided to explore its offerings instead. Now, as an acupuncturist with a private practice, she can work at a pace that suits her style.

For students, the first two years of college are a great time to make reality checks into a subject before declaring a major. One student who loved visiting planetariums took just one class in astronomy before she discovered that this major would entail more time hitting the science books than gazing at the stars.

I: Integrity. Because Renaissance Souls can be tempted by a host of interests—including those that aren't in line with their top values—it can help to write down *why* you find this particular Focal Point potentially worthwhile. Does it improve your sense of playfulness? Will this activity be a source of inspiration to your children? Will it provide an outlet for your sense of color and design? Taking the time to write out your reasons for pursuing an interest can help you stick with the most soul-affirming choices—and understand when you've been mistakenly pursuing a value you don't genuinely prize.

S: Specificity. Saying you want to be a "helpful, caring person" isn't enough. Helpful to whom? Caring about what? How? A Focal Point statement that says, "I want to help people" is less helpful than "I want to work at a hospice, helping children who are dying to lessen their fears by drawing pictures with them." Only when you have a specific statement will you be able to know when you are being successful in pursuit of this Focal Point.

In this regard, it's important to remember that success can be a sensitive topic for Renaissance Souls, since we are so often accused of the kinds of qualities—distractibility, restlessness, even flakiness—that undermine conventional notions of achievement. At this point in the PRISM test, it's useful to recall one of the characteristics of Renaissance Souls: We define success differently from other people. We understand that sometimes success rests not in the product but in the process. So as you define success for your Focal Point, ask yourself what's *really* important. Do you want to develop housing sites throughout your city, mastering fresh challenges and building on your knowledge until you're the head of a multimillion-dollar company? Fantastic! Or would you prefer to buy just one home site and learn how the building process works? Great! Either approach is legitimate.

You can also use this element of the PRISM test to check for goals that are *too* narrowly defined, thereby cutting off your full range of ambitions. Donald, a mailman, had always been frustrated by having to choose between gloves that kept him warm and gloves that allowed him to actually maneuver his fingers. So Donald decided one of his Renaissance Focal

Points would be designing warm, functional gloves. When Donald put his Focal Point statement through this part of the PRISM test, he found that he'd been *too* specific in his expression of success. He was interested in developing an entire line of functional outerwear, not gloves alone.

No matter how you define your dreams, it is specificity that will lend them shape and dimension. When you are specific about what constitutes success, you can articulate your desires to yourself—and to others, so that they can offer appropriate assistance. Lesli, a Renaissance Soul who's a fitness fanatic, notes:

> When I was attracted to a new sport, I used to say something at dinner like, 'Oh, I think I'll take up yoga for a while.' And everybody would smile and go back to their meals. But lately I've started to create very specific goals, like running a mini-marathon, for myself. And when I announce *those* goals, my family rallies around me, asking about my progress and offering to help babysit my daughter so I can go on long runs. They've enjoyed playing a role in my activities, even though they know that those activities are constantly changing.

M: Measurability. Every Focal Point statement must include a date and other relevant numbers. How many hours, products, or professional degrees? Simply stating that you want to work in a hospice—without setting a target date—will not bring forth a sense of urgency and commitment. "Soon" or "later this year" is *not* a useful deadline. Do you want to volunteer at that hospice starting next week, work part-time there next semester when your kid is in school, or get a degree as an art therapist and be director of the place five years from now?

At this point, some Renaissance Souls hear alarm bells ringing in their heads. "I'm going to get pinned down, fenced in, walled off!" you may be thinking. This is a normal Renaissance Soul reaction, brought on by repeated experiences with overly strict, inflexible schemes. You wanted to take gymnastics lessons when you were a kid—and your parents insisted you had to stick with it for at least a year, long after you'd perfected your handspring and were ready to move on. Or you took a goal-setting class and *forced* yourself to lay out that required five-year plan for your antiques store. But little over three years later, you moved into auctioneering, and that discarded plan looked like more evidence of failure.

It's okay to get the jitters when setting dates. Set them anyway. Just keep them realistic: Maybe you'll want to finish up a Focal Point within months, not years. Remember, the whole point of this process is to help you focus successfully on several interests at once. Dates help create a map, allowing you to take solid steps toward passionate productivity.

A DIFFERENT WAY OF SEEING

*B*efore you put a Focal Point statement through the PRISM test, a final word of caution. If you have previously encountered goal-setting strategies in your life, chances are that you were taught to see them as ways to achieve the biggest, most spectacular result in the shortest time possible. But the PRISM test is not meant to groom you for a race. Instead, it should open a window onto a fuller life.

So as you view your Focal Point through the lenses of

price, reality, integrity, specificity, and measurability, it is especially important for you to keep your whole self in mind. Take
time to consider your nature. Do you enjoy spontaneity, or ad-
justing your daily chores according to what your body and
mind require on any given day? Then don't set deadlines that
require you to stay on task every minute. Is your budget
squeezed? Don't take on massive debt. Are you more productive under pressure? Then by all means, challenge yourself
with deadlines that are tight but fair.

THE PRISM TEST

Now it's time for you to take the PRISM test. You'll want lots of paper for
this one. Write down each of the PRISM questions as listed below and give
yourself plenty of time to come up with answers. Some of you might need
days or even weeks to complete the necessary research, but your new sense
of certainty will make the time you spend on the PRISM test worth every
minute.

Here's the PRISM test once more:

Price: What will it cost you to get to your Focal Point?

Reality: What will you need to do on a daily basis if you engage this
Focal Point?

Integrity: Why do you find this Focal Point worthwhile?

Specificity: Can you define your Focal Point in specific terms?

Measurability: How will you measure success at your Focal Point? What
is your deadline? How many hours a day do you want to spend? How
many products do you want to make?

COMMITMENT GETS EASIER:
THE INTENTIONS PROCESS

You may have so little practice with true commitment that you've never picked up some of the basic skills needed for genuine stick-to-itiveness. Over the years of working with people around their Focal Points, however, I have identified a key that makes the process of commitment much easier.

What is this key? *Becoming honest and practical about our intentions.* The intentions process begins by acknowledging a continuing fact of Renaissance Soul life: Moving forward Renaissance-Soul style is a mixed bag. Yes, you have the fun of pointing yourself in brand-new directions. Like the explorers of the Italian Renaissance, you may discover new worlds, visions, and even riches on your adventures. But by heading for the unknown, you may also open the door to fear, discomfort, and growing pains.

One client of mine, Lynne, was a highly disciplined and persistent inventor. But, oh, did Lynne have trouble trusting others. She was so scared someone might steal her ideas that initially she couldn't even contemplate sharing her drawings with a mentor or asking for advice from an expert at the local small business center. Unless she could become more trusting, her projects would never see the light of day.

Joanne, a talented watercolorist, realized she needed to become more hard-nosed. People in her small community were constantly beseeching her to take them on as private students or offer children's art classes in her home. And her extended family, who did not consider painting "real work," always expected her to help them out by playing chauffeur or hostess or family therapist. Having been raised to please and serve and put her own needs last, it was hard to say no when there was so much pressure to yield with a yes. But then what happened to her time for painting?

Jim, who had decided to leave his highly successful construction business for a start-up career helping small businesses go digital, knew plenty about being hard-nosed from his years in his family's competitive business. "But," he said, "I've never started a business before—my dad had the hard work done before I was old enough to come on board. And knowing me, I'm going to be very impatient with the 'it takes three years for a new business to break even' kind of messages I hear everywhere. I'm afraid I'll just run back to the big bucks and the family pressures, even when the best part of me knows that would be a big mistake!"

Lynne, Joanne, and Jim are brave people. Instead of playing things safe, they put themselves in positions that are not completely comfortable—where their Focal Points required them to develop extra resources of trust, assertiveness, or patience. That's where intentions come in. Intentions are inner qualities you'll need to successfully pursue your interests, and identifying them will help you outline some of the steps needed to carry through with your Focal Point commitments.

On the opposite page is a list of possible intentions. Take a look at them and pick two that are both *critical* to the success of your Focal Point and *hard* for you personally. If you are sociable by nature but have trouble keeping your project's budget under control, you don't need to "intend" to be outgoing. Instead, you need to focus on becoming economical enough to make your Focal Point a reality.

I INTEND TO BE . . .

Assertive	Generous	Precise
Bold	Genuine	Prolific
Brave	Hard-nosed	Reliable
Caring	Honest	Resilient
Centered	Humble	Smart
Confident	Humorous	Studious
Cooperative	Imaginative	Systematic
Creative	Light	Thick-skinned
Dedicated	Mellow	Thorough
Determined	Nervy	Tolerant
Disciplined	Open	Trusting
Economical	Original	Understanding
Efficient	Organized	Vigorous
Energetic	Outgoing	Vulnerable
Flexible	Outrageous	Willing
Focused	Persistent	

My client Jason, who wanted to build a birch-bark canoe in time for a fortieth-anniversary trip he and his wife were taking to Maine, spelled out his two intentions this way:

I intend to be *brave* enough in *the way I admit what I don't know about building in general, let alone canoe building*, to get what I want from this Focal Point.

I intend to be *energetic* enough in *the way I handle the physical challenges involved in building a canoe* to get what I want from this Focal Point.

Carol had long wanted to bring a group of women together to create handmade quilts to give out at the children's cancer ward as Christmas gifts. But she hated the thought of approaching women she didn't know about the project. And she worried that she wouldn't be able to keep the quilting supplies from overtaking her house. Here are the intentions she identified:

> I intend to be *nervy* enough *in the way I ask other women to join this project* to get what I want from this Focal Point.
>
> I intend to be *systematic* enough *in the way I organize the materials we're going to use each week* to get what I want from this Focal Point.

Here's a set of intentions from Adele, who wanted to open a part-time, nonprofit tax counseling service.

> I intend to be *understanding* enough *in the way I respond to people's ignorance and lack of disciplined money management* to get what I want from this Focal Point.
>
> I intend to be *studious* enough *in the way I learn everything I need to learn about running a nonprofit* to get what I want from this Focal Point.

Now it's your turn to fill in the blanks:

I intend to be _____ enough _____ to get what I want from this Focal Point.

I intend to be _____ enough _____ _____ to get what I want from this Focal Point.

INTENTION MARKERS

*T*o turn your good intentions into concrete actions, you'll need to identify behaviors that will let you know you're on the right track. Intention *markers* show specific ways that you will follow through on your intentions. Although they are not end points in the themselves, upon reaching them you may take pride in having completed one leg of the journey. You may choose as many or as few intention markers as you like. Just make sure to include a time period for their completion.

Let's look again at Jason as an example:

INTENTION: I intend to be *brave* enough *in the way I admit what I don't know about building in general, let alone canoe building*, to get what I want from this Focal Point.

Intention Marker: I will share with my therapist each week anything I have observed about my willingness to be a beginner or my resistance to asking for help around things I don't quite get.

Intention Marker: I will sign up at the high school for the next Beginning Carpentry night class even though everyone in it will be half my age, and I'll attend regularly.

INTENTION: I intend to be *energetic* enough *in the way I handle the physical challenges involved in building a canoe* to get what I want from this Focal Point.

Intention Marker: This week I will start working out at the Y to increase the strength in my upper body and thighs. I'll exercise for at least an hour, four times a week, right after I walk the dog in the mornings.

Having such specific markers for his intentions has helped Jason stay focused on being brave and energetic, two qualities that don't come easily for him but which he knows he needs to hone if he is to build the canoe in time for that trip to Maine. Now he knows exactly what he wants to be doing and when!

Here's how Carol structured her intention markers:

INTENTION: I intend to be *nervy* enough *in the way I ask other women to join this project* to get what I want from this Focal Point.

Intention Marker: I will have a brainstorming party ten days from now with at least three friends to come up with nervy ways to present this idea to possible quilters.

INTENTION: I intend to be *systematic* enough *in the way I organize the materials we're going to use each week* to get what I want from this Focal Point.

Intention Marker: I will go to flea markets this Saturday and next to find an inexpensive cabinet with plenty of storage space to keep our quilting materials in. I will have it cleaned up and clearly labeled by our first session six weeks from tomorrow.

Intention Marker: I will hire Patsy from Quilters' Corner for two hours to help me determine exactly how much of which supplies and fabrics we'll need. I will call her tonight and make an appointment for the earliest time she has available.

Adele's intention markers were more numerous, rigorous, and detailed. This was appropriate because she liked to pursue her Focal Points sequentially; she wouldn't have any other Focal Points to manage while she got her tax counseling service under way. Her tax counseling service would also be a demanding, longer-term undertaking.

INTENTION: I intend to be *understanding* enough *in the way I respond to people's ignorance and lack of disciplined money management* to get what I want from this Focal Point.

Intention Marker: Beginning Saturday after next, I will read one trade paperback a week on popular money management so I become familiar in advance with the types of mistakes uninformed people make and why.

Intention Marker: By Wednesday I will sign up for my company's eight-week fall course on communication skills.

INTENTION: I intend to be *studious* enough *in the way I learn everything I need to learn about running a nonprofit* to get what I want from this Focal Point.

Intention Marker: I will attend this Saturday's Small Business Administration workshop.

Intention Marker: Starting next week, I will spend at least six hours a week for the next five weeks reading material relevant to setting up a nonprofit in this state.

Intention Marker: Starting next week, I will take two people experienced in not-for-profit work to lunch each week, bring my tape recorder, and pick their

brains for the pertinent insights that don't tend to
make it to the printed page. I will continue this process
until I have spoken to ten people.

As you dream up your intention markers, keep the ancient
Greek saying in mind: *know thyself.* There are people who get
a thrill from juggling dozens of intention markers at once.
Having a wide variety of tasks brings them energy, while the
specific, time-limited nature of the goals channels those energies in a satisfying way. But I know plenty of others who
would rather take their variety in smaller doses. So make sure
the dates you choose are reasonable and allow for a pace of living that suits your style. Stagger your dates, giving yourself
enough time to reach each marker. Vary the level of intensity
for each Focal Point. You may have some markers that require
large blocks of time; others can be bite-sized items that you
can accomplish quickly or even on the fly.

BE AWARE: SOME FACTORS ARE
OUTSIDE YOUR CONTROL

It's important for you to remember that there are factors
truly outside your control that affect whether, when, and
how you achieve your goals. As someone who may have spent
a lifetime being criticized for not staying on track, you need
to be fully conscious of this seemingly obvious but often-
overlooked fact. Illness strikes, family duties call, an organization crumbles, a fickle public fails to provide a market for
your work . . . and suddenly it is less possible to fulfill your
Focal Points than it once seemed. Without the tools offered
in this chapter that provide opportunities to measure your

incremental accomplishments along the way, you are likely to define insurmountable obstacles not as bad luck—but as proof that you deserve that infamous "jack-of-all-trades, master of none" label, or that, once again, you've made the wrong choice. The intentions process offers an alternative to the black-or-white, succeed-or-fail vision of the world. Instead, it helps you take measure of the smaller victories.

Once my clients have worked their way through this set of steps, they are raring to go. But not before they toss out one big question: "Margaret, how do I find the time to get all this done?" We'll tackle that in the next chapter.

TEN

Time-Management Magic for Renaissance Souls

I have to admit, I'm both excited out of my mind and terrified by the whole idea of being a Renaissance Soul. I love all these new ideas I'm generating about finally pursuing the passions in my life, but I can't help wondering how I am going to get it all done.

—*Molly, thirty-seven*

*Y*our delight in going with the flow, in responding to what interests you at the moment, means that iron-clad daily schedules don't work very well for you. Perhaps you've bought fancy Daytimer books or set up snazzy computer calendars, complete with bells and whistles to remind you to do something at a particular time, but you have struggled to stick with these tools. Even when you have your day neatly mapped out, you may find that your creative energy is sluggish during the hour you've appointed for generating business ideas. And since you often work in areas that are new to you, you may find yourself having to respond to deadlines you've just learned about at the last minute. You're in the process of building your portfolio as a printmaker, say, and in a visit to the art museum you learn about a juried show you'd like to enter. But there's a hitch. You'll have to get your slides to the judges in two days. Which will it be—the schedule you'd previously constructed for cleaning out the flat files in your studio, or the inevitable whirlwind of activity as you work like the devil to get those slides in on time? I know you know the answer.

It's very important for you not to micromanage your time, or to schedule yourself so tightly that you can't respond to opportunities. You need to design your life not by the minute or hour, but by the week or month—and by what really matters to you. You need a set of strategies that will let you respond to your energies and opportunities, while preventing you from chasing a zillion rainbows at once.

In this chapter I will share some of my favorite strategies with you. They are exciting, logical, and well tested by your fellow Renaissance Souls. After even just a few weeks of use, these strategies will seem second nature to you. But you will need to be patient with yourself as you begin to integrate them into your life. Absorb a step and move on to the next only when you're ready to learn something more. And don't worry about getting it "exactly right." I can guarantee you, from years of experience, that all Renaissance Souls end up following these ideas their own way.

THE FOCAL POINTS NOTEBOOK

The first step in learning to manage your time is to set up a Focal Points notebook for yourself. Divide it into several

sections, one for each Renaissance Focal Point. As you gather
more information about each Focal Point, turning the idea
over in your head, reading, brainstorming with friends, talking to mentors, creating intention markers, and so on, you'll
find yourself with plenty of activities you'll want to under-
take in relation to each Focal Point. When you think of one,
jot it down in the appropriate section of your notebook. I prefer a three-ring binder with pocketed dividers. Others use
spiral-bound notebooks, and many forgo the physical notebook altogether in favor of a computer file. Don't get too hung
up on the format: Whatever works is fine. The key is having a
separate place for listing any and every book to read, item to
purchase, call to make, or flower bed to dig for each of your
Focal Points.

For your Focal Points notebook to work, though, it *absolutely has to have* one more section than you have Focal
Points. Why? So that you have someplace to list all the fun, intriguing, compelling, interesting, worthwhile new interests
that you dream about. That way, focusing won't make you feel
that you're permanently losing out on other possibilities.

THE FOCAL POINTS WORKSHEET

Set aside a time each week (I happen to like early Sunday
mornings) to review each section of your notebook. After
crossing off any items that you've completed or that may have
become irrelevant, note the ones that are in most need of your
attention during the upcoming week. Use the Focal Points
Worksheet to list these activities. I've provided a blank worksheet on page 230, which you may copy and use as needed.

Let's return briefly to Richard, the Renaissance Soul with
passions for four Fs: fathering, the flute, fix-it projects, and col-

lecting farm implements. Richard decided to use a loose-leaf notebook for his Focal Points, and the time he chose to review it each week was Sunday night. On a Sunday night three weeks before Christmas, Richard took out his Focal Point notebook and a fresh worksheet. On the sheet he listed several items under his fathering Focal Point: He wanted to buy a Christmas tree with his son, help him wrap presents that needed to get in the mail, arrange playdates over the holidays, and spend time each evening reading together. Under his flute Focal Point he also listed a variety of activities, including attending the final rehearsal for Handel's *Messiah*, practicing for his next lesson, fixing his music stand, and recording the PBS special on indigenous flutists. But since December is not a particularly good time of year for collecting farm implements, all he listed under that Focal Point for the week was getting on the mailing list of an auction barn and booking an early-bird reservation at the motel near his favorite spring flea market. And given that both of his first Focal Points had four tasks for the week, all he put under fix-its was watching *This Old House* one night.

FOCAL POINTS WORKSHEET

Activities for the Week of _____

FOCAL POINT 1

1 ....
2 ....
3 ....
4 ....

FOCAL POINT 2

1 ....
2 ....
3 ....
4 ....

FOCAL POINT 3

1 ....
2 ....
3 ....
4 ....

FOCAL POINT 4

1 ....
2 ....
3 ....
4 ....

WORKING WITH YOUR CALENDAR

*O*nce you've filled in your worksheet, you're ready to sit down with a calendar. For this purpose, a week-by-week calendar is usually best. Take a look at your worksheet and note which activities can be performed only at specific times. Your weekly writing group may meet on Wednesday mornings from nine until eleven-thirty. So you'd block out that time on your calendar, just as you've probably always done.

Okay, okay, I know. This sounds just like all the other time-management tools you've tried. "List what needs to be done, pick the ones that need to be done this week, put them in a calendar, and do them!" But here's the pivotal difference between that "normal" time-management approach and the one that works for Renaissance Souls: Many of the items on your worksheet can probably be performed at a variety of times. But they cannot be done *equally* well at those different times. Remember, Renaissance Souls work best when we can match our activities to our energy flow. There are some times when we can get on that phone, make those networking calls, and feel delightfully energized while doing it. Other times we prefer to sit alone at the computer for hours on end, blissfully content. What we *can't* do is make those outreach calls effectively when we are in a solitary writing mood, and we can rarely force ourselves to sit and write anything useful when we are full of social energy.

All the standard time-management programs say to block in writing time on a specific day at a specific time, though, and to do the same for networking. This may look good in theory—but often you may fail to accomplish the assigned task. And how does that make you feel? Scattered and undisciplined.

Once again, that familiar voice whispers: *You just don't have what it takes.*

To silence this voice, I suggest that you mark your calendar with what I call Focal Point calendar blocks. These calendar blocks are chunks of time that are roped off for the pursuit of your chosen interests—but they do *not* require you to decide in advance which items on your worksheet you'll address during these times. Some of your calendar blocks each week should take up long stretches of time; others should be shorter. Say, for example, that Richard blocks off Thursday evening, December 11, from nine to ten p.m. as one of his Focal Point calendar blocks. Around nine, he looks at his worksheet and sees that he hasn't yet finished practicing for Handel's *Messiah,* watched the episode of *This Old House* that he recorded on Tuesday, or fixed his music stand. He takes a moment to decide which of these three activities appeals to him *at the moment.* He doesn't have to make a half-hearted, unproductive attempt at doing—or avoiding!—a predetermined activity that doesn't suit his energy. Instead, he looks over a limited, entirely manageable number of choices. Happily, he can go with the flow *and* know that whatever he chooses is directly connected to at least one of his Focal Points. This positive feeling increases his confidence, which brews up more energy to keep him moving forward.

When I first began blocking off my Focal Point time, I would encounter people who wanted me to do something else—have lunch, babysit, or whatever. Initially, before I had truly plunged into the Focal Points process, I found to my dismay that I tended to give that time away much too quickly. This only delayed full engagement with my Focal Points. To preserve my time, I started telling these people that I was sorry but that I had a dentist's appointment. This excuse kept friends and colleagues from pressing me to give up my "free"

time in favor of them. Or I wrote "appointment" or "commitment" on my calendar, to remind myself to hold firm against
any outside intrusions.

If a friend wants to have dinner and you've had your fill
of socializing lately, explain that you're sorry but you have an
appointment scheduled. If the friend is someone you'd really
like to see, try to reschedule your "appointment." Can you
move the three-hour calendar block to some other time in the
week? If not, then explain that you're sorry; you're unable to
change your appointment. And if the friend is coming from
out of town and is superimportant to you, of course you'll cancel your "appointment" altogether—just as you might cancel
a dentist visit for the same reason. Then you can mentally
make a note to mark out additional calendar blocks in subse-
quent weeks to catch up.

One of the things about the notebook and calendar blocks
that works so well is that they help you maintain a balance of
activities. It didn't matter that Richard focused more on fathering than fix-its that given week in December, because the
notebook helped him keep track of ideas for *all* his Focal
Points. Another way to make sure that you aren't spending all
your time on one Focal Point and neglecting others is to color-
code each focus area and use a matching highlighting pen to
indicate on your calendar which Focal Point you've pursued on
any given day. Every so often, you can glance over your calendar and notice whether one particular color predominates or if
another is missing in action. So if that dear friend from
Botswana causes you to skip over your cooking Focal Point this
week, that's fine—so long as the color code for that Focal Point
shows up at other times in the month.

As a Renaissance Soul, you understand what novelist Faith
Baldwin meant when she said, "Time is a dressmaker specializing in alterations." Consequently, it's perfectly normal for

your scheduled calendar blocks to undergo frequent reviews and revisions, especially when you're starting a new Focal Point and feeling around for its particular demands. But even with all this system's built-in flexibility, it's a practical way to organize your time. It's *much* more satisfying than the un-steady feeling that comes from simply responding to any of a dozen interests that beckon you on a given day.

A word of caution. At the beginning of this process, Focal Point time can feel like free time. This is when painting or singing or brainstorming is pure fun and no stress. But as you become more enmeshed in these activities, you'll find that Focal Point work isn't always a joyful release. You'll find yourself struggling to master a difficult technique or performing hum-drum tasks such as calling the Chamber of Commerce about festivals where your band can perform. So you must not think of your Focal Points as downtime. Be sure your life also includes enough time for true relaxation and goofing around. Block downtime out on your calendar if that proves helpful.

TOO LITTLE TIME!

$\mathcal{I}$ began the last paragraph with "A word of caution." I want to begin this one with a word of empathy. We've all heard the phrase "sandwich generation," referring to those of you simul-taneously dealing with your children and your elders. Diapers, carpooling, teenage hormones, or filling out forms for college *plus* filling pillboxes, making care plans, putting in eye drops, and even rearranging things so a widowed relative can live with you. How on earth are you supposed to fit in "enough time for true relaxation"? You can't—certainly not as much time as you deserve! However, here are two things that may help:

1. Recognize that during this particular stage of your life, *family* is your umbrella passion. True, not every minute you spend caring for your kids and elders qualifies as a passion moment. Children and elderly parents, once they're born or aging, are basically an ongoing given; often we do what we do for them without much choice. Give yourself credit for honoring these obligations now, but remember that *now* is only *a part* of your life! (When you forget this, redo the "Give Me Time!" exercise on page 40.)

2. Discover opportunities to build things that nourish *you* into the time you spend with family. One of my fondest memories of my mother's last year was walking with her under autumn maples. It was always something that I enjoyed doing, and I realized that it was also a great way for her to get some exercise while spending time with me. Though wary about falling, she suddenly acted like a kid, kicking leaves high into the air! She loved being out in the fall and so did I.

I know these are fairly basic suggestions. However, if they help you remember your needs aren't going to be overlooked *forever*, they'll have done their job! Now get a refreshing drink and ignore the upcoming section on page 237 about having too *much* time.

ENJOY YOUR M AND M's

*W*hen Renaissance Souls think about their new time-management tools, I see them both light up with appreciation and physically relax. But then they ask me something along the lines of, "But shouldn't I figure out how much time I need for the rest of my obligations, before I go giving myself Focal Point time?" After all, all my clients have busy lives already. Many are tempted to figure out just how much time they need for their existing commitments and to work with what's left over.

But I know from experience that this approach doesn't work. That's because tasks expand to fill the time allotted to them. If you say, "I've got to clean the house this weekend," it can take you all Saturday and Sunday to clean and you still may not be done. (You may even have made more of a mess because you pulled all the boxes out of the hall closet and brought up all the recyclables from that basement corner.) By Sunday night, there's no "leftover" time for your Focal Points. Yet the obvious alternative—to avoid this kind of chore overflow by assigning a specific amount of time to every task or errand in your life—is unappealing and unlikely to work.

With these realities in mind, I devised a technique for discovering how much Focal Point time is both **Meaningful** and **Manageable** for you. I call it "enjoying your M and M's." It asks you to reverse the process my clients attempted. Instead of trying to wrap your Focal Points around your ever-expanding list of chores and personal needs, your *first* step is to identify how much time you'd like to devote to your Focal Points. Only then do you determine whether you have enough hours left over for life's other obligations. As a final step, you balance out the two sets of demands. At the end of the process, you can be confident that you're devoting enough time to Focal Points so that your pursuit of them is meaningful—but not so *much* time that the rest of your life becomes unmanageable.

Let me show you how two Renaissance Souls learned to enjoy their M and M's. Ellie, an enthusiastic woman who loves to throw herself into whatever she does, began by thinking for a bit about how much time she'd like to spend doing each Focal Point. She then made this ambitious list:

Focal Point #1 (Embroidery): about 7 hours a week

Focal Point #2 (Working with developmentally delayed teens): about 20 hours a week

Focal Point #3 (Hosting a jazz program on college radio station): about 20 hours a week

Focal Point #4 (Training with her Master's swim team): about 10 hours a week

Now Ellie needs to see if those numbers are realistic. She goes through a very simple process—one that doesn't require her to figure out exactly how long it takes her to clean the house. All she has to do is jot down the total numbers of hours in a week (168). Then she thinks about how much sleep she averages a week (in her case about 8 hours per night, or 56 hours of sleep total) and how much time she spends at her job, including commuting time (in her case, 50 hours). Although Ellie would like to change jobs eventually, she works with the numbers that reflect her life as it is *now*. (If you are a student, then you'd include time needed for studying and going to class instead of—or in addition to—time for work.) Ellie then adds her sleep and work hours together (106) and subtracts that figure from the total number of hours in the week, leaving her 62 hours to play with.

Now she looks back to her Focal Point numbers. Hmmmm. If she adds her M and M approximate weekly hours (7 + 20 + 10 + 20), they use up 57 of the 62 hours she has left to play with. *That leaves her only 5 hours for everything else in her life!* Not a very tenable scenario. There's no way she'll have enough time to clean the house, prepare meals, hang out with friends and family, do errands, and enjoy life's small details.

So what does Ellie do at this point? She goes back and reevaluates her M and M numbers. She can lower her embroidery Focal Point to 4 hours a week. But her other activities are not so easy to cut back on, because the organization for developmentally disabled teens, the radio station, and the Master's swim team all require a minimum number of hours from their participants per week. So Ellie decides that she will work with the teenagers only during the summer, when the organization usually needs extra volunteers to replace staff members who are on vacation. She'll host the radio show during the academic school year only, when demand for disc jockeys is highest. She'll leave the swim-team numbers as they are.

Now her schedule looks something like this:

Total Number of Hours in a Week: **168**
Hours of sleep required (8 × 7)   <u>56</u>
Remaining Hours   **112**
Hours required by current paying
job including commute   <u>−50</u>
Remaining Hours   **62**
Total Number of M and M hours as
currently estimated (4 + 10 + 20)   <u>−34</u>
Remaining Hours (4 hours a day!)   *28*

Now, 28 hours a week, 4 hours a day, for "everything else" looks a lot more doable, doesn't it? In some weeks, those 28 hours will allow for one of those giant weekend housecleanings, while during other weeks entertaining friends will use up more of that time. But no matter what occurs during the rest of her life, *each week will include 34 hours of Focal Point time.* Allocating her time in this way assures Ellie of meaningful, manageable blocks of time to pursue her passions.

$\mathcal{E}$llie was overly enthusiastic in her initial estimates of Focal Point time. But it's also possible to err in the other direction, as my young friend Carl did. Here are the M and M numbers he first wrote down:

Focal Point #1 (Managing my portfolio): 3
Focal Point #2 (Working on the governor's campaign): 9
Focal Point #3 (Improving my tennis game): 6
Focal Point #4 (Attending Business Network International meetings): 5

Now Carl looks at whether these numbers leave an appropriate amount of time for his other pursuits:

Total Number of Hours in a Week:	**168**
Hours of sleep required (7 × 7)	<u>49</u>
Remaining Hours	**119**
Hours required by current paying job (Carl works at home)	−<u>27</u>
Remaining Hours	**92**
Total number of M and M hours as currently estimated (3 + 9 + 6 + 5)	−<u>23</u>
Remaining Hours	*69*

With 69 extra hours in the week, Carl probably has a *surplus* of time on his hands. He might want to reevaluate his M and M numbers. He could easily make himself more valuable to the governor's campaign (and therefore more noteworthy as well) by tripling the number of hours he volunteers there *and*, depending on his mood, energy, or the stock market any given week, throw in another morning of tennis, another evening at BNI meetings, or more hours on financial matters. Even with both these changes, he'd still be left with 48 hours each week. Now *that* makes more sense. Carl knows that with almost 7 hours remaining each day, he can handle his other needs and responsibilities. And he's confident that he can zero in on his Focal Points.

Here's a form you can use to determine your own M and M's.

YOUR M AND M WORKSHEET

Use a pencil so you can adjust your numbers as needed.

First, name each of your Focal Points and estimate how much time would be both meaningful and manageable for each.

Focal Point 1 _____ Hours/Week: ____

Focal Point 2 _____ Hours/Week: ____

Focal Point 3 _____ Hours/Week: ____

Focal Point 4 _____ Hours/Week: ____

Focal Point 5 _____ Hours/Week: ____

Total M and M Hours/Week: ____

Next, fill in the blanks below, subtracting where indicated.

Total Number of Hours in a Week: **168**

Hours of sleep required per week: − ____

Remaining Hours   ____

Hours required by current paying
job, including commute: − ____

Remaining Hours   ____

Total Number of M and M hours as
currently estimated: − ____

Total Remaining Hours   ____

Now, evaluate the number of hours you have remaining in each week. Does it leave too much or too little time to complete all the nonwork, non–Focal Point activities in your life? If so, revisit the first step and refigure your Focal Point numbers until you find a winning balance.

Recently a friend shared a story with me that vividly illustrates the importance of thinking about your Focal Points before you start in on your "shoulds." In this story a professor walks into his classroom carrying a glass jar with four large beautiful rocks in it. Holding it up for the students to see, he asks, "Is this jar full?" "Well, yeah," the students respond, puzzled by a question with such an obvious answer. The professor then opens a bag he's brought with him and begins pouring gravel into the jar. Once the gravel has sought out every nook and cranny it can find, the professor asks, "Now is this jar full?" Sensing a trick question, the students remain silent. The professor opens another bag and begins pouring sand into the jar with the four rocks and the gravel. Once the sand has filtered down around the rocks and the gravel, he repeats his question: "Now is this jar full?" A few students, now looking at a really full jar and seeing that the professor has no more bags, nod their heads, only to be puzzled when the professor leaves the room. A few moments later he returns with a pitcher full of water. Without comment, he pours water into the jar and the kids stare as the sand soaks up the liquid. Then the professor drives his lesson on priorities home: "If the gravel and the sand and the water go into the jar first, will there be enough space for the rocks?" Your Focal Point M and M times are your beautiful rocks: Put them into your jar of life first. The housecleaning (gravel), errand running (sand), and lawn maintenance (water) will still find their way into your days, I guarantee it.

MANAGING DISTRACTIONS

Even after blocking out time for Focal Points, it can still be difficult to settle down. So many interesting possibilities call out—the cookbooks on the kitchen counter, the riding lawn mower that's in need of a tune-up—possibly distracting you from making full use of your designated Focal Point time. This is especially true for the many Renaissance Souls who work at home or gravitate toward interests that require a great deal of self-direction. Here are some tips for keeping distractions at bay.

Location, location, location! When I started doing research for my business, I fell into a pattern you might recognize: I would select a book from the shelf near my desk and then head for a cozy reading chair in the living room. But on my way over, I'd see the computer and think, "While I'm here, I should probably do a quick e-mail check, in case that magazine reference has arrived." Then, while waiting for my computer to boot up, I'd get the bright idea to be "efficient" and do the laundry while reading. So I'd go to the kitchen to collect dishtowels for the wash and there I'd see that some of the flowers in the vase had wilted. So I'd step outside to bring in some fresh ones from the garden. . . . And so it went, with the phone ringing or the Federal Express man knocking at the door—and before I knew it my Focal Point reading time had evaporated.

Here's the solution that saved me: I changed location. I found a friend who spent afternoons at the office and did my reading in her living room, not mine. Sitting in her house, it was completely inappropriate for me to answer her telephone, run around looking for her laundry, or decide her flower arrangements were unsatisfactory.

"Why not go to the library?" my sister-in-law asked me when I told her about this arrangement. "That's where I go." Why not go to the library? Because to Renaissance Souls, a library is like a candy store. Send us there and we'll get more distracted than ever! So if for some reason it didn't work at my friend's or if I didn't have time to go back and forth, I would create the same effect for myself by staying at home and turning a chair toward a neutral corner. The only trick is to get to that corner without bumping into all the distractions between it and me. This is where the NO! NO! NO! rule comes in handy.

The NO! NO! NO! rule. This rule is helpful both when you are trying to get *to* your ideal location and once you have arrived. Say you are walking out of your house to go to your friend's home to study for your real-estate test. On your way out, you see that a snow shovel has not been returned to the shed. You are, of course, tempted to put it back where it belongs. Then, seeing all that stuff in the shed, you wonder what day the church white elephant sale is. So before getting into your car, you "quickly" pull out your smartphone "just" to check the date. Likewise, if you are working at home, you may well find yourself "just taking a peek" when you hear the mail being delivered or "happening to notice" a new e-mail in your inbox. If you recognize these patterns, you'll want to master the NO! NO! NO! rule. Any time you find yourself doing anything but what you planned to do during this Focal Point time, you must STOP. Do not pass Go, do not give in to whatever temptation is calling you. Instead get in the habit of stopping to say NO! NO! NO!—and saying it out loud—when you get distracted. This will give you the solid stretches of time that we all need for success.

The No Exceptions! rule. While the previous tips can help you fend off immediate distractions, you may need a more powerful tool to maintain commitment over the long haul. Any and every journey has its exciting moments and its stretches of slower, more frustrating terrain. And for Renaissance Souls, who are most interested in the new and the different, those stretches can become detours. I may start on a fiction-writing scheme, for example, but sticking to it when I hit a dry spell can be very hard, especially if I suddenly hear a new gardening project calling. While the NO! NO! NO! rule can help me resist the lure of a ringing phone after I've sat down to write, the No Exceptions! rule can help me continue to pick up the proverbial pen, week after week after week.

I've culled the No Exceptions! rule from the works of the philosopher William James, who developed a three-pronged strategy for people who were seriously committed to making a change. The first prong is to make the change immediately. The second is to make the change flamboyantly. The third is to make no exceptions. When I first read about this third prong, it angered me. I—along with many of my clients— have worked hard to avoid this all-or-nothing thinking. "Do it every day, every week, every year, forever and ever—or you've blown it!" is the kind of motto that undermines many a Renaissance Soul.

But as I thought about it, I realized that the challenge implicit in James's suggestion is to reframe the desired goal in such a way that it's both realistic and practical to make no exceptions. For example, I firmly believe that the only thing we *must* do every day of our lives is breathe. So if, in conjunction with one of my Renaissance Focal Points, I set up a writing program that requires me to write a scene every single day, the odds that I could continue with No Exceptions! would be low. However, if I laid down a minimum writing requirement of four writing sessions per week, I could then take the No Exceptions! challenge far more seriously and meet that minimum requirement every single week. True, a stint in the hospital or a death in the family would qualify as a legitimate exception to the No Exceptions! rule. But in the normal scheme of things, I found I had enough flexibility *and* enough of a commitment to get me through the first couple of months. When I knew that I had a busy weekend up ahead, I'd try that much harder to get in my "required" four sessions early in the week. The real reward, however, came as the pride of my continually extending streak of commitment helped me through the rough patches that in the past would have de-railed my Renaissance Soul. When you have eleven or thirteen or seventeen straight weeks of No Exceptions! under your belt, you become more and more motivated to keep your streak alive.

Multitask in one direction. Renaissance Souls are masters of multitasking. It is a gift that enables us to accomplish much. But I hope I've made it clear that we absolutely must not use this gift during Focal Point time. No doing the laundry while trying to write poetry. No checking e-mail while designing your darkroom. However, there is nothing wrong with multi-tasking our Focal Point activities into *other* activities. If I happen to be on a three-hour drive home from visiting a friend, there's nothing that says I can't listen to Spanish tapes in the car, if learning Spanish is one of my Focal Points. Nor is it a problem for me to pick up those tapes from the library when I am there to take a neighbor's child to story hour. Multitasking works one way, but not the other.

Renaissance rewards. Whether it's buying a DVD box set af-ter ten weeks of following the No Exceptions! rule, or treating yourself to a short walk through the park after you've gotten up the nerve to make a difficult phone call, rewards can rein-force a new life design, especially one that's so different from what we've been taught is "right." For my part, I like to identify at least one positive action I've taken each day and put a fun or attractive sticker on my calendar before I go to sleep that night.

Checking off items on a daily "to do" list is another kind of reward. If you follow the suggestions in this chapter, you'll experience the satisfaction of crossing items off your Focal Points worksheet each week. But many of us, whether Renaissance Souls or otherwise, also keep a daily checklist of things to do—not just Focal Point work but household errands and other activities as well. Here's a fun way to make this list more beneficial to your Renaissance Soul: in addition to all the humdrum activities such as "mow the lawn," include things like "take a risk," "ask for help," "chant NO! NO! NO! if distracted." Knowing that you'll receive the reward of checking these helpful new behaviors off at the end of the day can play a large part in improving the speed with which they become second nature.

LIVE WITH AN ABUNDANCE OF TIME

*D*o you often think about efficiency? About getting several items accomplished each day? Of how to get more done? The time-management strategies discussed here can help you make good use of your time. But as a Renaissance Soul, drawn to many different life experiences, you may want to reconsider your attitude toward time altogether.

"Time is money," we like to say, and this attitude permeates our language: Time (like money) is something to manage, to spend, to save. Or is it? Richard Leider and David Shapiro enchanted me with a twist on the popular hourglass analogy in their book *Repacking Your Bags*. Why, they ask, do we always picture ourselves living in the top half of the hourglass,

---

FRESH IDEAS FOR YOUR DAILY "TO DO" LIST

- Ask myself what my mentor would do in my shoes.
- Increase my concentration by changing location.
- Chant NO! NO! NO! as needed.
- Honor my commitment to the No Exceptions! rule.
- Take a risk.
- Ask for help.
- Take a spontaneous action.
- Live with an abundance of time.

where time is always running out? Instead, why don't we imagine ourselves in the bottom of the hourglass? There, every minute is followed by another minute that comes pouring in. Every hour is followed by another hour, and every day is just the first of many days to come. . . . With a bottom-of-the-hourglass perspective, we can thoroughly enjoy our piano lessons, the basketball time with the kids, and the visit with dear aunt Joyce (who doesn't move all that quickly anymore) as each event unfolds. We don't have to worry about time being "spent" or "lost."

At a conference I attended recently, a speaker shared this story: A brain surgeon must perform a critical element of an emergency operation and he has only three minutes to save most of his patient's cognitive functions. The doctor is frantically giving directions to the various medical personnel in the operating room when one of the hospital's most outstanding surgeons enters and steps to his side. The venerable doctor speaks slowly and clearly: "Dr. Morgan, you only have three minutes. You better slow down." What a wise perspective to carry with us into our life designs.

I find that I am truly a different person, more generous, more spontaneous, more kindhearted, and more open to new ideas and experiences, when I have a sense of time in its abundance. By putting this item—"live with an abundance of time"—on my list of things to do, I can check off another victory when I have accomplished less, not more! True, I don't go to everything that's "interesting"; I don't see every movie that gets a good review; I don't join as many things as I used to; my house goes longer between cleanings. But I *do* have time for that impromptu long phone call with a potential contact or that walk up the hill to witness an unprecedented visit by a mama bear and her cubs. My daily checklist literally includes a place to check off items such as "Did something impromptu" and "Felt relaxed about time today." I appreciate soprano Leontyne Price's insight that the ultimate sign of being successful is the luxury to give yourself the time to do what you want to do.

TOO MUCH TIME!

If you're a Renaissance Soul with "too much time," you're probably in one of three situations:

1. *Laid off.* You've got empty hours you didn't expect and wish would end. Even if the "boss" who laid you off is yourself, because the economy made you close your business, the issues are the same. Your expenses are premised on your paycheck or monthly profits. What do you do when that's gone and your unemployment runs out?

2. *Grad.* When you finished school, you expected to work in your field. Then the economy crashed and any opportunity for an entry-level job seemed to disappear. You're ready to earn a living, but how can you when no one's hiring new grads?

3. *Retiree.* You probably figured free time would be great, right? Surprisingly, however, when you *are* retired, you may travel, garden, or play golf for a time, but you may also feel lost without structure or accountability to shape your days.

Clearly, the feelings you have and solutions you need when you have "too much time" depend on why. However, unless you *chose* to retire, your first concerns will be financial: How to repay my school loans, support my family, or keep my house? Fortunately these issues are being discussed all the time, since so many face them. Here I'm specifically addressing those of you facing these issues but *fortunate* enough to be Renaissance Souls. Being one can be a real plus, and the tools this book gives you can give you a leg up in these tough times!

An Unexpected First Step for Renaissance Souls

Having too much time on your hands, with no say in the matter, does not feel like freedom. You want to continue doing *X*; the economy says no. You may feel discouraged, even depressed, none of which leaves you with the energy or creativity so key to your Renaissance Soul. After all, when things are going well, you *love* to eat from your four-flavor sampler; you get *excited* by the variety of hats your umbrella passion lets you wear!

But if having too much time on your hands kills your Renaissance Soul creative spirit and drains your enthusiasm, what can you do? Find a magic wand to make you feel enthusiastic and excited again? No, just the opposite. You need a fabulous pity party! Feel glum, be mad, and go into a first-class funk!

I'm serious. If you don't acknowledge how *awful* things feel right now, you're not likely to have a tomorrow any different from today—even though this is something that, as a Renaissance Soul, you do very well! Your gut knows your life's going to change; after all, the only thing *you're* going to do every day for the rest of your life is breathe.

So you *know* a different tomorrow's coming, which means a new challenge, a new something to sink your teeth into with the Renaissance Soul energy that "magically" reappears when you've had your pity party and are moving again. Moving with the powerful tools this chapter on time management for Renaissance Souls gives you.

Four Focal Points Plus!

So what tools do you apply in your new situation of having too much time and too little money? Earlier in this chapter I talked of handling about four Focal Points at a time (or four subsets of an umbrella passion). But you've got *more* time now and *more* to accomplish. So I'm going to suggest you zero in on five key areas. Plus I'm going to show you how to take advantage of Focal Points you had while you were still in school or working. As you think about these different areas, you'll need the M and M approach for figuring out how much time to spend on what (page 235), and the Focal Point blocking tool (page 231) to accomplish what you want without feeling boxed in.

The first three Focal Point areas are pretty basic:

1. Read the most contemporary information you can find on job hunting and interviewing, as well as alternative books focusing on making a living without even having a job.

2. Follow through on the ideas you found most helpful; intentions and intention markers (see page 217) can help here!

3. Address your financial situation.

The fourth Focal Point tends to get easily overlooked by Renaissance Souls so eager to get back to their passions. I remember a cartoon from when I was growing up. It shows a laid-off father, who comes home and yells at his wife, who gets mad at the child, who then kicks the dog. That is *one* way of using your unwanted free time. But it is far more sensible to make it your fourth Focal Point to spend quality time with your partner, kids, and/or friends while you have "extra" time.

The areas I've listed so far apply to anyone who's looking for new work. The *difference* is the use of the Renaissance Focal Point approach to get done all that you want to get done. Remember, as a Renaissance Soul, you work best when you 1) block out times to do tasks but 2) have *flexibility* in choosing which blocks you use for which tasks. What you want to accomplish and the energy you have to accomplish it should match as closely as possible.

Now on to the fifth Focal Point, which can give your Renaissance Soul a real edge! To get this, collect *all* your Focal Point ideas. Not just the four you were happily working on before you lost your job/closed your business/graduated, but also those in the fifth section of the notebook (see page 228), with its list of every idea that's come to you as a possible future Focal Point. Once you have all these ideas spread out around you, you're going to use them to your advantage in two ways. The first is to avoid what I call rut-mode; the second is to make you shine in the most critical aspect of getting ahead in this economy!

Focal Point Edge #1: Avoiding Rut-Mode

Many people who can't work at the job or business they were doing before, or can't break into the field they've been studying, unconsciously limit themselves to looking in the same direction. In a sense, all the eggs they're familiar with and have been thinking about are in one basket.

But that's not you! Your mind has been thinking in lots of different directions, listing Focal Point ideas so exciting "you'd even pay to do them" and "you'd go on doing them even if you won the lottery." Often those ideas weren't brand-new either; they were connected in some way to something you'd already enjoyed doing. Take my client Eric. Given his limited skills, he'd likely have stayed unemployed if he hadn't been a Renaissance Soul. He'd worked most of his adult life in an Ohio factory, hammering out train parts. The company moved abroad, leaving a skeleton crew working nine-hour days to close up. Eric, a crew member, just worked, ate, and crashed. No thinking about Focal Points except on Sundays, when he continued to relax restoring an old Edsel sedan.

Then the factory closed, leaving Eric with lots of time and little money. Friends in rut-mode urged him to look for Help Wanted ads for the train work he'd been doing. Since that form of work was no longer being done in the US, he would have still been looking by the time his unemployment ran out.

But what happened? Eric had his pity party, looked over his pre-overtime four flavors, and found only the Edsel still spoke to him. Then he looked at the (absolutely necessary!) fifth section with its list of possible *future* Focal Points. His eyes lit up. "I remember this guy! He was on TV, using that wild new machine I wanted to learn. Wonder if I still can?"

The Renaissance Soul in Eric had been rekindled! He

checked at the community college to see if anyone knew about the machine; no one did. But a guy told him about a training program for fixing and restoring broken kitchen appliances, "since nowadays folks aren't sure about paying for new ones. It pays pretty well, too, if you can handle electrical stuff."

"Fix? Restore? Electrical? I'm doing that with the Edsel, so I bet I could catch on about appliances. After all, I do love learning new stuff." Because Eric was a Renaissance Soul, with possible Focal Point passions already listed in his notebook, he'd broken out of rut-mode! He didn't have to look for work that didn't exist: he was on to something far more likely.

Focal Point Edge #2: Being Unforgettable

When people talk about landing a job, they often say, "It's not *what* you know; it's *who* you know." Today you need to add a third phrase: "*and* who remembers they know you!" Why? Because your future employer is likely to hire you *before* he's even written a job ad! What do I mean? If you want a meaningful job, you can't be excited when you see it posted. You have to be excited about it, period!

Compare Bill and Ann's situations. Job hunting "for ages," Bill's gotten discouraged by the minimal (if any) response he's gotten to his resumes. In fact, by now he *hates* job hunting; he'll text, watch TV, anything *not* to think about it. Ann's been out of school equally long, has no responses to her applications, and also hates thinking about job hunting. But what *does* she think about? Having reviewed all her Focal Points, Ann's spotted one or more of them that still call her name. In fact, they excite her enough she has trouble not thinking about them.

Is that so different from thinking about texting or TV? Yes. To understand why, check out the following scenario:

PROJECT MANAGER: Given what's holding us back, we really
need somebody who's interested in, and skilled at, doing X.

SUPERVISOR: *I* know someone like that. I saw my neighbor's
daughter Ann yesterday while in line at the store. She told
me how much she loves developing X for the Chamber of
Commerce, especially because it ties in with Y, a course she
loved in college. "Plus they let me organize things, which
I'm addicted to doing!"

REGIONAL MANAGER: Sounds like just what we need. Tell her
to call HR; I'll give them a heads up. . . .

Sure, that's a pretty stilted skit, and others may have been
doing X at the Chamber and Y in school. But since X and Y
were truly related to Ann's Focal Points, when she was talking
with the supervisor, her eyes were shining, her voice was full
of enthusiasm, and she made good sense. And what did that do
for her? *It made her memorable!*

Bill may have seen the ad and applied, but, by thinking of
and talking about her Focal Point passions, Ann had gotten
there first. As I said, it's not what you know, but who you know
and who remembers they know you!

But What If You're Retired?

So many of the time-management tools here are for folks
wanting to get back into the workforce (or in for the first time)!
But what if you're among the Renaissance Souls who've finally
gotten *out* of it? You've done your dream projects—organized
the closets, built the deck, visited the kids, perhaps even taken
a cruise. But now what? You've weeks, months, years stretching
out ahead of you. Great, right?

Perhaps for you it is. But maybe, like many retirees, you've
found it unsettling to have left your work-related identity and

schedule; you begin looking at your calendar's empty pages with mixed feelings. Lack of structure, lack of accountability, and/or lack of connection can cause this. Luckily, addressing the first two can fix the third and, as a Renaissance Soul, you have special time-management skills to help with both.

Structure. Before worrying about *lack* of structure, remember for *you* too much structure can be worse. Don't sign up for lots of projects and classes only to rebel when your schedule feels tighter than when you worked. That's the gift of the Focal Point blocking strategy: your calendar pages aren't empty, but you're not facing "You have to do *this* at *this* time!" hell.

That said, it's good to do things that *benefit* from structure. Love to sing? Join a local chorus. Want to learn Spanish? Take a class. Remember, you're no longer worried about a GPA; if you want to visit relatives for ten days, just go! In fact, keep flexibility a priority: this may not be the time to sign up for any year-long commitment with weekly responsibilities. Instead, enjoy being free during the day and join a book club, writing group, or a world issues discussion. Such activities not only contribute structure but minimize loneliness. And, if you don't feel like going out into the rain on a given day, the flexible approach lets you stay home with a different Focal Point.

Accountability. In the short run, the structure of the intentions process (page 217) can really help here, showing you the progress you're making, giving you deadlines to aim for. For bigger projects, don't forget the Specificity and Measurability parts of the PRISM Test you used to pick your Focal Points (page 213).

It's also good to be accountable to someone other than yourself. Some activities have external accountability built in:

Instead of just going out to take photos, see if you can join a photography club that requires you to submit X number of photos by Y date for an exhibit, or look for photo contest deadlines.

You can also get external accountability by checking in regularly with individuals open to this role. If you'd like to have people *specifically* acquainted with *each* of your Focal Points, take a look at the Who Can Help? tool (page 264). The information about mentors and coaches (page 167) offers additional options. One person on your list can also be a retired friend who is trying to get X done by Y time, while you're focusing on doing A by B. As long as you each report what you've done, it doesn't matter if you're doing different things! Spending time each week with folks who are holding you accountable is also a great way to increase social time.

REVISITING THE MAGIC WAND

In this chapter I've given you a time-management process designed for your personality, and for the situation you're in— too little time, too much. Ideally, with a magic wand like this, you'd wave it and your new Renaissance Soul life would appear instantly. Given that you're human, however, sometimes it's not that simple, no matter what the wand. That's why in the next chapter we'll look at ways to overcome momentum blockers that try to slow you down.

ELEVEN

Staying the Course: Overcoming Momentum Blockers

I've got my Focal Point notebook set up, and my Focal Point times blocked out—I love all that! But what other issues should I be thinking about as a Renaissance Soul? I figure being forewarned is forearmed, and I don't want to lose my new momentum.

—Jason, twenty-three

Nature abhors a straight line. Renaissance Souls do, too. So as a preparation for getting into action, you need to think about what you'll do when things don't go the way you anticipate, when the road zigs instead of zags. As Confucius said, "It does not matter how slowly you go, so long as you do not stop." That's why it's important that you identify and plan for roadblocks *before* you get thrown totally off course.

What can you do when you feel stumped, stymied, road-blocked, frozen? Think back on what's worked for you in the past, and have these strategies in mind when you run into trouble with one of your Focal Points. One of my clients knew, for example, that when he got bogged down writing proposals at work, all he had to do was leave his workspace and wash his face with cold water, to begin again with a fresh focus. He decided he could use this same strategy at home when he got stuck on the detailed blueprint work of one of his Focal Points, designing a small addition to his house. "As long as I remember the NO! NO! NO! rule while I'm getting that washcloth," he said with a knowing smile. Another client knew from past experience that she could rely on her friendship network in a pinch. So when she suddenly had to pull together an appropriate outfit for the opening of her first art exhibit, she didn't panic but used that strategy again, borrowing clothes from friends with more elegant wardrobes. When another client got frustrated trying to figure out how to put his new printer together for his memoir Focal Point, he drew on an old technique of calming himself down with quiet music and sitting in a comfortable chair before tackling the manual.

Everyone's different: what's important is to know, and list, the strategies that have worked for you before. There are no right or wrong answers: what's important is to have answers ahead of time, sets of steps already written out so that you can focus in on them immediately.

Consider the following strategies, all of which clients of mine have used to maintain their momentum:

+ When frustrated and tempted to give up, think what you'd say to a young child in such a situation.
+ If what you're doing makes you very tense, and you are alone, stand in some ridiculous position while you think about the problem: Laughter is a great antidote for tension.

+ If a key call makes you too nervous, pretend you're someone else making the call.
+ Put on lively music to get your energy flowing or calming music to tame your panic.
+ Think of someone who'd expect you to give up and prove that person wrong.
+ Create order in some small part of the area in which you are going to be tackling something difficult.
+ If you work best under pressure, have a movie or other event that begins at a specific time as your "reward deadline."
+ If you are afraid that you are going to make a mistake in one of your creative efforts and therefore keep procrastinating, remind yourself that the Amish deliberately put a mistake in every quilt to honor the fact that no human is perfect.

This chapter details many more strategies for adapting to the challenges that come your way.

MOMENTUM BLOCKER #1:
IT'S MORE THAN YOU CAN DO ALONE

Even Renaissance Souls who have carefully identified their Focal Points and discovered ways to manage their time can find themselves feeling overwhelmed every now and then. Perhaps one of your Focal Points suddenly takes off faster than you'd expected, and a given week now has more critical deadlines than you could have anticipated. Or a coworker is out sick, so your J-O-B hours increase during the very week when, as part of your quality parenting Focal Point, you've promised your eleven-year-old you'd attend an important

afternoon activity. At times like this you may well need outside support and help in order to move forward. Yet I don't
know how many times I've held this sort of conversation with
Renaissance Souls:

> ML: Is your partner/parent/coworker supportive of what you're
> trying to accomplish?
>
> RENAISSANCE SOUL: Oh yes!
>
> ML: Would he/she be willing to help you with this problem
> you're having?
>
> RENAISSANCE SOUL: Oh, I've tried. But it's hopeless. I'm better
> off just doing it myself.

We've all felt this way before. The "supportive" person
may pay lip service about assistance, but then fail to do the job,
or not do it right, or make a big deal about doing it, or do it
once but never offer to do it again even though the need hasn't
gone away. For a while, when I heard people bemoaning this
problem, I assumed it was just an inevitable part of life. But
then I started asking more questions, and I realized this wasn't
necessarily true. Sometimes the *way* we ask for and respond to
help may negatively affect the cooperation we receive.

In response to this momentum blocker, I developed the
Mirror, Mirror exercise. It's designed to improve your chances
of receiving cooperation by helping you focus in on what
doesn't work when asking for help. Obviously using this exercise won't magically turn anyone you ask into a paragon of cooperative virtue. But when I have used it with my clients, it's
amazing how often people suddenly get an "aha" look on their
faces and share something along these lines:

> ✦ "You know, now that I think about it, when I ask my
> teenage son to help with the laundry, I do just what I

hate having my supervisor do: I check every little thing he's done to be sure he's done it *my* way. I act like there's only one way to fold towels, one way to hang the boys' shirts on the line."

+ "When my boss went out on personal leave, she acted as if I didn't know a thing about writing loans. She spelled everything out in such detail I felt insulted. Does she think I know this little, two years out of grad school? That sure doesn't inspire me to want to cover for her in the future. But I wouldn't be surprised if *I* don't do that with the folks on the football boosters committee I chair for Rotary. I bet I'd get more help on my pet projects if, when I described a task, I gave them credit for having brains, too."

+ "I have two sisters. Both of them are busy career women who call me from time to time to rescue them from some overcommitment. I hadn't realized, until I did this exercise, that I always say yes to one and resist the other's requests. And you know what the difference is? One of them always asks in the whiniest, cranky-little-kid tone of voice, which just grates. And it hit me. When I'm really feeling overwhelmed, and need my husband to pick up some pieces for me, *that's* the very voice *I* resort to! I'm going to watch for that next time."

+ "When the Mirror, Mirror exercise suggested thinking of someone you don't like helping, it didn't take me a second to come up with my partner Jan. At first I couldn't imagine why. She is smart as a whip, so I was delighted she wanted to partner with me on this new venture of mine. But she often has to take off at the drop of a hat to care for her elderly mother.

In the beginning I was more than happy to take over for her at work. But you know what? Now she seems to just assume I will, and she doesn't even bother to thank me. Thinking about Jan made me realize something about our other partner, Kip. Kip's a real extrovert and so I've always assumed he doesn't mind being the one to handle all the networking gigs that are so important to our business. I just pass them on to him—and I don't think I've ever thanked him! Maybe that's why he's seemed so unresponsive lately. I really need to thank him."

So take a few minutes to do the following Mirror, Mirror exercise and see what comes up for you.

MIRROR, MIRROR

Think of several people you have resisted helping (a boss, a committee chair, a relative):

1 . . . .

2 . . . .

3 . . . .

    1. What contributed to making it difficult?

       A. The way they asked?

          i. Never

          ii. Indirectly

          iii. In a whining tone

          iv. Too often

          v. Assuming the only answer was yes

B. The way they described the task?

   i. Too vague

   ii. Too much detail

   iii. Without any context

   iv. Without any inspiring motivation

   v. With directions that were impossible to follow

C. Their expectations?

   i. Standards too high

   ii. Time frame unrealistic

   iii. As if the only right way is *their* way

D. Their assumptions?

   i. That you know more about something than you do

   ii. That you know less about something than you do

   iii. That you work for free

   iv. That you charge

   v. That you had nothing else planned for this time

E. Their feedback?

   i. None

   ii. Only negative

2. Jot down what this "mirror" suggests about how you would want to involve others in helping you move forward with your Renaissance Soul Focal Points:

....

....

....

....

Who Can Help?

When you just can't go it alone, it is also important to consider *whom* to ask for help. Many of us tend to ask the same people over and over, restricting ourselves to a few reliable souls who will love us "even if" we need a favor. Some people tighten the circle even further, feeling that they can ask only family members for favors. Another mistake, especially in business, is to look no further than our department or team. Or to assume that we can ask for help only when we can return the exact same favor.

It's not that Renaissance Souls necessarily need more help than other people. But one reason we're attracted to new interests is that we don't already know everything there is to know about doing them. So we're more likely than most to need a *variety* of favors.

This being the case, it's unrealistic for Renaissance Souls to expect we can rely on one or two people to provide the multiple kinds of help we're likely to need. Dr. Sidney Simon, an author, lecturer, and retired psychology professor, suggests that creative people are obliged to think about the different forms of support available and the variety of people with the wherewithal to provide it. Identifying sources of help *before* you are in a jam is another great strategy to use when you're feeling overwhelmed.

Here's a tool I've adapted from Dr. Simon's book *Getting Unstuck.* Whenever you start coaxing a new Focal Point to life, think about the categories of help you might need. For each category, come up with three friends, associates, or contacts who could supply it. (A person can supply more than one form of help, but remember that the point here is to avoid leaning on any one person so hard that you push him or her over the edge.) Rank each person 1, 2, or 3 according to his or her ability to give that help to you. Then, when that's what you need, call your number 1 candidate for that category, using the other two names as possible backups or ways to share the load. (Dr. Simon's opinion: If you can't think of three names, your standards are too high!) Whenever I find myself with a brand-new set of needs, I like to type up my list of go-to names and post them in a visible place.

Here are some help categories that frequently come up. By all means, feel free to add your own.

- Who is willing to share professional expertise? ("Can you look over this contract for me?")
- Whom can I trust for emotional support or friendly nudges? ("Will you call me Friday before my big interview?")
- Who can help with childcare or eldercare? ("Can you babysit the kids while I go to this unexpected meeting?")
- Who can watch the house, the pets, the plants, the yard? ("Could you pick up the mail while I attend a conference this weekend?")
- Who can offer computer/technical assistance? ("Can you help me understand this database program?")
- Who knows how to polish my image? ("Can you help me pick the right suit for this meeting?")
- Who will be my partner in an activity? ("Will you jog with me twice a week at the track?")

Clients who have used this strategy usually return with tales of success. One story I always remember fondly is Dr. Stephen's. At eighty-two, Dr. Stephen was one of my very oldest clients. He could no longer drive, had trouble hearing on the phone, needed to be accompanied when he traveled by plane, and had trouble reaching overhead cupboards in his house. This Renaissance Soul didn't want to let any of that stop him, but he didn't want to keep bothering people for help, either. I suggested that he make his own Who Can Help list. At our very next session he asked me with a twinkle in his eye: "You know what I like best about this? It doesn't just help me ask, it helps them answer."

Seeing that I wasn't quite following, he spelled out what he'd experienced.

Now, if I'm calling the first of the three people I have down for driving me to the doctor's, I can let them know that they don't need to feel obliged, since I have two other people I can still call. And if I'm on the last of my three possibilities, then I can say, 'Janet, I know you're busy, so I tried both Clark and Mrs. Elliot before I called to ask you this favor.' Then Janet knows I'm not just assuming she has time on her hands or that I'll assume that if she says 'yes' now, I'll count on her for all my following appointments as well. Do you know all the things I've managed to get help with this week? A member of my church is going to scan my photo for that new online column we've been talking about, my nephew drove me to the anthropology museum to pick up a piece of research documentation I needed, my neighbor got my cat delivered to the vet, and the college kid who mows the lawn at our condo came over to lower some of the shelves in my kitchen. I even got up the nerve to ask a volunteer at the senior center to deal with the Clark School for the Deaf about getting me a phone that's easier to use. To be honest, I'd been sort of avoiding getting going on the interviews for my column because the phone is so hard. That's five different people who have helped me out and I've got lots more ideas of how to use help next week.

If you find your momentum blocked because you can't manage to do everything you've included in your Renaissance Soul life design, outside help can really make a difference. And by thinking ahead about *how* and *whom* you can ask for that help, you're far more likely to get the results you seek.

MOMENTUM BLOCKER #2:
HELD HOSTAGE BY PERFECTIONISM

*O*n the way to Renaissance life design heaven, there is an old adage that trips up a lot of us: *If the job is worth doing, it's worth doing right.* Of course, the trap in this truth is the definition of "right." This leads us to perfectionism, the belief that anything short of perfect is *wrong.*

Now, not all Renaissance Souls are perfectionists, but a great many of us lean in that direction, myself included. And while perfectionism challenges Mozarts and Ben Franklins alike, it plays out especially powerfully with Renaissance Souls. A perfectionist inventor, for example, may need to send out a press release for his upcoming exhibit. If he is wired more like Mozart, it may not even occur to him to write his own: he thinks of himself "as an inventor, for heaven's sake, not a PR person!" Or he may try doing a press release briefly, but as soon as he realizes that he can't do it perfectly, he picks up the phone for help: the challenge serves to remind him that doing press releases is not his department.

But a perfectionist inventor who is wired more like Ben Franklin may decide that he can't send out any press releases for his upcoming show until he knows how to write the perfect press release. So instead of focusing on his inventions, he starts fussing with his writing, which, as a Renaissance Soul, he may also consider his department. And when he gets a draft done, he wants to set it up perfectly on his computer. But he doesn't know how to use the graphic design program on his machine perfectly, so off he goes to a desktop publishing workshop. For him, the challenges are intriguing, not red flags that he's out of his element. But by pursuing perfection in every direction, he's definitely allowed his inventing momentum to be blocked.

What do you do if you're a perfectionist as well as a Renaissance Soul? I learned long ago that it's impossible to talk perfectionists out of perfectionism. A far better strategy for adapting to roadblocks created by this character trait is to learn how to become a *perfect* perfectionist—someone who knows when a task demands 100 percent perfection, when it calls for 75 percent or 50 percent perfection, and when 25 percent perfection will do.

The following exercise, Being Perfect About Perfection, is designed to help you perfect *your* perfectionism.

BEING PERFECT ABOUT PERFECTION

Janet has the following tasks to perform:

1. Make supper for her toddlers before she and her partner go out
2. Write the cover letter for her grant proposal
3. Rake the last leaves away from the back corner of the yard
4. Check the math on her income tax return
5. Network by sending back her high school reunion form asking about her current work
6. Plan her outfit for a regional conference

SCENARIO ONE

Janet is an imperfect perfectionist. She expects to do each of the above as if her life depended or it. Consequently, she feels frantic, overwhelmed, and irritable. During the course of her day she mails the high school survey without a stamp, overlcoks the fact that one of the shoes that go with her outfit has a broken heel, doesn't push the defrost button on the microwave, leaves the grant proposal address at work, and forgets to bring the rake in from the backyard. . . .

SCENARIO TWO

Janet knows how to do perfectionism perfectly! Help her plan her work by sorting her tasks by number into their perfect categories:

25 percent perfection needed: _____

50 percent perfection needed: _____

75 percent perfection needed: _____

100 percent perfection needed: _____

What difference do you think being perfectly perfect will make to how Janet feels and functions in this scenario? Now list six tasks that you currently face and create a Scenario Two for yourself:

YOUR TASK   DEGREE OF PERFECTION NEEDED

1 . . . .

2 . . . .

3 . . . .

4 . . . .

5 . . . .

6 . . . .

MOMENTUM BLOCKER #3: UNEXPECTED BOREDOM

$\mathcal{C}$raig, a Renaissance Soul who liked to follow his Focal Points one at a time, had moved from his engineering position at the Department of Defense to a career as a high school math teacher. He'd experienced the alternating despair and anxiety that many first-year teachers report but had moved past it and into a period of delighted, creative immersion in his work. But now, eight years after he'd left the DOD, he was bored, and painfully so. If a parent took up five extra minutes during a conference, he had to quell his fury at being kept inside the classroom. He dreaded grading tests. "Sometimes I wish I could toss all the midterms up into the air and assign grades according to where they land," he confessed. "I find myself daydreaming about learning to pilot single-engine planes."

Craig was *not* suffering from a momentum blocker. It was just time to move on to a new Focal Point. He'd met his goal of teaching for at least three years, and now his boredom was like a green light flashing *go, go, go.*

But there is another kind of boredom, one of a much shorter duration. It's the kind that pops up right in the middle of the very Focal Point activity that seemed fine to you just a half hour ago when you saw Focal Point time blocked off in your date book and happily chose this activity from your weekly Focal Point worksheet. But now you feel bored and in need of doing something else.

Perhaps you head for the refrigerator? Turn on the television? Pick up the phone to call someone whose name pops into your head? Do you plop yourself down on the couch and turn your back on the world, escaping into sleep? Many of these behaviors are often associated with depression—and therefore make you *feel* depressed. Certainly they can be momentum blockers.

But you know what? They don't have to be. It's amazing what can happen when you consider this kind of boredom as a helpful, cautionary, yellow light—one that's designed to protect you from storming ahead in ways that can cause danger instead of progress. Maybe you have been overanalyzing something with your rational left brain, and it would be wise to give your creative right brain a chance at the challenge. Adaptability strategies that work well here include grabbing a short nap to see what new insights emerge while you're asleep, and taking a short walk outside, drinking in the natural world instead of chewing on a point of logic.

Or maybe you've been doing something past the point of freshness and the "yellow light" cautions you against continuing. All experienced Renaissance Souls know that a great adaptability strategy for this situation is turning to your weekly Focal Points Worksheet (see page 230). It's likely to include activities that you can match to the energy you happen to have at the moment and the time span available. So skip the judgments. Just let yourself do something else from your Focal Point list that absorbs you or gives you a break. You'll end up moving another Focal Point forward and may well find that your momentum for your original Focal Point comes roaring back.

MOMENTUM BLOCKER #4: MARRIED TO MOZART

Over the years I've definitely seen that many of my Ben Franklin clients find it hard to keep up their momentum when their loved ones are wired more like Mozart. (And I'm always amazed at how many couples seem to have one of each.)

Here's an example of how this momentum blocker can catch us unawares and even seem insurmountable. Jeanne, one of my clients, was a young, dynamic woman who'd been married for about two years when she came for her first session. At this point, she and her husband, Robert, were "happy as clams" designing and building a meticulous reproduction of an eighteenth-century New England farmhouse on a piece of land that had been in his family for generations. She had a particular decision to make, which I helped her with, and off she went.

A few years later, Jeanne called me again. At the start of our session, I casually asked how Robert was and was shocked by the look on Jeanne's face.

"We hardly know how to speak to each other," sighed this usually strong woman. She told me that she and Robert had felt like kindred spirits—"two souls on the same page"—as Jeanne put it, while they were dreaming about, designing, and building their house. "We had even agreed to cut back on the cost of our wedding and honeymoon, because our house dream seemed paramount to both of us," she said.

"So what happened?" I asked.

Jeanne's face fell. "I can't bear it. He wants to live there *forever*. He doesn't want to change a thing or go anywhere! He's totally *content*. And now that the house is all done, the project finished, I'm bored out of my gourd. I'm ready to build something else. Or at least move—I've been looking into contemporaries lately. And that isn't all. I'm excited about a job offer I have that involves potentially relocating to England. But what does Robert say? 'Jeanne, why did we spend all that time designing and building this house together if this isn't where we wanted to be?'"

Jeanne and Robert aren't the only couple I know who built a relationship around a shared passion, only to face challenges when one member is ready to move on to something new. This is particularly true for those Renaissance Souls who happen to follow their passions sequentially. Despite Jeanne's apparent surprise at Robert's contentment with the house, she had actually assumed from the very beginning that they would *both* live happily ever after in their new home. Only when they had successfully transformed their dream house into a reality did Jeanne find herself itching to move on. It was at this point that Jeanne realized that she and Robert weren't as similar as they had originally believed.

Fortunately, the story ends happily. Jeanne realized that her need for variety wasn't any better or worse than Robert's need to stay put. It just meant that, in order to maintain her momentum, Jeanne had to revisit the PRISM test. Clearly, taking a job that required her to relocate would strain her marriage, making the "price" (the *P* in PRISM) of this Focal Point too high. Yet Jeanne still yearned to visit worlds far beyond her reproduction farmhouse on the family homestead. So she took a job that let her travel a few months every year. Robert (a freelance writer who could work at home or on the road) sometimes accompanied Jeanne; other times he stayed contentedly at home while she was gone. The two of them had to work to determine just how long a separation each could take, and how they could trade off preferences between them. Like anything else in a meaningful relationship, such negotiating is challenging but doable.

The last photo Christmas card I got from Jeanne and Robert came from Tanzania. It showed them both beaming at me from a Habitat for Humanity project they were building together. "We took off three weeks around the holidays and we're having a ball!" Both of them had signed it.

Part V

Going Deeper

Margaret, I was so excited when we talked about the four Focal
Points idea. I thought I was itching to choose mine and get going.
But to be honest, I haven't even looked at my notes! Remember
how I had good reasons for not having done my "homework"
those first few times? Well, now I have to be straight with myself.
I may love the idea of being a Renaissance Soul, but something is
stopping me from actually getting off my butt. It's like I've hit
an invisible wall. Any suggestions?

—*Andy, twenty-five*

 hope that the previous chapters have shown you that
the Renaissance Soul has a normal, healthy set of per-
sonality traits. You've seen that it *is* possible to organize your
life even when so many things are worthy of your attention,
and that you can become good at what you love, even when

your loves keep changing. Not only is it possible for you to become an expert in your areas of interest; you can do as well or better financially by honoring your Renaissance Soul than by denying it. So you should now be eager to pull up your socks and get moving, right? Perhaps you are. But sometimes Renaissance Souls find themselves inexplicably stuck at this point, gunning their engines but uselessly spinning their wheels, unable to move forward.

Stefan was such a person. A few generations ago, his family immigrated from Stockholm, bringing a strong work ethic with them. The message had always been clear: "Work is hard, work is tough. That is what grown-ups do, and don't you even think of considering anything else!" Each generation heard the story of the one errant sheep in the family, Uncle Olaf, who dreamed of being an artist rather than a farmer. What happened to this fool? He lost an eye in World War I and then drank the family money away.

And what happened to Stefan after he identified his Renaissance Soul? Every time he grew even the slightest bit excited about something he loved, the old message of "Don't be such a fool!" would rear its ugly head. How did he respond? By immediately busying himself with so many (unsatisfying) chores that there was no time to even think about any sinful Renaissance Focal Points.

Stefan's anguish will probably ring bells with some of you. In this chapter I'll take a look at several problems that can dampen your fires and block the successful pursuit of your Focal Points. A few of these difficulties occur quite frequently and are usually temporary; the others often require more mindful intervention.

RESISTANCE AS AN OLD PROTECTIVE STRATEGY

*B*efore you could proudly identify yourself as a Renaissance Soul, were you unable to explain your personality traits to yourself, let alone those around you? If so, you may have unconsciously developed protective mechanisms to avoid being pinned down. For example, my client Tim would always come up with some reason he just couldn't follow through on whatever exciting ideas he came up with during his sessions. Over time, however, as Tim grew more comfortable with his identity as a Renaissance Soul, we examined these so-called reasons. He came to recognize that killing off every new suggestion had just been his way of resisting the dreaded career ladder. Tim was afraid that taking a suggestion seriously meant being prepared to follow through with it, which he was still unconsciously translating as "being stuck with it for life."

Tim harbored fears similar to those of a child who tells his mother that he'd like to take tap dancing. So the mom gets the kid into tap dancing. But, after a month or three, the kid understands how to make those neat sounds with his feet. Innocently he tells his mom he doesn't want to go on with the lessons. What response does he get from the frustrated parent who has paid for the lessons, bought the tap shoes, and lined up the whole carpooling arrangement? An exasperated, "But *you said* you wanted to take tap dancing!" By finding fault with the good ideas that came up in our sessions, Tim was essentially avoiding admitting that he'd like to "take tap dancing." Other clients have accomplished the same thing by procrastinating, forgetting key appointments, or losing their Focal Point notebooks.

With Tim's new awareness that liking something now did

not mean committing to it forever, his self-defeating pattern faded away, and soon Tim felt ready to take a stab at the items listed in his Focal Point notebook. Whenever he felt that familiar desire to push away a new idea, he looked back over his values exercises. If his idea reflected the values he'd identified, he could forge ahead with confidence. If he found that it did not, he could trust the process of rejecting that idea, knowing he was not just being negative out of habit.

OLD MESSAGES

Each of us has grown up with certain prescriptive ("You must do this!") or proscriptive ("You can't do that!") messages from our family and community. As you begin designing your life based on Renaissance Focal Points, you may find yourself stepping outside the lines laid down by these "rules." This is exhilarating for some; for others, it feels like a walk down the proverbial plank. You may find yourself struggling without even knowing why. That's because so many family expectations—about how much money you need to make, whether women can make it to the top, or whether you deserve to succeed if you're the youngest in the family—remain unspoken.

I had a client, Andrea, whose parents were both highly successful, prominent professors. Academia was their lifeblood; they had excelled in school since day one. They expected the same from their one and only child—their prize, their princess. Unfortunately Andrea went through school with an unusual learning disability that wasn't identified until her mid-twenties. This impairment turned the classroom into an extremely frustrating and unsafe place for her, and she turned to nature for solace. When she came to me, she knew that two of her key passions were bird-watching and wildlife identification. Andrea also knew that her parents saw that type of thing as nothing but a hobby for the elderly and infirm, so she continued to spend forty miserable hours a week in a huge windowless building making fund-raising calls. Why? Because the calls were for a university and thus safely connected her to academia as her family history required. Her parents could say proudly, "We teach at University *X* and our daughter is with University *Y*."

Another client I worked with recently, Jeanette, had a mother who rarely left home. Terrified of the world outside her house, Jeanette's mother focused all her energies on cooking and sewing for her family, as her mother had done before her. My client had seemingly broken that mold and was out in the world, working a demanding job. She saw little relation between her mother's world and her own until we discovered her mother's core expectation: "No one is supposed to be happier than poor, miserable me!" Mother was a victim of her agoraphobia, and all her children were to be victims of something also. So when Jeanette came to me, she could rattle off a litany of all the terrible things that were going on at work, and how unfair it all was, and how she couldn't change jobs because she was trapped for this and that reason. She could talk happily for hours about things she would have liked to do, if only she'd been luckier. The idea of actually changing any facet of her life, however, was clearly taboo. It was not surprising that, as Jeannette began to claim her Renaissance Soul, she found herself asking, "Margaret, why is it that I just can't seem to get started?"

The situations of Stefan, Andrea, and Jeanette stand out in my mind because their family expectations were so dramatic. But many of us have received messages, perhaps more subtly communicated, that waylay our best-laid plans. Maybe in your family "everyone" goes into law. On the other hand, maybe no one in your family would be "caught dead" in one of those "irrelevant, ivory tower" colleges. Maybe you grew up hearing that nobody sane would want to be an artist because they all starve. Or that "only sickos would want to be therapists." Was a practical career the be-all and end-all, or were accountants immediately assumed to be "boring"?

Identifying these messages often makes them much easier to address and overcome. Stefan used the exercises I will be sharing with you in this chapter to see that he wouldn't lose an eye, as Uncle Olaf had, if he took his fiddling seriously. Likewise, Andrea found that doing the exercises gave her enough clarity to bring up the ever-present but never-discussed elephant in the room and finally hash out her lack of interest in a university setting with her parents. During that discussion, she shared her own interests and her plans for following them. Neither parent was exactly thrilled, but Andrea was freed. In Jeanette's case, once she could clearly read the message her mother had handed down, we looked at ways she could show compassion for her mother without having to stay miserable herself. Jeanette ended up spending a set time each week with her mother, listening sympathetically to her endless litany of "poor ME"s and then spent the rest of time designing her own life with conviction rather than guilt.

Assumptions about Money

Speaking of messages, we all certainly have received messages about financial success. Was monetary reward the only one that counted in your family? Or were rich people always presumed to be selfish, evil, greedy, and unhappy? Perhaps you grew up unconsciously or consciously assuming that if you became wealthy and successful, others would envy you, talk about you behind your back, and only pretend to be your friend so they could get things from you. Or perhaps it was the one rich member of your family who was admired and catered to and emulated whenever possible. Some of us were told over and over again that money is the root of all evil and cannot buy happiness, while others heard that without money, life isn't worth living!

The message—or combination of contradictory messages—you received about this emotionally loaded subject certainly affects how you design your life. Those, for example, who feel that success brings envy or false friends may often unconsciously limit their Renaissance Focal Points to things they know they won't be wildly (and dangerously) successful at. This is an unfortunate but understandable distortion. Identifying which of these messages may be getting in your way can direct you toward the reading material, workshops, or therapist who can help you look at the issue from healthier perspectives.

Gender Stereotyping

Sometimes the family messages—about money or careers or other subjects—are applied only to one sex. For many women born in the 1930s and '40s, girls had a very prescribed path: marry, have children, and, if financially necessary, work either as a nurse or a teacher. In Stefan's family, the assumption was that all boy children were headed for a lifetime of farming. These examples may seem outdated. But there are two things to keep in mind here. One is that the messages we carry around in our heads often gained a firm footing early on in our lives, and they were passed down to our parents and teachers many decades before that. If our parents or grandparents grew up reading books like *The Organization Man* and going to movies like *The Man in the Gray Flannel Suit*, and if they handed down those values to their kids, then *we* may still be carrying around the old cradle-to-grave, company loyalty, one-job-for-life mind-set, even though we may never have heard of that book or that movie ourselves. The second is that more contemporary messages may be equally oppressive. Not all women need to climb to the top any more than all women need to stay home. Not all men need to identify drumming in a rock band as one of their Renaissance Focal Points just because it's now okay that some grown-up men do.

Sibling Position

Not only can you be influenced by whether you came into this world as a boy or a girl, you can also be affected by where you fit into your family's chain of siblings. Oldest children frequently pick up different pictures of themselves and what's expected of them than youngest children do. Oldest boys are often expected to be very responsible, practical, and serious about their schoolwork. Often it's assumed that oldest girls will play the part of caregiver, attending to younger children and often to the needs of an overworked mother as well. On the other hand, youngest children may still feel that as adults they just don't know "enough" or they may still expect not to be taken seriously. I have last-born clients who, in their forties and fifties, still consider acting "cute" or "adorable" the most reliable skill they have for achieving things in life. And middle children have another story to tell. They may frantically pursue, or be overly afraid of, positions that put them in the spotlight, since they so rarely experienced such attention as children. And "only" children need to think about whether they grew up too quickly, eagerly attaching themselves to the interests of their parents who were the only playmates they had. Or perhaps they were kept "the precious little one" way too long, making them less confident now about deciding anything much for themselves.

Immigrant/Outsider Assumptions

Sometimes we are blocked by the sense that we do not belong, that we are defined as "outside" of the areas our soul would like to pursue. This problem often resonates strongly with immigrants and their children, but it is not limited to that group. It can affect any of us who feel that we do not know how to dress right or spell well enough or speak properly. It also includes anyone who may feel that, due to their race, religion, sex, class, or sexual preference, they are not welcome where they would like to be.

Unfortunately, there is a realistic basis for many of these feelings of exclusion, which can be quite painful. But talking with peers or joining relevant support and activist groups can sometimes help. The more you can take advantage of such help, the easier it will be to move on to more successful life design.

REWRITING OLD MESSAGES

If family or societal messages are limiting you, it's time to recognize that fact. Fortunately, there are many excellent strategies you can use on your own to help overcome distorted messages. Therapists may suggest them; many self-help books include them. When old messages crank up their forbidding, angry voices, you can also try a process I call Evaluating Old Messages. Let me show you how it worked for Amos, a bright and multitalented client of mine.

Amos was the first person from his blue-collar family to

consider applying for a management position. His fellow workers and family members had actively encouraged him to go for an opening at his workplace. The idea excited Amos, but still he found himself not moving forward on his application. He came to me for coaching.

What Amos felt blocked from doing—seeking a promotion into management—was clear. So we began by jotting down any and all negative thoughts that popped up about himself and/or the state of the world when he thought about taking the action at hand. Amos's list looked like this:

1. It's selfish to care about success.
2. I can't dress right for those big meetings.
3. Go into management? That's joining the people who discriminated against my grandfather!
4. My spelling's lousy. They'd know I didn't belong.
5. You have to sell out to move up.

When Amos finished sharing these negative thoughts with me, he was quite surprised. "Wow, I didn't even know I was thinking all that. No wonder I've been stalling." And then he added a little sadly, "Well, I guess that's the end of *that* idea."

Fortunately we were not at the end of the process. We went on to identify the assumptions that underlay each negative message. These are often generalizations about human nature or the state of the world ("No one will love me if I'm the boss" or "Real women should be able to handle a career *and* motherhood"). As Amos and I talked, his assumptions emerged. He put them in parentheses after each message:

1. It's selfish to care about success. **(All successful people are selfish.)**

2. I can't dress right for those big meetings. (**Those people know something I don't know.**)
3. Go into management? That's joining the people who discriminated against my grandfather! (**Everyone in management has to discriminate.**)
4. My spelling's lousy. They'd know I didn't belong. (**Bosses naturally spell better than blue-collar guys like me.**)
5. You have to sell out to move up. (**Promotions aren't based on who you really are or what skills you actually have.**)

"Yeah, so what?" Amos challenged. But we weren't done. It was time to code each negative thought according to the following system. I told Amos he could use more than one of the code letters if more than one applied.

+ Does my adult self truly believe the statement I've written down to be absolutely true? If not, code it with an *X.*
+ Could I *learn* to do this if it's important to me? If so, code it with an *L.*
+ Is there some way I can *modify* this "fact" about the world; is there some way in which it doesn't have to apply to me? If so, code it with an *M.*

Looking his list over, Amos decided that he didn't really believe numbers 1, 3, or 5, so he gave them each an *X.* He felt he could learn how to dress, so he gave number 2 an *L.* He also figured that he could learn to spell better or use a spell-checking program or dictionary if he decided it was important to him, so he gave number 4 an *L* also. And, rereading his list,

Amos quickly added an *M* next to the *X* of number 5. "Maybe some people would sell out to move up, but I put my honor ahead of my wallet. I feel sure of that."

"I'm beginning to get it," he said, smiling at me.

But I knew one last step would solidify things for Amos: I asked him to write a summary statement incorporating his new awareness. Here's the paragraph Amos came up with:

> I have good skills and I know I could plan good projects. But you have to be in management to plan projects. So I'm going to do what I need to do to get this promotion. I'll get advice about my clothes and learn how to write stuff that isn't full of spelling mistakes. And I'll apply for this promotion based on the skills I have. When I'm in my new job, I'll still be me and will treat people as fairly and unselfishly as I can.

Getting all these old messages out into the open changed Amos's feelings about moving ahead entirely. Whenever he felt himself wavering, he simply read and reread this simple paragraph.

CREATIVE FEAR AND ANXIETY

As you let go of the familiar and reach for something new, you may experience some unsettling symptoms. Your appetite may change; you may find yourself hyperalert at night or sleeping all morning long; your heart may pound; you may think your digestive system is turning inside out. This is to say: you may be afraid. Fear is an absolutely normal, absolutely human response to the unknown. Stress hormones like adrenaline and cortisol are built right into our nervous systems to mobilize us against anything we perceive as danger. So there is no point in trying to eliminate fear entirely. If you are trying something new, you may be excited, you may be thrilled, you may have been waiting for this opportunity all your life—and you may be afraid as well.

We *all* experience fear, including specialists who are presenting their dissertations or interviewing for their first career-ladder positions. But fear is a frequent traveling companion particularly for those of us who like to set our caps for new directions, or who may well try inventing our own business rather than settling into a corporate slot. Why? Because we are constantly changing our situation, our position, our "label" in life, and change involves fear. Over and over, I hear Renaissance Souls speak of the fear that they'll lose their footing, that doors may close on them, or that they may have burned their bridges. The images are strong and scary. One alternative image I like is that of the leap through midair made by circus artists as they swing from one trapeze to the next. Scary, yes, but also sublime.

If the trapeze-artist metaphor is a little too daring for your style, try picturing a lobster instead, snug and protected in its familiar shell. But for the lobster to grow, it must break open that rigid shell to make room for the new one growing beneath it. Once the old shell has been broken, the lobster has nothing but its newly revealed shell, thin as a membrane, to protect it. It would be right for the lobster to fear this change of shell, because at this point it is extremely vulnerable. But this vulnerable state is the prerequisite for growing into a larger creature. In time the shell will harden and mature. If the lobster refused to break open the shell it knew originally, it would only succeed in stunting its growth. This is what happens to Renaissance Souls who succumb to rationalizations such as "This just isn't a good time for me" or "I can't afford it right now" or "I'm too busy as it is" in order to avoid facing the fear that accompanies transitions.

Put Fear to Work

Although fear can never be eliminated, I know a few tricks for taming it. Recognize that you have a choice. You can choose to let fear paralyze you, limiting yourself to what feels comfortable. You can talk a blue streak about what you are going to do "someday" or what you could do "if only." You can procrastinate, work below your capabilities, and never, ever try anything that isn't one hundred percent guaranteed to give you a safe landing. Or you can tap into fear as a source of energy, using it to jump-start yourself into effective preparation.

Let's say, for example, that you need to make a short but very public announcement in connection with one of your Renaissance Focal Points, and that you have never done anything like this before. What are your choices? You can say, "I just don't know how to do that!" and stay home. Or, opting for preparation instead of paralysis, you can ask yourself: *What exactly are my fears? What are those fears telling me about how to prepare for this announcement?*

Are you afraid of tripping over your words? Practice giving your announcement until uttering the words becomes second nature. Then close your eyes and simply imagine yourself speaking with ease. Maybe you can even imagine that things don't go well—your voice starts to quaver—and plan how you'll handle the situation.

Are you worried that something will go wrong with the equipment? Then plan to drive to the place where you'll be speaking early, so you can adjust the height of the rostrum and microphone and make sure no staticky noises emit from the sound system.

Worried that your mind will go blank at the big moment? Then plan to bring large three-by-five-inch note cards to help you recall your message.

Whichever steps you take, you can be grateful to your fear for prompting them. As Julia Cameron, the author of *The Artist's Way*, reminds us, "Anxiety is fuel. We can use it to write with, paint with, work with."

Name the fear, break it down into specific worries, and then let those worries teach you how to prepare. The following chart offers some examples of popular fears and how to turn them into instruments of progress. These examples show you how to make fear work in your favor. There are three steps involved: naming the fear, breaking it down into specific worries, and deciding how to prepare yourself to handle your anxiety.

In addition to practical steps such as these, you can also calm yourself by doing something a little more fun and a little less logical: repeating a relevant, goofy, religious, or sacrilegious phrase over and over as you begin whatever task that has you terrified. Writer, performer, and entrepreneur Carol Lloyd speaks on behalf of the silly mantra: "By silently chanting, 'Y'all are worms' or 'Blessed be' or 'Sweet stinker' (or some stronger language), you can cut through the paralyzing panic of anticipation and move forward. Your irreverent mantra will occupy your conscious mind while you let a deeper part of yourself take over and do the work."

Sometimes a quiet visualization is more appropriate. Picture all your fears as hard hailstones, falling down on you from above. Then, breathing deeply, imagine that the hurtling hail melts into a soft, early spring rain. Continue your slow breathing as you picture the gentle water nourishing one emerging crocus after another, until there's an entire field of new growth, bursting forth with energy and promise.

EXAMPLES OF PUTTING FEAR TO WORK

FEAR	BREAK IT DOWN	PREPARE
I hate picking up the telephone and asking for something.	I don't like to call people unless I can say that so-and-so referred me.	I'll ask around at church and see if I can't find someone who knows the person I'm trying to reach and who will let me use his or her name. Then I can say, "Trish Hammer suggested I give you a call."
	I never know what to say if I get an answering machine, so I leave dorky messages.	I can jot down key answering message points before I dial.
	I don't feel up-to-date enough on business trends. Suppose they refer to some current bestseller that I haven't even heard of!	I can think through an honest but comfortable response such as "I must admit I've been so busy expanding my business, I've let my reading slide. That sounds fascinating, though. Can you give me the author's name again?" And/or I can make a point of glancing at the Sunday business section and the nonfiction bestseller list for fifteen minutes each week to reduce this anxiety.
If I get this analyst's position on Wall Street, I'll make more money than any of my friends from college do. Will they still like me?	People only like people who are equally or less successful than they are.	My cousin Frank, who runs a multimillion-dollar business, is a role model to me—and his financial status doesn't affect how much I like fishing with

		him. Which reminds me: I should make sure I spend some of my rare free time doing things like fishing with my college friends.
I'm afraid of injuring myself while exercising.	What if I pull a muscle like my friend Jackie did?	I can stretch before I exercise and I can build up my exercise regimen slowly and carefully (plus I need to remind myself I'm more likely to pull a muscle just running for a bus if I don't exercise!).
Will I have a clue how to handle the money part of my new business?	How will I know what to charge for my products?	I can go to a variety of sales venues to see what similar goods are selling for.
	I've heard record keeping for small businesses is really complicated. What if I mess it all up?	I could call our local Chamber of Commerce for guidance. And I can ask my sister-in-law Betty how she dealt with money when she started her computer consulting business.
What if I get the VP job —and I just can't play the role?	I'll have to go on business trips. How would I hide my fear of flying?	I remember reading something about hypnosis helping with phobias. I could check online or ask my brother to ask his therapist.
	How would I dress the part? I've been in stay-at-home-mom clothes for so long, I haven't a clue what to wear!	What are friends for, after all? Plus I can look at catalogs and magazines for inspiration on new styles.

Transforming the Fear of Failure into the Gift of Failure

The idea that you can transform fear into a gift applies especially to the familiar old fear that you won't succeed. So many of us deny ourselves the chance to try new things because we fear failure. Yet you may look back at struggles in your life, projects or plans that ostensibly ended poorly, only to recognize that those "failures" included gifts you later appreciated. My client Stuart, a film editor, had just such an experience. Raised in a family where boys didn't cry and "I can do it myself!" was the family mantra, he prided himself on his ability to tackle any ticklish project the movie studio handed him and make it work. "I always identified with the lone sheriff who rides into town and single-handedly beats the bad guy," he told me. "Everyone knew I could do it." So Stuart's friends and family encouraged him when he came up with a film project he wanted to develop on his own. But what happened? Stuart's great idea collided with rough economic times and ran into real financial difficulty. In fact, it never ended up seeing the light of day. The sheriff didn't win. But what is Stuart's take on that "failure"?

> Margaret, before we came to that dismal day when I had to lay everyone off and tell my wife the money we'd put in was a total loss, something else had happened. I had been forced by the very severity of the situation to put aside my pride, my upbringing if you will, and actually *ask for help*. Not just from banks—I'd done that before—but from people I knew! From friends and family. Even from my dad! And they came through for me. With ideas. With contacts. Even with money. Not enough to save the project, as it turned out, but in a way that still just turned my head

around. If the film had made me a million, or a billion, I wouldn't have gotten as much out of it as I got from being forced to ask. It took failing to let me get in my gut that two or four or fourteen heads can be better than one. I've never gone into another project without a true team, and what a difference that has made in my life!

OR DO YOU FEAR SUCCESS?

At almost every workshop I've given, someone has said, "But what about those of us who fear success instead of failure? I don't know how many times people have told me it's my fear of success that makes me jump ship every time I seem to be getting near the top." Others in the room nod their head in pained agreement. In response, I tell them about clients and friends who truly are afraid of success. They don't want to outstrip a parent, or they have long-standing negative associations with the experience of being praised (which may have felt like coercion to them when they were children). They may also have forbidding "rules" associated with success, such as "everyone will be jealous of me" or "I'll have money and become 'the enemy.'" For many of these clients the suggestions in this chapter prove very helpful; for others, working with a therapist may prove beneficial.

For most Renaissance Souls, however, the answer to the question "Do I fear success?" is a blunt No! I say this for two reasons. First, people who are afraid of success protect themselves by being solid failures, not by working hard until they're "near the top." Second, Renaissance Souls jump ship when we have things so successfully figured out that little remains to challenge us. We are no more afraid of our success than the molting lobster is afraid of his old, confining shell. We aren't unnerved by success. We just outgrow it!

NO MOTIVATIONAL ENERGY

This problem is potentially more devastating than being chained to old messages or feeling vulnerable and afraid during times of change. It involves an inability to feel excited about *anything*, even after you've identified yourself as a Renaissance Soul. Nothing, absolutely nothing, lights your fire. If, while reading the following pages, a light bulb goes off in your head, you may wish to seek professional medical or therapeutic assistance to get you past this roadblock.

Unfortunate Timing

Sometimes, just when you hope to move forward with an exciting new life design, you find yourself with additional responsibilities you didn't necessarily choose: living with a seriously sick family member, caring for aging parents, or facing overwhelming responsibilities at work in the wake of layoffs. Shouldering these burdens is difficult work, and you may be left with little energy for pursuing your true interests.

Ironically, however, it is often in the aftermath of major change or loss that we are forced to reexamine our choices. And we may just not be ready. *To the extent possible*, try to channel any remaining energies into making your situation less overwhelming. If that can't be done, allow yourself the time to ride out these rough seas. If you are suffering from a loss, bear in mind that grief often doesn't disappear half as fast as our society seems to expect. Just because it's been six

months since an injury left you with compromised function-
ing or a year since the death of a loved one doesn't mean that
you will necessarily be ready to bound ahead in new directions. In fact, recent research has shown the anniversaries of
difficult events may haunt us for years.

Whether dealing with added responsibilities or potent
losses, it is important to remember you can give yourself permission to leave your Renaissance Focal Point work for a few
months, or longer if needed. Letting yourself off the hook in
such situations is not a sign of failure but a guarantee that
when the situation is more favorable, you will be able to return to your Focal Points with renewed enthusiasm.

Undiagnosed Illness

Sometimes people flounder about for months or even years
with persistent medical symptoms that are mistaken for career anxiety or simple malingering. If you understand the
concept of identifying and combining key interests but just
don't have the energy or interest to do so, you might consider
scheduling a thorough physical. Untreated chronic disorders
such as anemia, chronic fatigue syndrome, untreated thyroid
conditions, seasonal affective disorder, menopausal or peri-
menopausal symptoms, or immune-deficiency problems can
make a person too exhausted to conjure up a creative new life.
In a parallel vein, medications, especially in combination, can
leave you unusually sleepy or anxious. Check with your doctor
if you're taking several pills at once (but don't stop using any
of them except on direct medical orders).

Chronic depression can prevent anyone's light from shining. Dr. Carol Eikleberry, in her book *The Career Guide for
Creative and Unconventional People,* points out that depression
doesn't always come with a clear label. She mentions clients

"who didn't think they were depressed because they weren't sad. But they did feel empty or numb, or very tired." Depressed people may mistake this kind of apathy, in which they may sleep much of the day away, watch endless television, and generally do as little as possible, for a character flaw. Sometimes depression takes the form of grueling rounds of insomnia instead. Other depressed people may not pay much attention to personal hygiene or maintaining their surroundings. My years of experience with struggling clients bears out Dr. Eikleberry's observation that "if you are not moving forward . . . because you are too tired to move anywhere, you may need treatment for depression as a first step."

Past Trauma

I have had clients who were in good shape and who hadn't suffered any significant losses in their lives in the last few years, who nevertheless had difficulty getting excited about beginning anything, even after grasping that they were Renaissance Souls. In these cases, it often turned out their personal history included factors that were holding them back in the present. Abuse, war trauma, rape, and other horrors can strongly affect how freely and joyfully you approach the design of your Renaissance Soul life. Without addressing this complex psychological phenomenon at great length here, let me just highlight four ways in which it can interfere with life-design work.

Purposely preoccupied. Have you developed a pattern of always staying super-busy or super-vigilant or super-in-control, either to keep yourself from remembering, or because you believe such behavior will somehow protect you from a repetition of the traumatic experience? If so, the energy available for creatively thinking about your interests is probably running low or has been diverted elsewhere. Does the following complaint of my client Deborah resonate with you?

> I always think finding more free time is the way to get on with writing my poetry. But then, when I do take a weekend to myself, or a vacation, it never turns out like I expect. There I am, sitting on the deck serenely overlooking the beautiful lake I've paid so much to see, an ideal setting for getting back in touch with my creative self. But what happens? Sitting doing nothing makes me antsy and I immediately grab for the nearest book. Or I get on the phone and call people when I thought I'd come to escape the phone. Sometimes I even find myself creating new tasks for myself, like sending postcards to everyone I've ever heard of, just to avoid being alone with myself with time to actually think or feel. I come home so frustrated.

Of course, not everyone who likes to stay on the go has suffered from a trauma; some of us were simply born busy. But novelist Connie May Fowler described busyness as avoidance when she wrote, "If I busy myself with something, maybe I can prevent even one tear from trickling down my face." When you bury yourself in activity to avoid a traumatic home situation or to keep your mind clear of painful thoughts, you can seem highly successful to others. But you might choose to spend your time in ways that are more meaningful to *you* if you felt safe enough to do so. Addressing this behavior pattern will help you pursue Focal Points that make sense to you.

All-or-nothing thinking. I have had clients who as children were traumatized by alcoholics, had an emotionally abusive

"crazy" parent, or who were physically or sexually abused in
some way. As children, all of them had a family secret to keep.
And often the thing about keeping secrets is that either we
keep them or we don't. Usually there isn't a whole lot of space
in between. One of the insidious repercussions when the middle ground is unfamiliar terrain is that the pattern of all-or-
nothing thinking continues into adulthood. You may fear that
if you get excited about your Renaissance Soul activities, then
all you'll ever do is play, and you'll never, ever again be responsible. You "know" that either you should want to pursue every
speaking gig that comes your way or you should give them all
up. It may be hard for you to believe you can do some and not
others, that you can choose Renaissance Focal Points you'd enjoy and still carry out other types of activities you've committed to as well.

Hiding secrets, seeking approval. If you were abused as a
child, you may well believe the bad things that were done to
you happened because you were inherently bad or had done
something terribly wrong. You didn't have the ability and
information at a young age to understand that things like alco-
holism, mental illness, plant closings, racism, physical health
issues, homophobia, or the general stress factors of everyday
life could cause adults to treat you badly. Consequently you
tended to blame things on yourself. And unfortunately, until
and unless the truth of the situation is uncovered and named,
you can carry that mistaken shame forward with you for many
years. This can leave you believing that anyone who really gets
to know you will discover your horrible inner secret. To hide
that secret, you may pursue destructive paths to external approval, producing the sad success of a Marilyn Monroe or Elvis
Presley. Novelist Ursula Hegi wrote vividly of the power of
such shame when she described a character for whom "the

shame settled somewhere low in her belly, a familiar presence that claimed any food she ate before it could nourish her." Such low self-esteem and shame is hardly a healthy soil in which to grow your dreams: the "fertilizer" of therapeutic help is highly recommended here.

The cloak of invisibility. While some people may respond to abuse or other traumas by seeking approval, others may feel that if they can just make themselves fat enough or thin enough or dumb enough or silent and inconsequential enough, no one will notice them and they will be safe from further abuse. Thus they cut themselves off from some of their greatest gifts and passions, and are wise to seek good counseling as part of pursuing their life design.

For those who suffer from trauma, depression, and other serious problems, there is hope. Every community has therapists who are skilled in a variety of helpful, healing approaches to the difficulties I've touched on here. There have also been major breakthroughs in the availability of herbal and synthetic antidepressants, so that most people can find one that suits their personal constitution and doesn't produce crippling side effects. Most communities also now have a variety of free or inexpensive support groups, including those for children of alcoholics and for survivors of sexual abuse, listed in their local papers. I've personally seen clients and had friends who have wisely and bravely asked for help. Now they are lit up with a fresh sense of possibility.

Experience tells me that Renaissance Souls who come up against less entrenched troubles, such as old messages, can overcome them—often on their own. When the problem doesn't run as deep as major depression, the solution is some-

times as simple as recognizing those defeating, endlessly repeating tapes for what they are. A little self-awareness and a
lick of courage can go a long way toward generating more
truthful habits of thought. Therapy is another helpful option
when you're struggling with old messages and other painful
blocks. Whichever tools you use, you will know when you've
been successful by your refreshed yearning for directed action.

It's a great feeling when your wheels stop spinning in one
place and start to move you closer to all the things you want to
be doing. Have a grand adventure.

CONCLUSION

Be a Role Model!

My grandfather created an achievement award for me when I was in high school to honor and give recognition to all the ways I was expressing myself. He hired a calligrapher to list all the activities I'd done in high school (including volunteering in a hospital, editing the yearbook, investing my earnings, sewing, performing in the church choir, sailing, organizing the senior farewell dance, and participating in the student council). I have my award hanging in my closet where, at sixty-three years of age, I still see it as I get dressed every morning!

—*Sandra, sixty-three*

$\int$f your parents had understood how to encourage and support a Renaissance child, how would your life have been different?

If your high school guidance counselor had not insisted on a single answer to the questions "What do you want to be when you

---

PAST, PRESENT, AND FUTURE RENAISSANCE SOULS

Past. Tam Wing Kwong, born in China in the late 1800s, could literally play every instrument in the Chinese orchestra. In addition, he became both a chemist and an owner of a trading business, while "on the side" he wrote a Chinese-English dictionary and invented a new form of calligraphy and a telegraph system.

In the 1920s, Tam Wing Kwong founded a school in Hong Kong, one of the first to recognize the interconnection of mind, body, and spirit. And whose fund-raising efforts made this the only free school in the province? None other than Renaissance Soul Tam Wing Kwong!

Present. Steve John has been a nuclear physicist; a principal in a consulting firm; director of an international pharmaceutical company; and senior vice president of a Wall Street financial firm. He holds a CPA and an MBA, and has a PhD in organizational development. In his off hours, John sails and restores classic cars. For his next project, he plans to direct a documentary on the ethical Arthur Andersen employees who lost their livelihoods.

Future. In 2003, my local library displayed the poem on the opposite page by middle-school student Hannah Brassard. Accompanying the poem was a picture of her hands.

grow up?" or "What do you think you'll want to major in when you get to college?" how would your life have been different?

Would your work life have been more productive if your employers knew how to make the very best use of your interest in the new and the different?

Would your relationships with your friends, your partner, your siblings be more positive if they didn't keep wishing you'd figure out the one thing you wanted to do with your life?

If your answer to any (or all) of the above questions is *yes*,

> HANDS
>
> I am an artist sketching on a piece of paper.
> I am a basketball player swishing the ball.
> I am an American waving a flag on the 4th of July.
>
> I am a pianist playing notes on the piano.
> I am a swimmer diving into a cold pool.
> I am a soccer player sprinting on the dewy grass.
>
> I am Irish, celebrating St. Patrick's Day.
> I am a skier speeding down the slope.
> I am a singer following along with the chorus.
>
> I am an author creating ideas on a page.
> I am a reader flipping pages of a book.
> I am a rainbow arching in the sky.
>
> —*Hannah Brassard*

then consider starting your own informal education campaign, so that future swans will face fewer of these obstacles.

HOW CAN YOU HELP?

Share your own story with the people closest to you. Tell them how identifying yourself as a Renaissance Soul has changed how you feel about yourself and your life's possibilities.

You can share this book and the www.RenaissanceSouls.com Web site as well. As we all do our work of spreading the truth about Renaissance Souls, this site can serve as a source of Renaissance Soul buddies, mentors, coaches, and peer groups from around the country.

And as you continue on your life's varied journey, I invite you to share with me new insights, examples, or stories you believe will help other Renaissance Souls get unstuck. You can reach me via www.RenaissanceSouls.com, and I will do my best to spread what you share via that Web site, talks and workshops that I give, and future editions of this book.

BE A ROLE MODEL

One of the best things you can do for other Renaissance Souls is to keep growing. And keep changing. As Renaissance Souls become more comfortable with their new identities, shame lifts and something more positive settles in its place. "I'm sick and tired of not being who I am!" we exclaim. This kind of honesty inevitably works its magic on others, who will find the courage to announce: "I'm finding a way out of this cubby-hole, career-ladder existence. I want to nourish *all* of my selves." Others get up the nerve to proclaim, "It *does* make sense—at least for me—to study acupuncture *and* write *and* design my own log home!"

As the truth about Renaissance Souls spreads, more of us will begin to grasp that honest self-acceptance is crucial to our sanity, our sense of well-being, and the contributions we can make to the world. Teachers, employers, and loved ones will begin to accept that there is nothing wrong in our pursuing diverse interests; quite the opposite. We have a right to pursue the variety and combination of activities we feel enthusiastic about. It is good to remember—and to tell others—that the word "enthusiasm" comes from the Greek word *entheos*, which means "filled with God."

You are blessed to be a Renaissance Soul. I hope you'll share those blessings with the world.

RELEVANT READINGS

For Renaissance Souls with a Creative Bent

Cameron, Julia. *Vein of Gold: A Journey to Your Creative Heart.* New York: Jeremy P. Tarcher, 1996.

Capacchione, Lucia. *Visioning: 10 Steps to Designing the Life of Your Dreams.* New York: Jeremy P. Tarcher, 2000.

Eikleberry, Carol. *The Career Guide for Creative and Unconventional People.* Berkeley, CA: Ten Speed Press, 1995.

Fritz, Robert. *Creating: A Practical Guide to the Creative Process and How to Use It to Create Anything—A Work of Art, a Relationship, a Career or a Better Life.* New York: Ballantine Books, 1993.

Lloyd, Carol. *Creating a Life Worth Living: A Practical Course in Career Design for Artists, Innovators, and Others Aspiring to a Creative Life.* New York: HarperPerennial, 1997.

For Entrepreneurial Renaissance Souls

Alexander, Shoshana. *Women's Ventures, Women's Visions: 29 Inspiring Stories from Women Who Started Their Own Businesses.* Freedom, CA: The Crossing Press, 1997. <u>Note:</u> Renaissance Soul men have also found this book very inspiring.

Edwards, Paul. *The Best Home Businesses for the 21st Century: The Inside Information You Need to Know to Select a Home-Based Business That's Right for You.* New York: Jeremy P. Tarcher, 1999.

Gurvis, Sandra. *Careers for Nonconformists: A Practical Guide to Finding and Developing a Career Outside the Mainstream.* New York: Marlowe & Company, 2000.

Reinhold, Barbara B. *Free to Succeed: Designing the Life You Want in the New Free Agent Economy.* New York: PenguinPutnam/ Plume, 2001.

SARK. *Make Your Creative Dreams Real: A Plan for Procrastinators, Perfectionists, Busy People, and People Who Would Really Rather Sleep All Day.* New York: Fireside, 2004.

Tam, Marilyn. *How to Use What You've Got to Get What You Want.* San Diego, CA: Jodere Group, 2003.

Toms, Justine Willis, and Michael Toms. *True Work: The Sacred Dimension of Earning a Living.* New York: Bell Tower, 1998.

Winter, Barbara. *Making a Living Without a Job: Winning Ways for Creating Work That You Love.* New York: Bantam, 1993.

Inspiring Help for Getting Your Renaissance Life Going

Bronson, Po. *What Should I Do with My Life?* New York: Random House, 2002.

Falter-Barns, Suzanne. *How Much Joy Can You Stand?: A Creative Guide to Facing Your Fear and Making Your Dreams Come True.* New York: Ballantine Wellspring, 2000.

Jarow, Rick. *Creating the Work You Love: Courage, Commitment, and Career.* Rochester, VT: Destiny Books, 1995.

Louden, Jennifer. *The Comfort Queen's Guide to Life: Create All That You Need with Just What You've Got.* Easton, PA: Harmony Press, 2000.

McWilliams, Peter. *Do It! Let's Get Off Our But's.* Los Angeles, CA: Prelude Press, 1994.

Richardson, Cheryl. *Take Time for Your Life.* New York: Broadway, 1999.

Sher, Barbara. *Wishcraft: How to Get What You Really Want.* New York: Ballantine, 1979. <u>Note:</u> The *craft* portion of this book is relevant here, when applied to all our goal<u>S!</u>

Young, Valerie. *Finding Your True Calling: The Handbook for People Who Still Don't Know What They Want to Be When They Grow Up But Can't Wait to Find Out.* Northampton, MA: Changing Course, 2002.

Personal Issues

Aron, Elaine. *The Highly Sensitive Person: How to Thrive When the World Overwhelms You.* New York: Broadway, 1996.

Barnett, Rosalind, and Caryl Rivers. *Same Difference: How Gender Myths Are Hurting Our Relationships, Our Children, and Our Jobs.* New York: Basic Books, 2004.

Bass, Ellen, and Laura Davis. *The Courage to Heal: A Guide for Women Survivors of Child Sexual Abuse.* New York: Perennial Library, 1994.

Carson, Rick. *Taming Your Gremlin: A Surprisingly Simple Method for Getting Out of Your Own Way.* New York: HarperCollins/ Perennial Currents, 2003.

Hallowell, Edward, and John J. Ratey. *Driven to Distraction: Recognizing and Coping with ADD from Childhood Through Adulthood.* New York: Simon & Schuster, 1995.

Jeffers, Susan. *Feel the Fear and Do It Anyway.* New York: Ballantine Books, 1988.

Kelly, Kate, and Peggy Ramundo. *You Mean I'm Not Lazy, Stupid or Crazy?!: A Self-Help Book for Adults with Attention Deficit Disorder.* New York: Scribner, 1996.

Markova, Dawna. *No Enemies Within: A Creative Process for Discovering What's Right About What's Wrong.* Emeryville, CA: Conari Press, 1994.

Norem, Julie. *The Positive Power of Negative Thinking: Using Defensive Pessimism to Harness Anxiety and Perform at Your Peak.* New York: Basic Books, 2002.

Simon, Sidney, and Suzanne Simon. *Forgiveness: How to Make Peace with Your Past and Get on with Your Life.* New York: Warner Books Inc., 1991.

Stoddard, Alexandra. *The Art of the Possible: The Path from Perfectionism to Balance and Freedom.* New York: William Morrow and Company, Inc., 1995.

Sully, Susan. *The Late Bloomer's Guide to Success at Any Age.* New York: Quill/HarperCollins, 2000.

SO WHAT'S NEXT?

✓ Do you want a Renaissance Soul as your life coach?

✓ Do you want to know about upcoming Renaissance Soul workshops and gatherings?

✓ Would you like to be connected with other Renaissance Souls?

✓ Do you have Renaissance Soul stories of your own to share?

Visit www.RenaissanceSouls.com.

Also feel free to get in touch with Margaret Lobenstine at margloben@ToGetUnstuck.com.

YOUR RENAISSANCE SOUL
NOTEBOOK

Consider the following pages to be your own personal Renaissance Soul notebook. Take notes as you read, jot down your thoughts and inspirations . . . These pages are yours to use as you wish.

ACKNOWLEDGMENTS

$\mathcal{W}$hile this book was written by an early-childhood teacher, a motivational speaker, a bed-and-breakfast owner, a life coach, a literacy specialist, an activist, a family business consultant, and a book author—namely Renaissance Soul me, it never would have been possible if it hadn't been for the help I received.

First and foremost I need to thank all the wonderful, honest, puzzled, inspiring Renaissance Soul clients and workshop participants with whom I've been blessed to cross paths, and the busy Renaissance Souls who gave up precious time to be interviewed for this book. By sharing your struggles, your creativity, your questions, and your triumphs, you taught me both why this book is so necessary and what it needed to include.

I also can't thank enough the folks who first helped spread the word about Renaissance Souls through their groundbreaking newspaper, magazine, and Web site articles, and initial workshop invitations; my amazing support team of readers/advice/encouragement givers; my dear friends/clients who may not have read rough drafts but helped keep me going through it all; my fellow writers and National Writers' Union colleagues who gave me inspiration, contract advice, and great contacts; the gifted computer people who made so much possible; and my extended family who lovingly heard about this project at *every* family gathering and lots of times in between. To list everyone by name would take pages, but you know who you are!

It is also important to recognize that every step forward is built on those that have gone before. In alphabetical order, my incredible mentors include Shoshana Alexander, Elaine Aron, Suzanne Falter-Barnes, Po Bronson, Shel Horowitz, Rick Jarow, Jennifer Louden, Tom Plaut, Barbara Reinhold, Cheryl Richardson, Joel Roberts, SARK, Barbara Sher, Sid Simon, Judith Sturnick, Marilyn Tam, Justine and Michael Toms, Barbara Winter, and Valerie Young.

You wouldn't be holding this book in your hands if it weren't for its publishing team: Kris Puopolo, my enthusiastic and supportive editor at Broadway Books and the hardworking people with whom she works; Betsy Amster, the agent with every connection one could ever need; Laura Bellotti, my encouraging book proposal guide and editor; and, *so key*, Leigh Ann Hirschman, the talented and reliable freelance editor whose wonderfully gifted work smoothed out *all* my rough drafts, making it possible for this book to see the light of day.

INDEX

ABOUT THE AUTHOR

Margaret Lobenstine has a master's degree in education and has been a career counselor for twenty years. Before that she was one of the founders of the bed-and-breakfast movement in the United States and ran an apprenticeship program for potential innkeepers. It was in her work with them that she realized that many people try to escape their careers because they have a variety of interests that one job doesn't satisfy. She works in person or by phone with people all over America. In addition, because being wired to pursue many interests rather than just "settling down" with one is a *human* characteristic, not only an American one, Margaret also works with clients from as varied places as Dubai, India, Norway, Russia, Brazil, Australia, Italy, South Africa, China, France, Japan, England, Guatemala, and Switzerland. She is also helping expand the number of life coaches who can work effectively with Renaissance Souls by offering a nine-CD set, *Coaching the Renaissance Soul: The Guide to Working With Clients Who Have "Too Many Interests" To Pick Just One*, available from her website, www.RenaissanceSouls.com. You can reach Margaret by e-mail (margloben@togetunstuck.com) or phone (413-253-7693). She'd be delighted to hear from you! She presents her Renaissance Soul workshop at a wide variety of venues. This is her first book.